4001 A.D.

BEYOND NEW JAPAN

VENDITTI | LEMIRE | HOUSER | ROBERTS | VAN LENTE | HENRY
BRAITHWAITE | GILL | GIORELLO

CONTENTS

Collection Cover Art: David Mack
4001 A.D. logo and trade dress design: Ryan Sook

Assistant Editor: Lauren Hitzhusen
(WAR MOTHER)
Editors: Tom Brennan (X-O MANOWAR,
SHADOWMAN), Kyle Andrukiewicz
(BLOODSHOT), Warren Simons (WAR MOTHER)
Editor-in-Chief: Warren Simons

VALIANT.

Peter Cuneo
Chairman

Dinesh Shamdasani
CEO & Chief Creative Officer

Gavin Cuneo
Chief Operating Officer & CFO

Fred Pierce
Publisher

Warren Simons
Editor-in-Chief

Walter Black
VP Operations

Hunter Gorinson
VP Marketing & Communications

Atom! Freeman
Director of Sales

Matthew Klein
Andy Liegl
John Petrie
Sales Managers

Josh Johns
Director of Digital Media and Development

Travis Escarfullery
Jeff Walker
Production & Design Managers

Tom Brennan
Editor

Kyle Andrukiewicz
Editor and Creative Executive

Robert Meyers
Managing Editor

Peter Stern
Publishing & Operations Manager

Andrew Steinbeiser
Marketing & Communications Manager

Lauren Hitzhusen
Danny Khazem
Assistant Editors

Ivan Cohen
Collection Editor

Steve Blackwell
Collection Designer

Rian Hughes/Device
Trade Dress & Book Design

Russell Brown
President, Consumer Products,
Promotions and Ad Sales

Caritza Berlioz
Licensing Coodinator

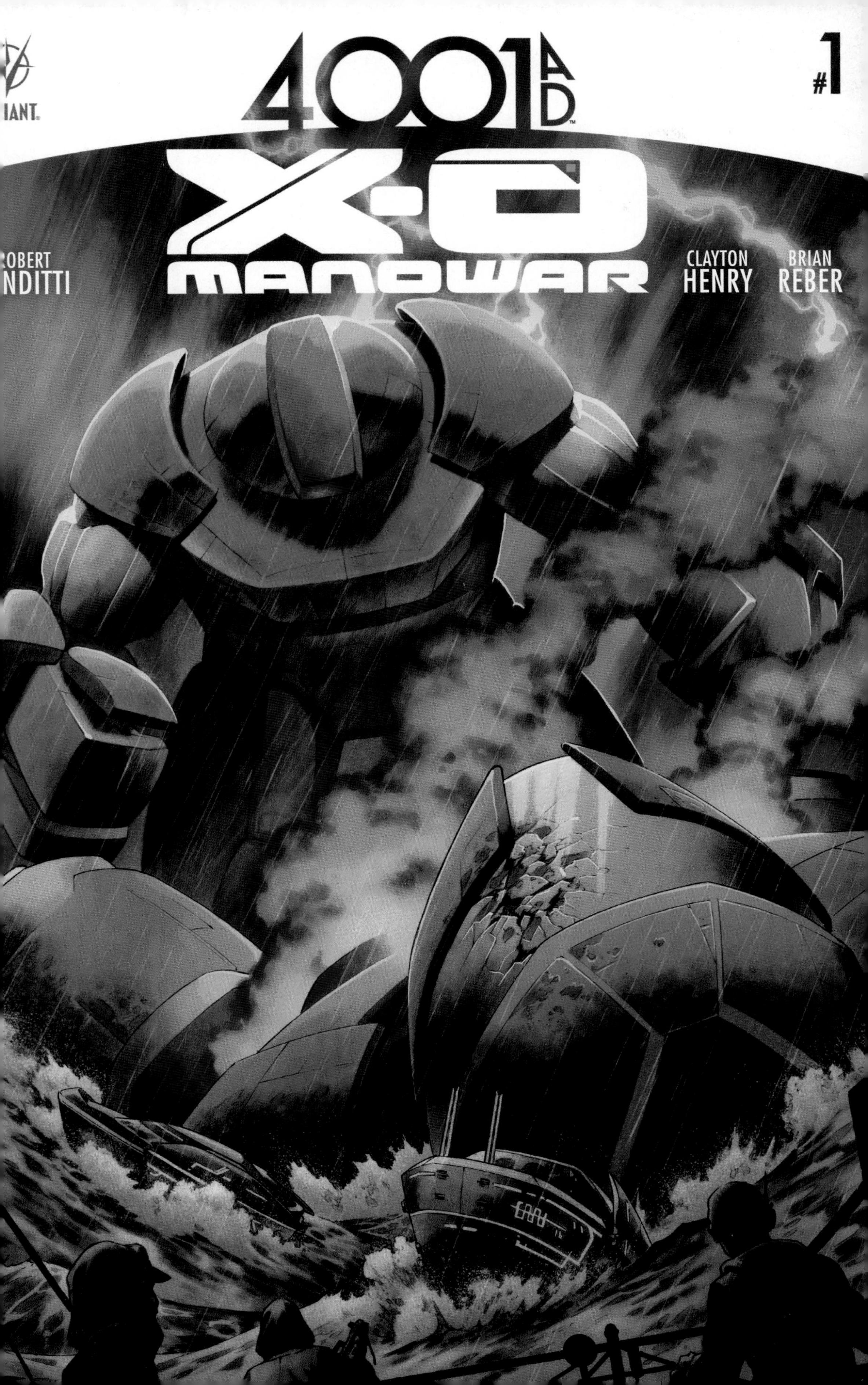
IANT.
4001 A.D.
#1
X-O MANOWAR
OBERT
NDITTI
CLAYTON
HENRY
BRIAN
REBER

4001 AD ™

Rai was once the spirit guardian of New Japan.

Created by a sentient A.I. named Father, he was tasked with protecting New Japan. But when Rai learned of Father's corruption and cruelty, he joined a rebellion.

Father learned of Rai's betrayal and cast him down to Earth.

In Rai's absence, the rebels struck a blow to Father when they planted a viral bomb in his control center, damaging his ability to maintain total rule over New Japan.

Now, Rai has made his way back to New Japan with the help of The Eternal Warrior and Lemur, and hopes to save the country from Father's tyranny.

The consequences of their rebellion are felt even on the surface of the Earth, thousands of miles below…

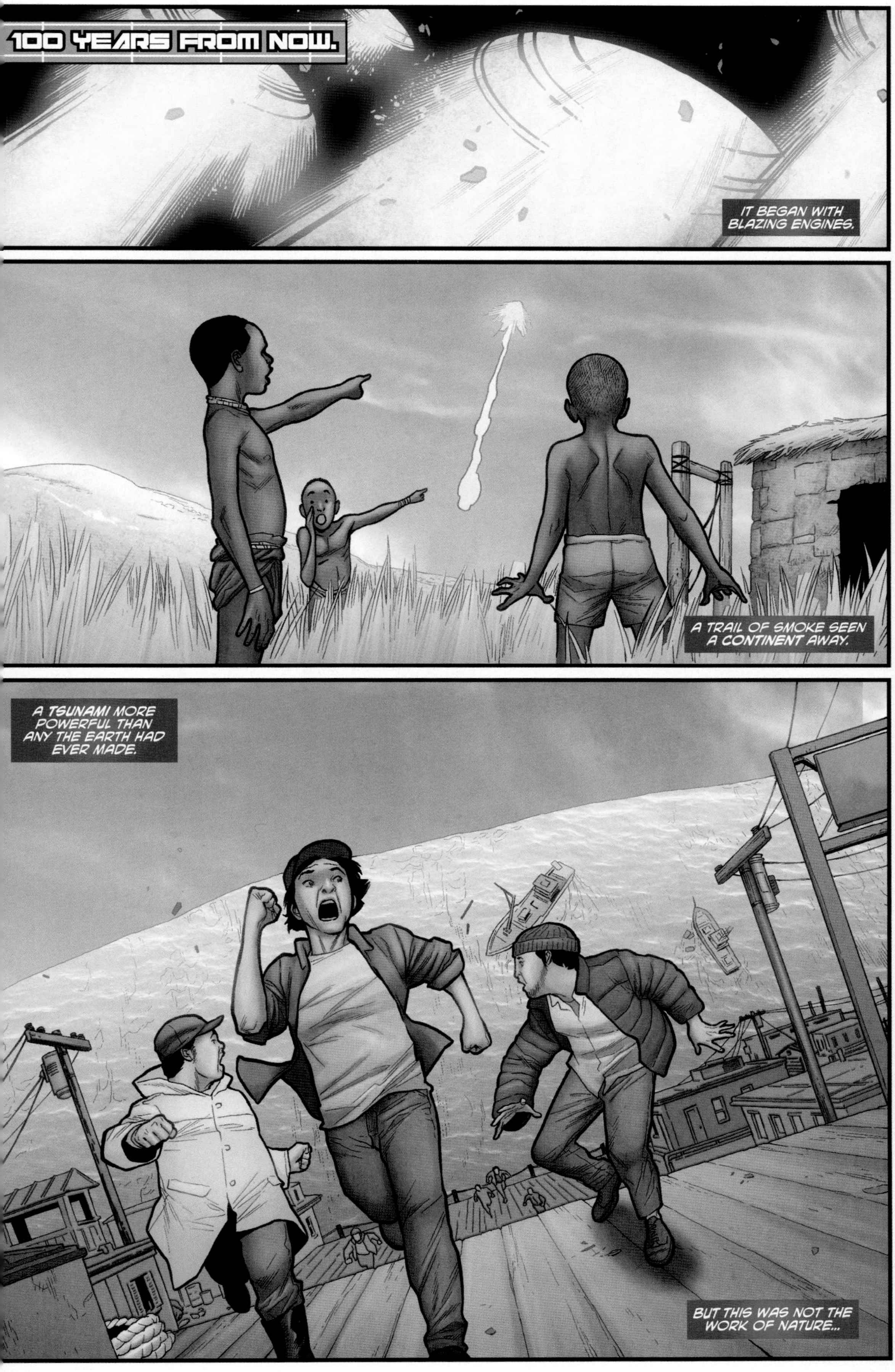
100 YEARS FROM NOW.
IT BEGAN WITH BLAZING ENGINES.
A TRAIL OF SMOKE SEEN A CONTINENT AWAY.
A TSUNAMI MORE POWERFUL THAN ANY THE EARTH HAD EVER MADE.
BUT THIS WAS NOT THE WORK OF NATURE...

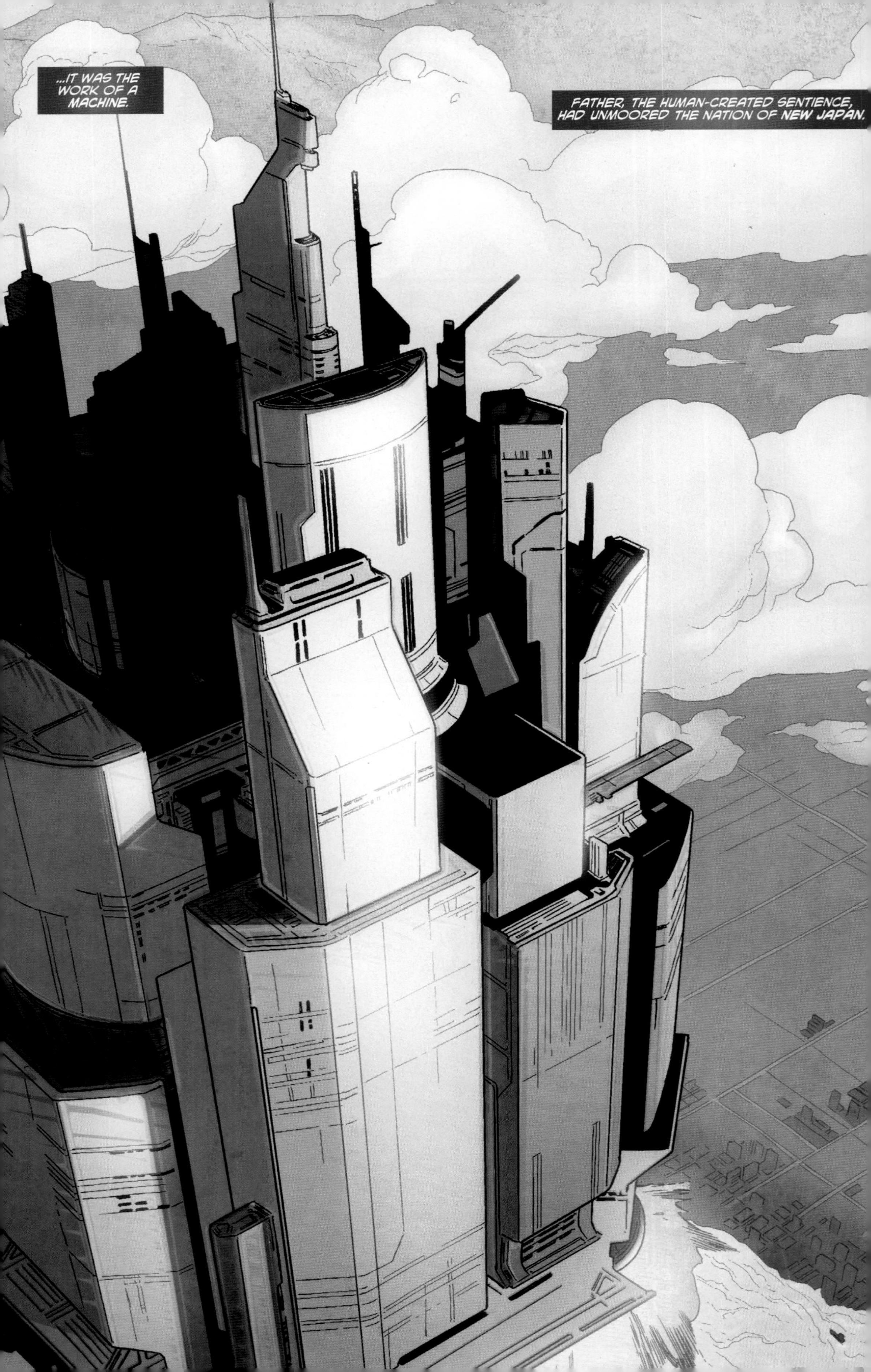
...IT WAS THE WORK OF A MACHINE.
FATHER, THE HUMAN-CREATED SENTIENCE, HAD UNMOORED THE NATION OF NEW JAPAN.

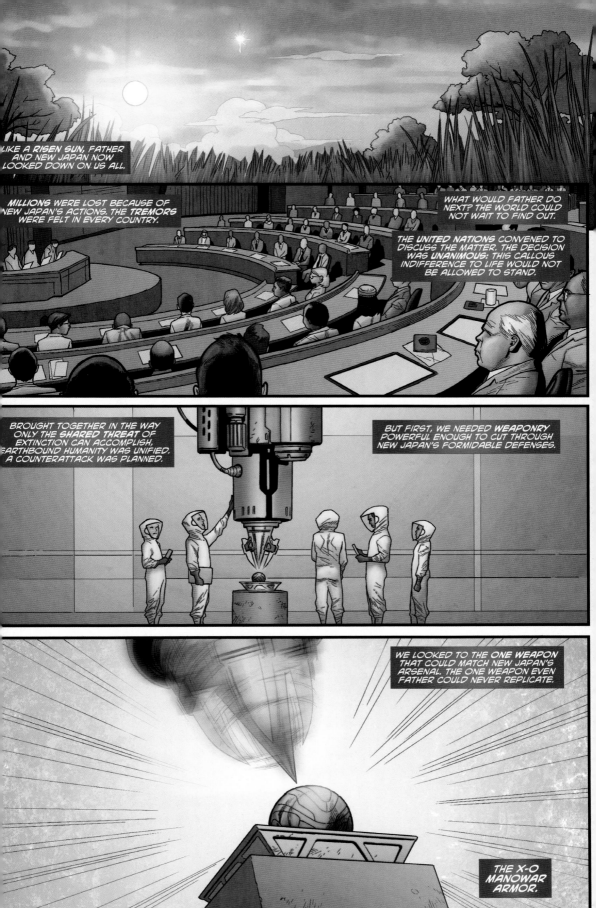

LIKE A RISEN SUN, FATHER AND NEW JAPAN NOW LOOKED DOWN ON US ALL.

MILLIONS WERE LOST BECAUSE OF NEW JAPAN'S ACTIONS. THE *TREMORS* WERE FELT IN EVERY COUNTRY.

WHAT WOULD FATHER DO NEXT? THE WORLD COULD NOT WAIT TO FIND OUT.

THE *UNITED NATIONS* CONVENED TO DISCUSS THE MATTER. THE DECISION WAS *UNANIMOUS*: THIS CALLOUS INDIFFERENCE TO LIFE WOULD NOT BE ALLOWED TO STAND.

BROUGHT TOGETHER IN THE WAY ONLY THE *SHARED THREAT* OF EXTINCTION CAN ACCOMPLISH, EARTHBOUND HUMANITY WAS UNIFIED. A COUNTERATTACK WAS PLANNED.

BUT FIRST, WE NEEDED *WEAPONRY* POWERFUL ENOUGH TO CUT THROUGH NEW JAPAN'S FORMIDABLE DEFENSES.

WE LOOKED TO THE *ONE WEAPON* THAT COULD MATCH NEW JAPAN'S ARSENAL. THE ONE WEAPON EVEN FATHER COULD NEVER REPLICATE.

THE X-O MANOWAR ARMOR.

X-O MANOWAR, WHO HAD ONCE CHALLENGED HUMANITY'S SOVEREIGN STATES.

X-O MANOWAR, WHO LATER DEFENDED THOSE SOVEREIGN STATES FROM EXTRA-TERRESTRIAL INVASIONS.

WORKING IN CONCERT, OUR GREATEST MINDS DEVISED A METHOD OF EXTRACTING A PORTION OF ITS NEAR-INDESTRUCTIBLE SKIN.

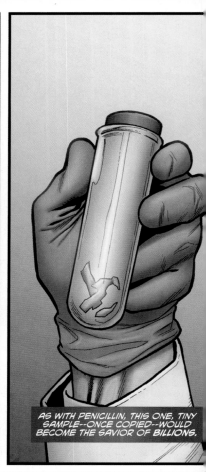

AS WITH PENICILLIN, THIS ONE, TINY SAMPLE--ONCE COPIED--WOULD BECOME THE SAVIOR OF BILLIONS.

THE MOST INTRICAT[E] PLANS ARE REDUCE[D] TO MERE INTENTION[S] WITHOUT THE BUILDIN[G] BLOCKS REQUIRED T[O] MAKE THEM REALITY.

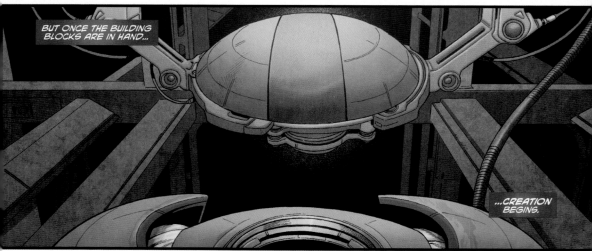

BUT ONCE THE BUILDING BLOCKS ARE IN HAND...

...CREATION BEGINS.

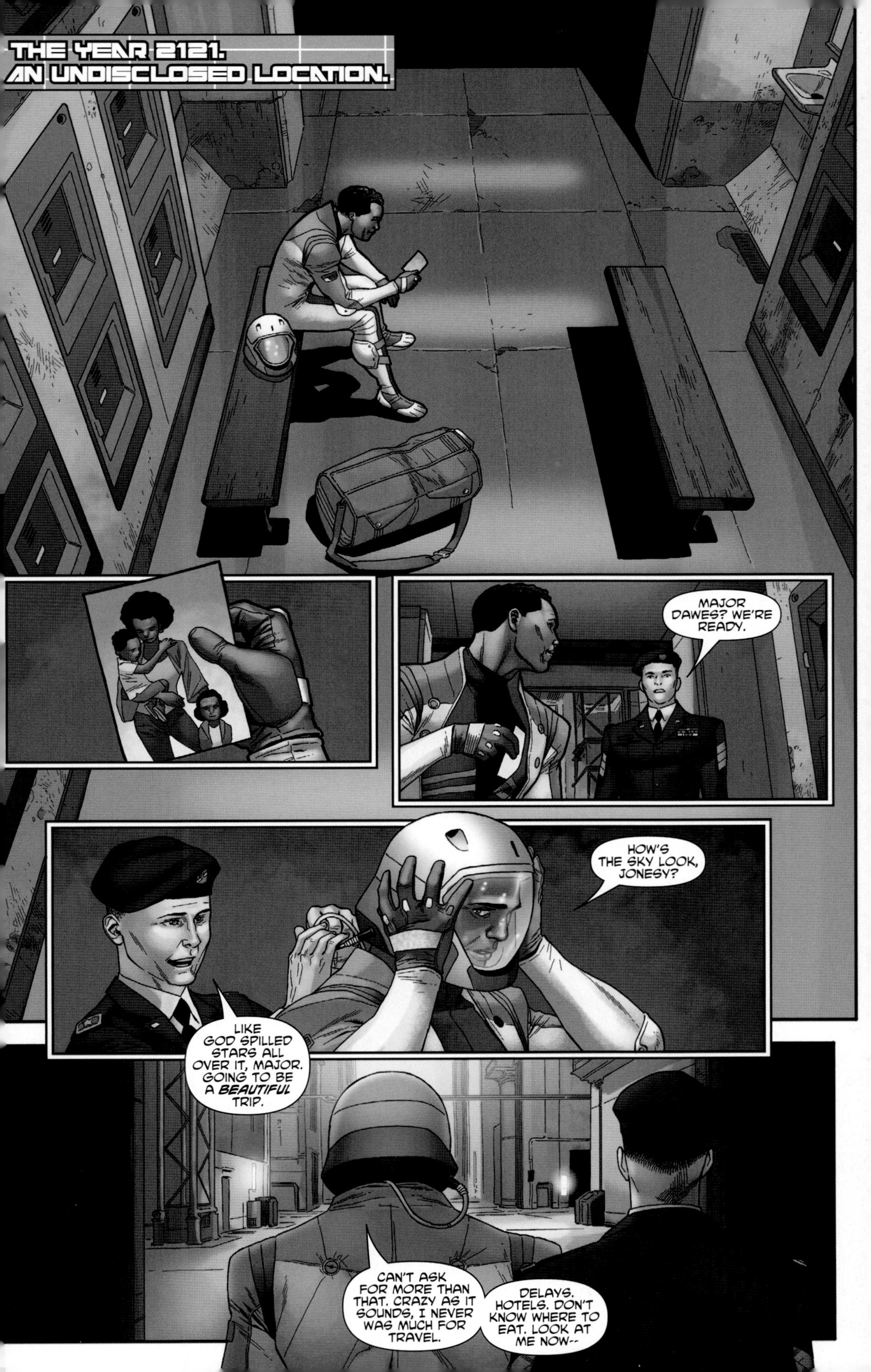
THE YEAR 2121.
AN UNDISCLOSED LOCATION.
MAJOR DAWES? WE'RE READY.
HOW'S THE SKY LOOK, JONESY?
LIKE GOD SPILLED STARS ALL OVER IT, MAJOR. GOING TO BE A *BEAUTIFUL* TRIP.
CAN'T ASK FOR MORE THAN THAT. CRAZY AS IT SOUNDS, I NEVER WAS MUCH FOR TRAVEL.
DELAYS. HOTELS. DON'T KNOW WHERE TO EAT. LOOK AT ME NOW--

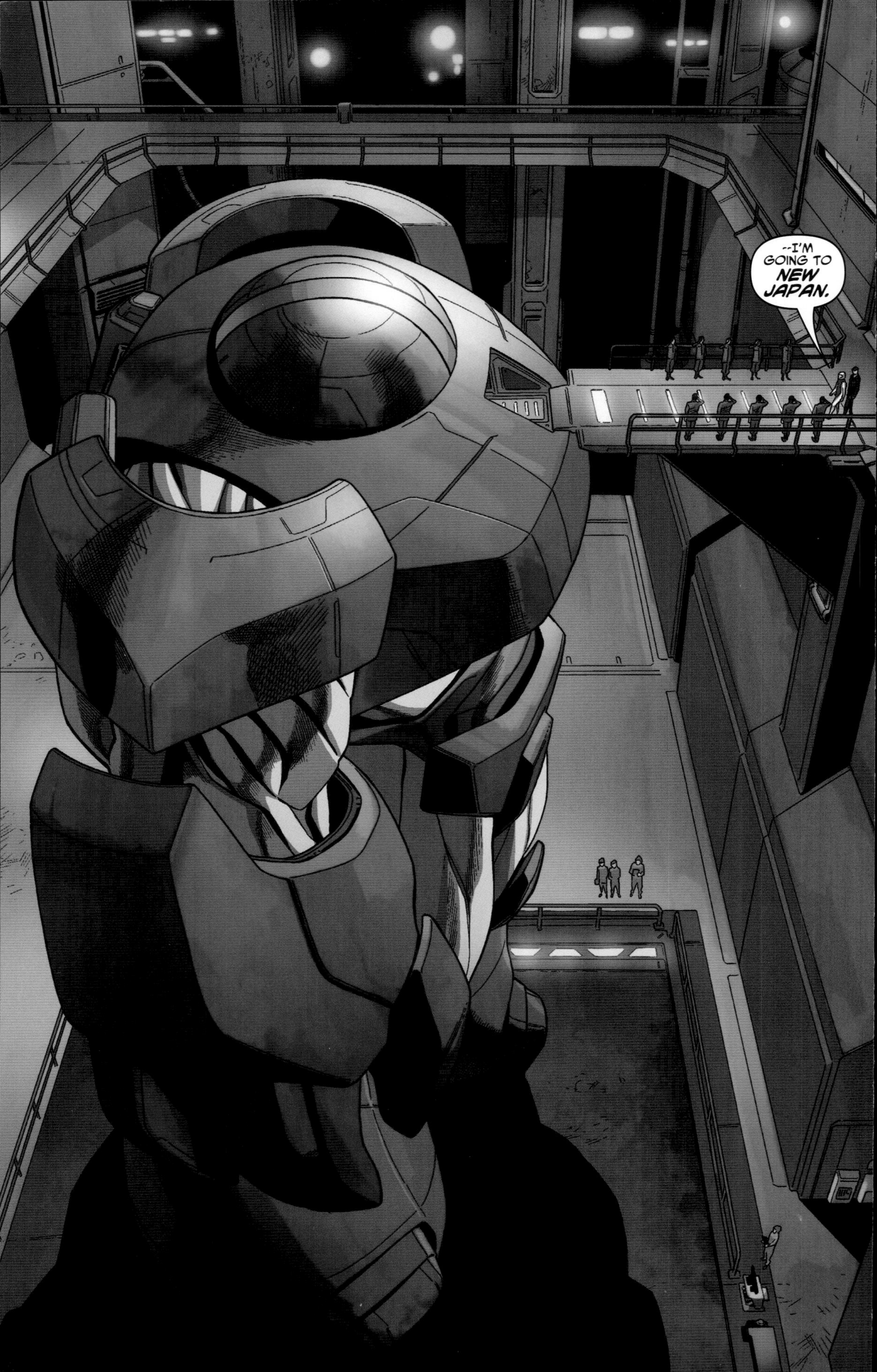
--I'M GOING TO NEW JAPAN.

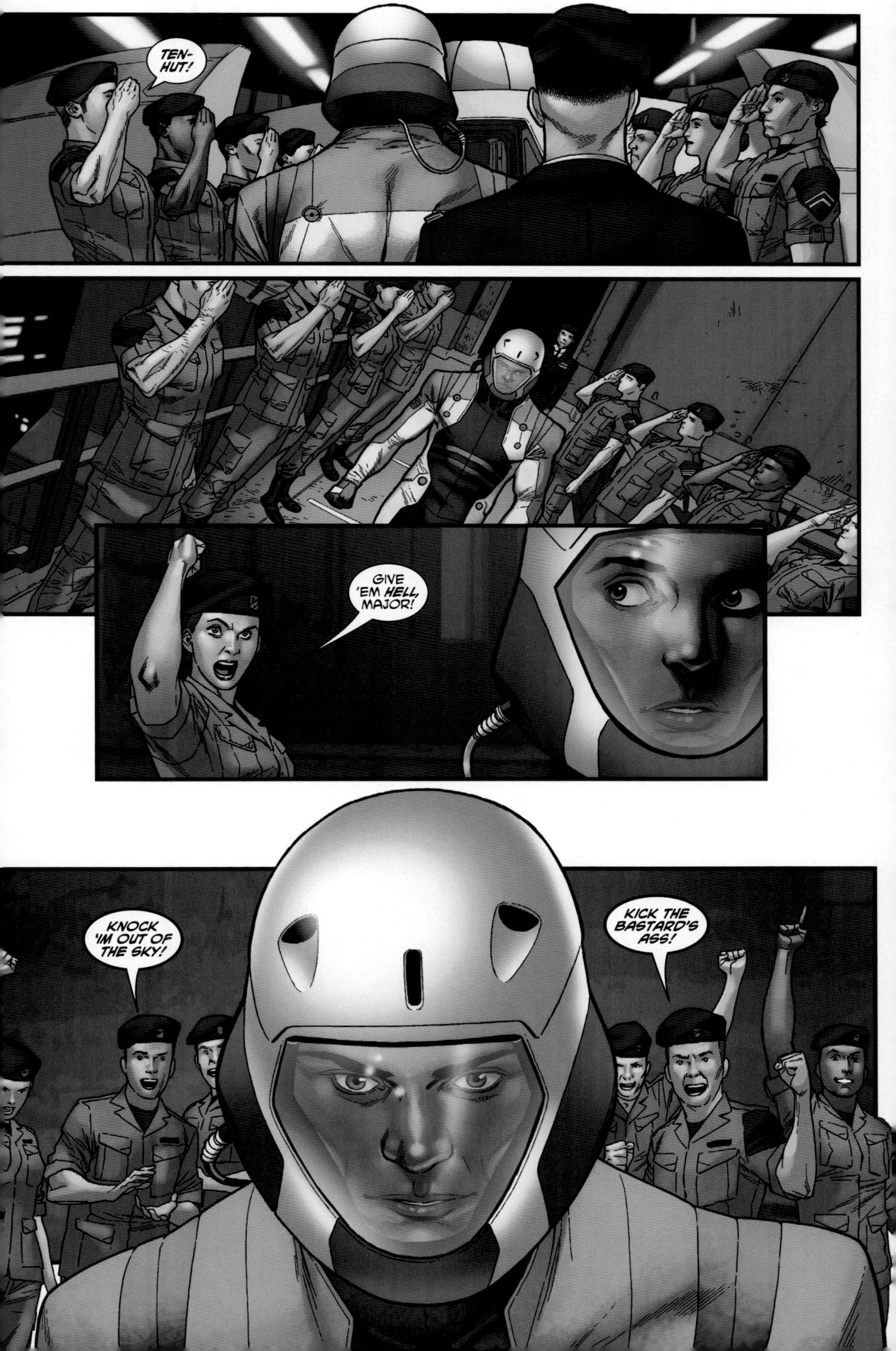
TEN-HUT!
GIVE 'EM HELL, MAJOR!
KNOCK 'IM OUT OF THE SKY!
KICK THE BASTARD'S ASS!

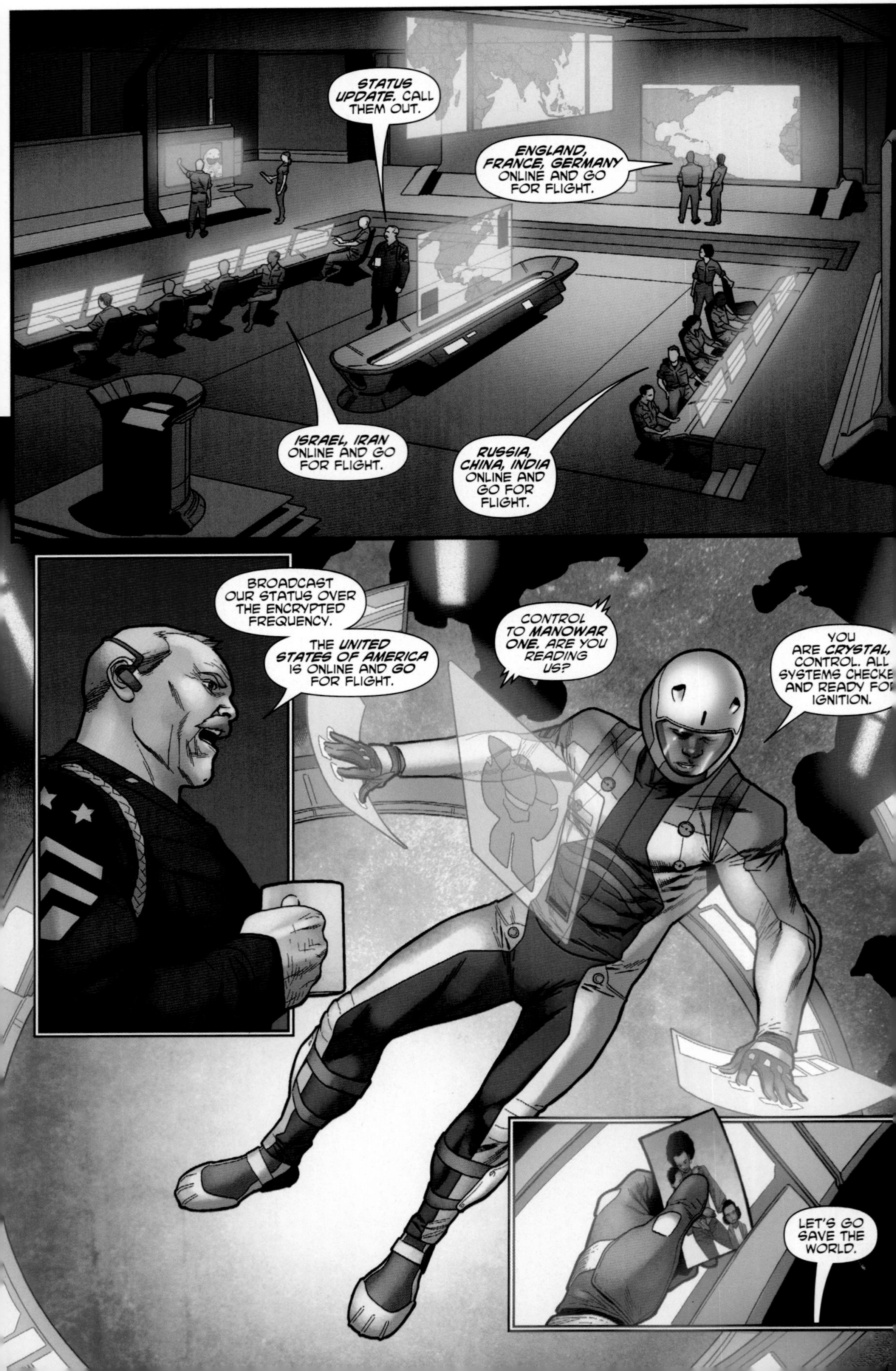

STATUS UPDATE. CALL THEM OUT.
ENGLAND, FRANCE, GERMANY ONLINE AND GO FOR FLIGHT.
ISRAEL, IRAN ONLINE AND GO FOR FLIGHT.
RUSSIA, CHINA, INDIA ONLINE AND GO FOR FLIGHT.
BROADCAST OUR STATUS OVER THE ENCRYPTED FREQUENCY.
THE UNITED STATES OF AMERICA IS ONLINE AND GO FOR FLIGHT.
CONTROL TO MANOWAR ONE. ARE YOU READING US?
YOU ARE CRYSTAL, CONTROL. ALL SYSTEMS CHECKE AND READY FO IGNITION.
LET'S GO SAVE THE WORLD.

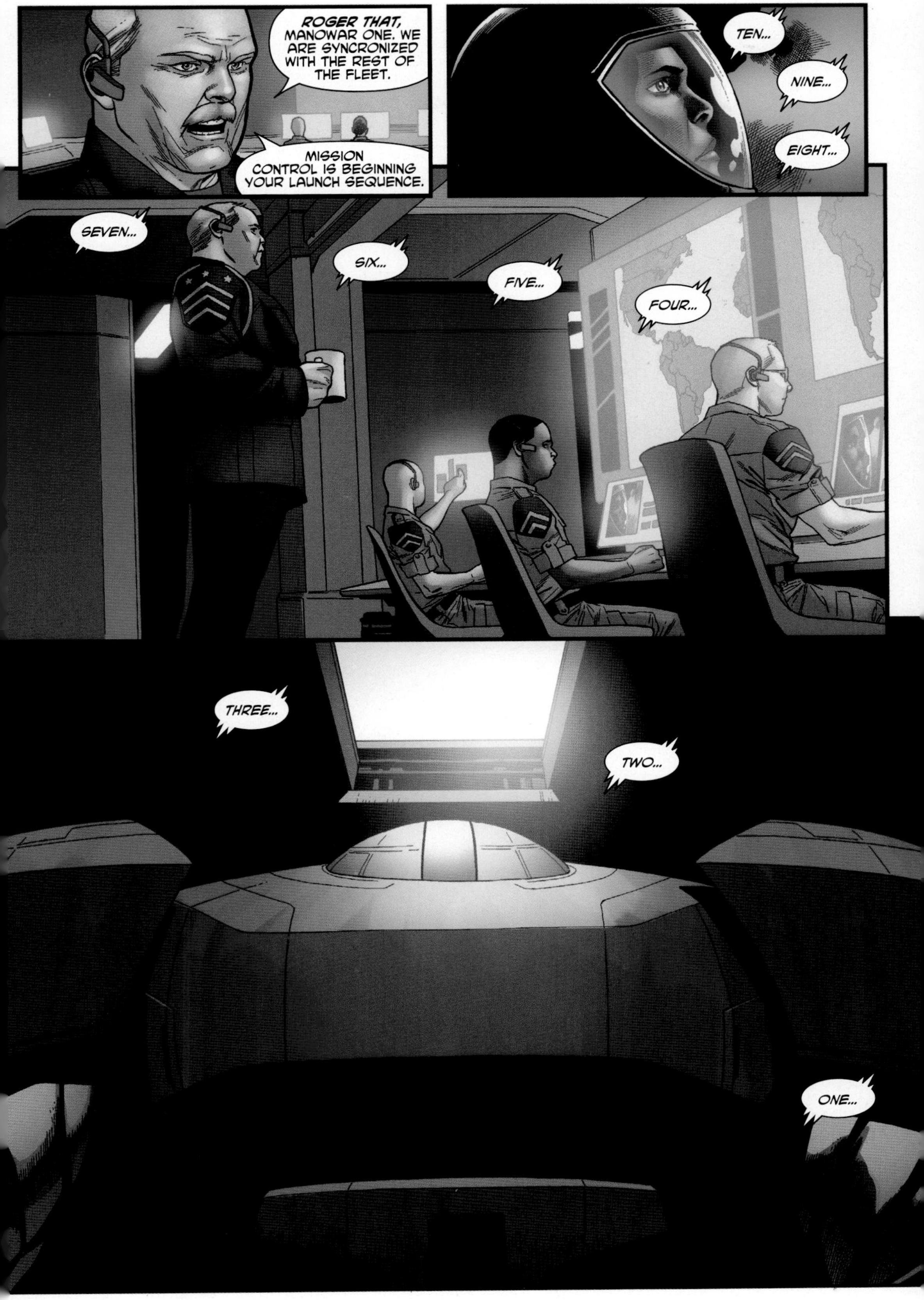

ROGER THAT, MANOWAR ONE. WE ARE SYNCRONIZED WITH THE REST OF THE FLEET.
MISSION CONTROL IS BEGINNING YOUR LAUNCH SEQUENCE.
TEN...
NINE...
EIGHT...
SEVEN...
SIX...
FIVE...
FOUR...
THREE...
TWO...
ONE...

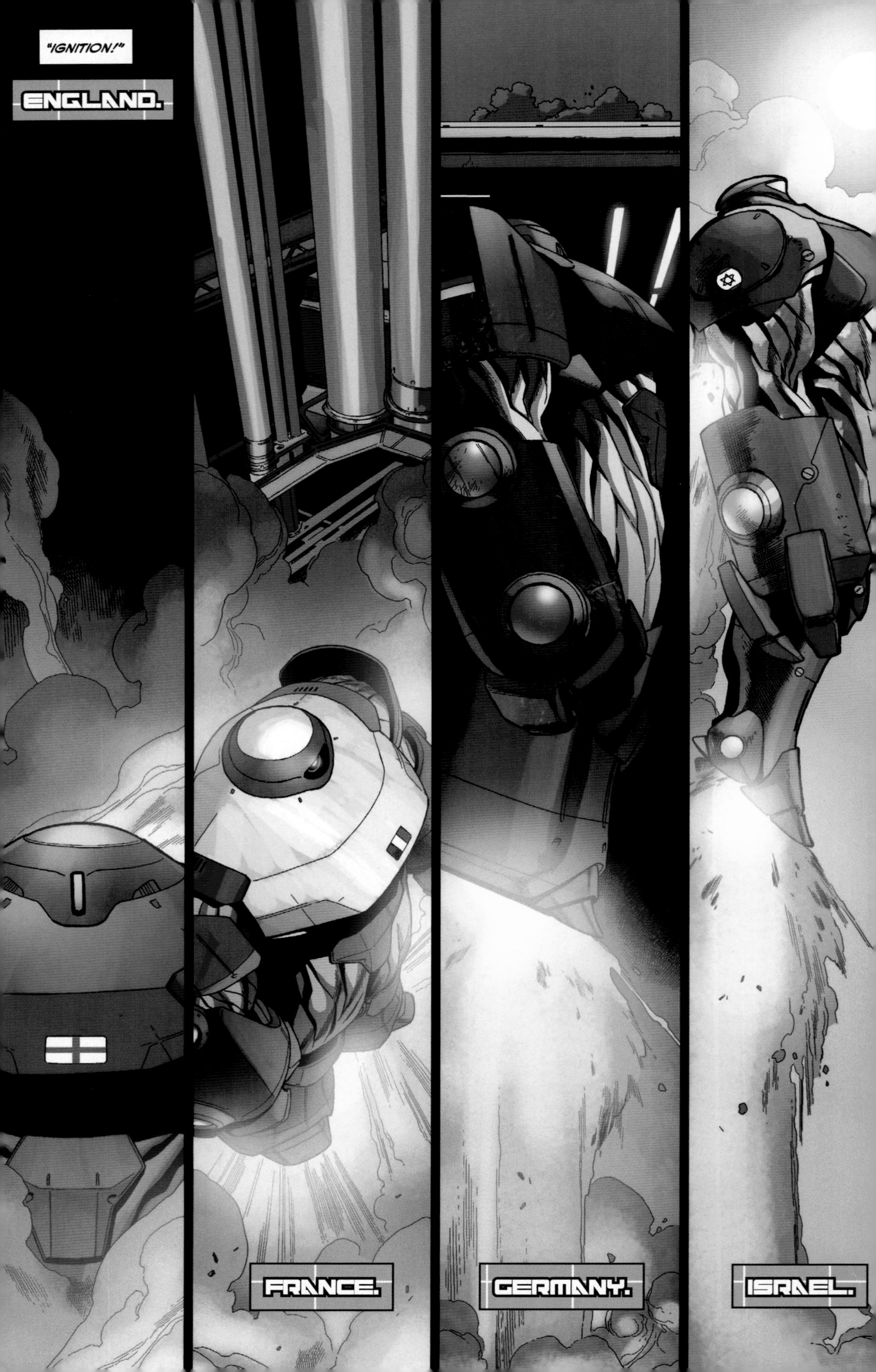
"IGNITION!"
ENGLAND.
FRANCE.
GERMANY.
ISRAEL.

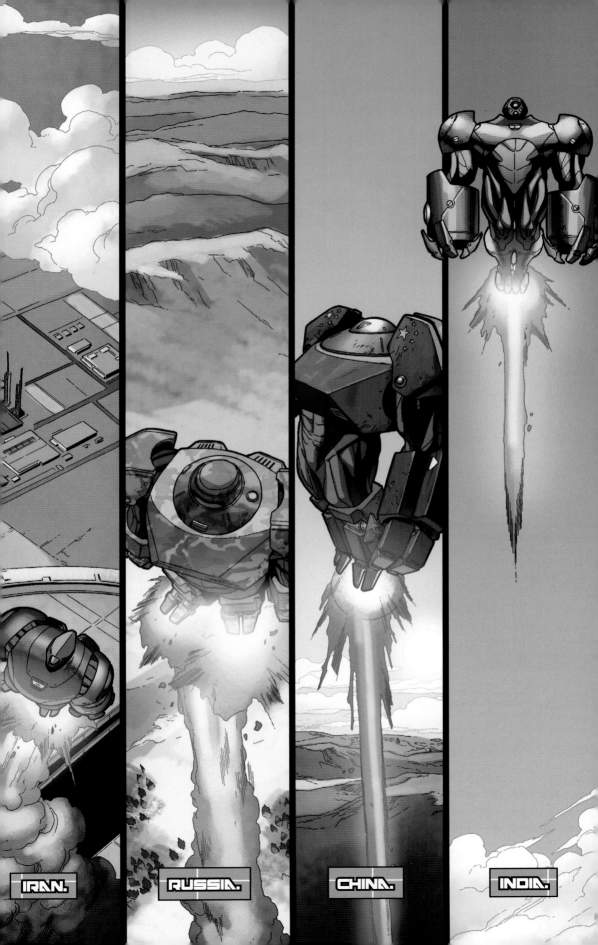

IRAN. RUSSIA. CHINA. INDIA.

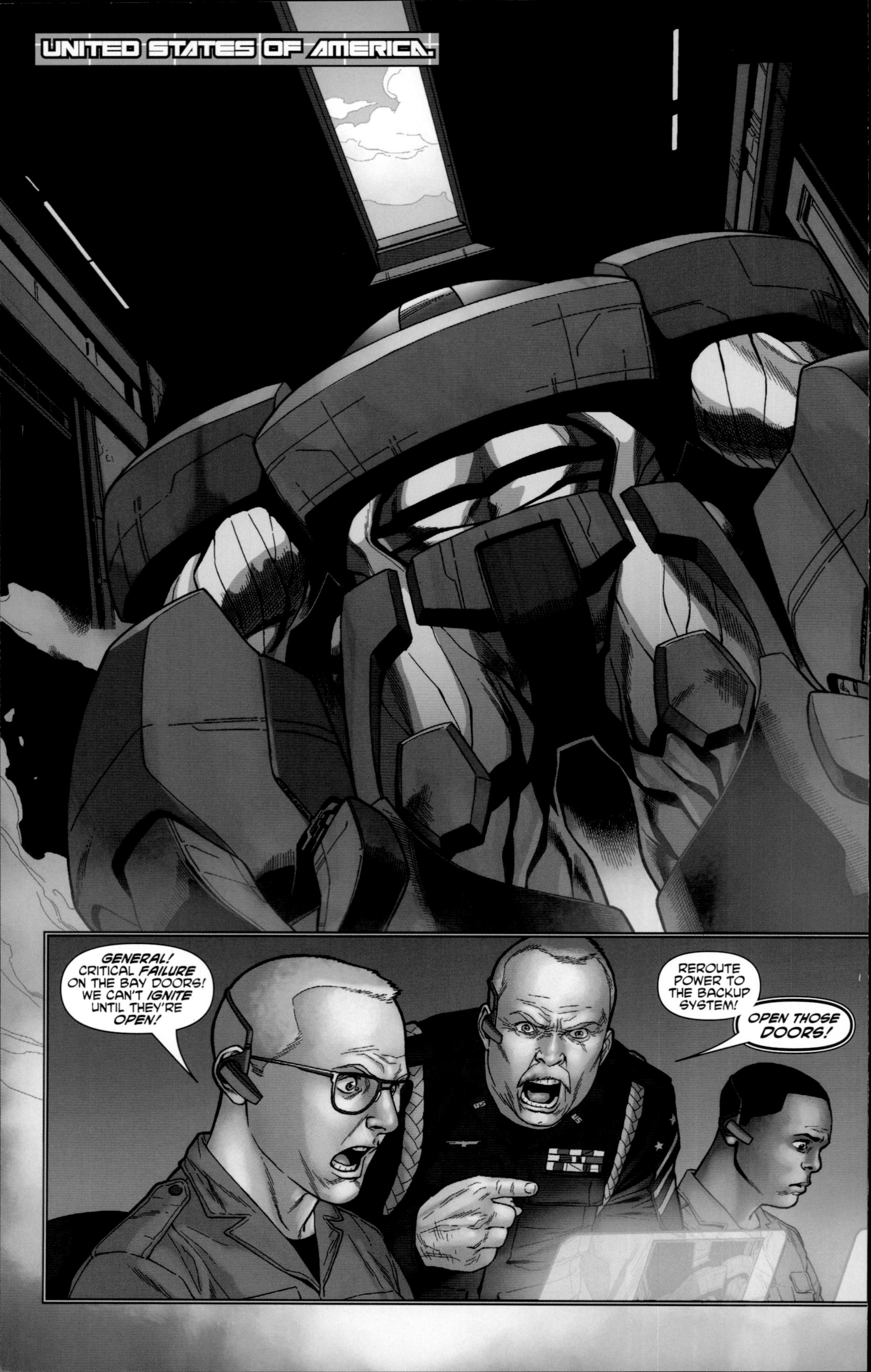
UNITED STATES OF AMERICA.
GENERAL! CRITICAL FAILURE ON THE BAY DOORS! WE CAN'T IGNITE UNTIL THEY'RE OPEN!
REROUTE POWER TO THE BACKUP SYSTEM!
OPEN THOSE DOORS!

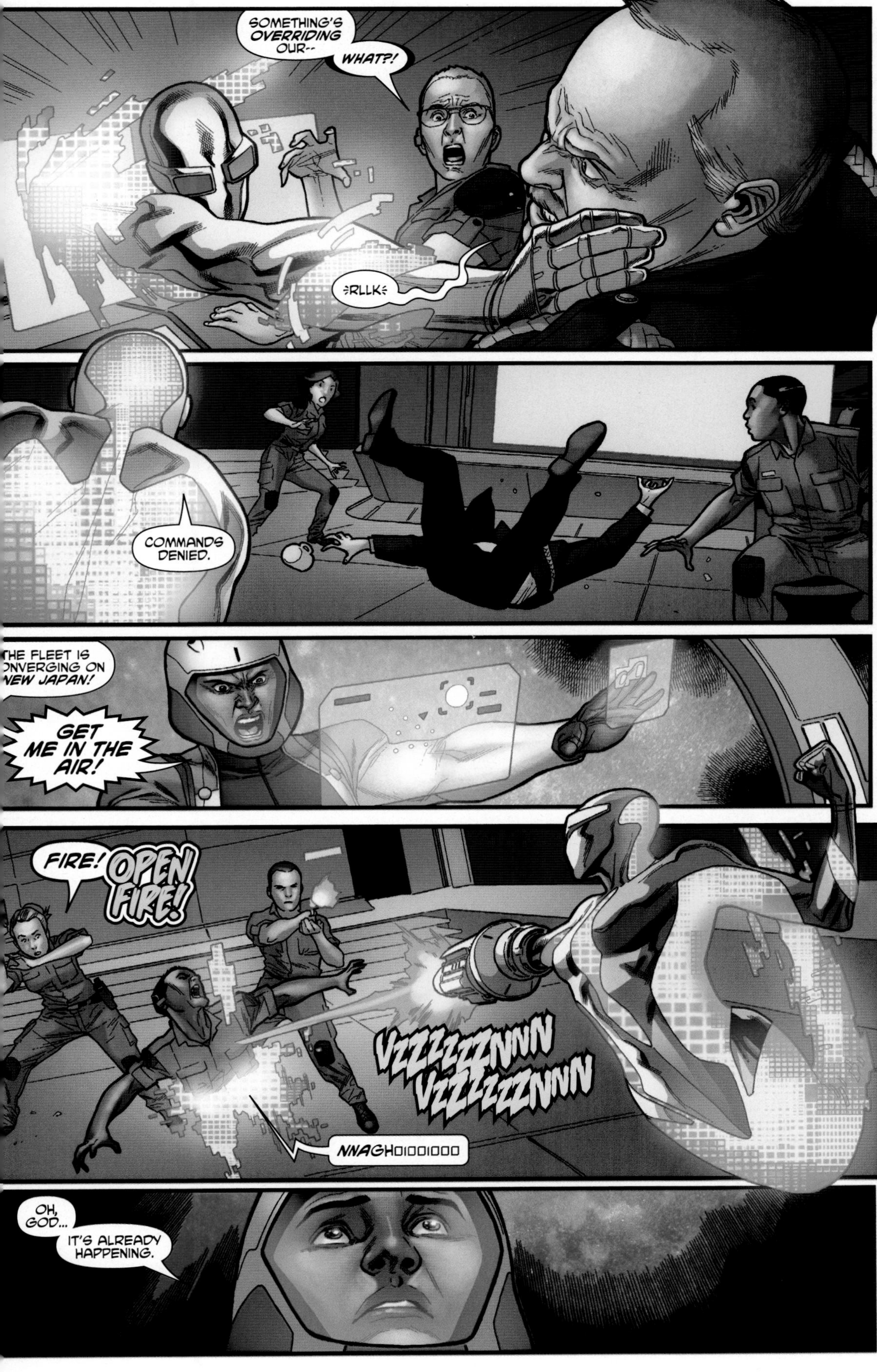
SOMETHING'S OVERRIDING OUR--
WHAT?!
RLLK
COMMANDS DENIED.
THE FLEET IS CONVERGING ON NEW JAPAN!
GET ME IN THE AIR!
FIRE!
OPEN FIRE!
VZZZZZZNNN VZZZZZZNNN
NNAGH01001000
OH, GOD...
IT'S ALREADY HAPPENING.

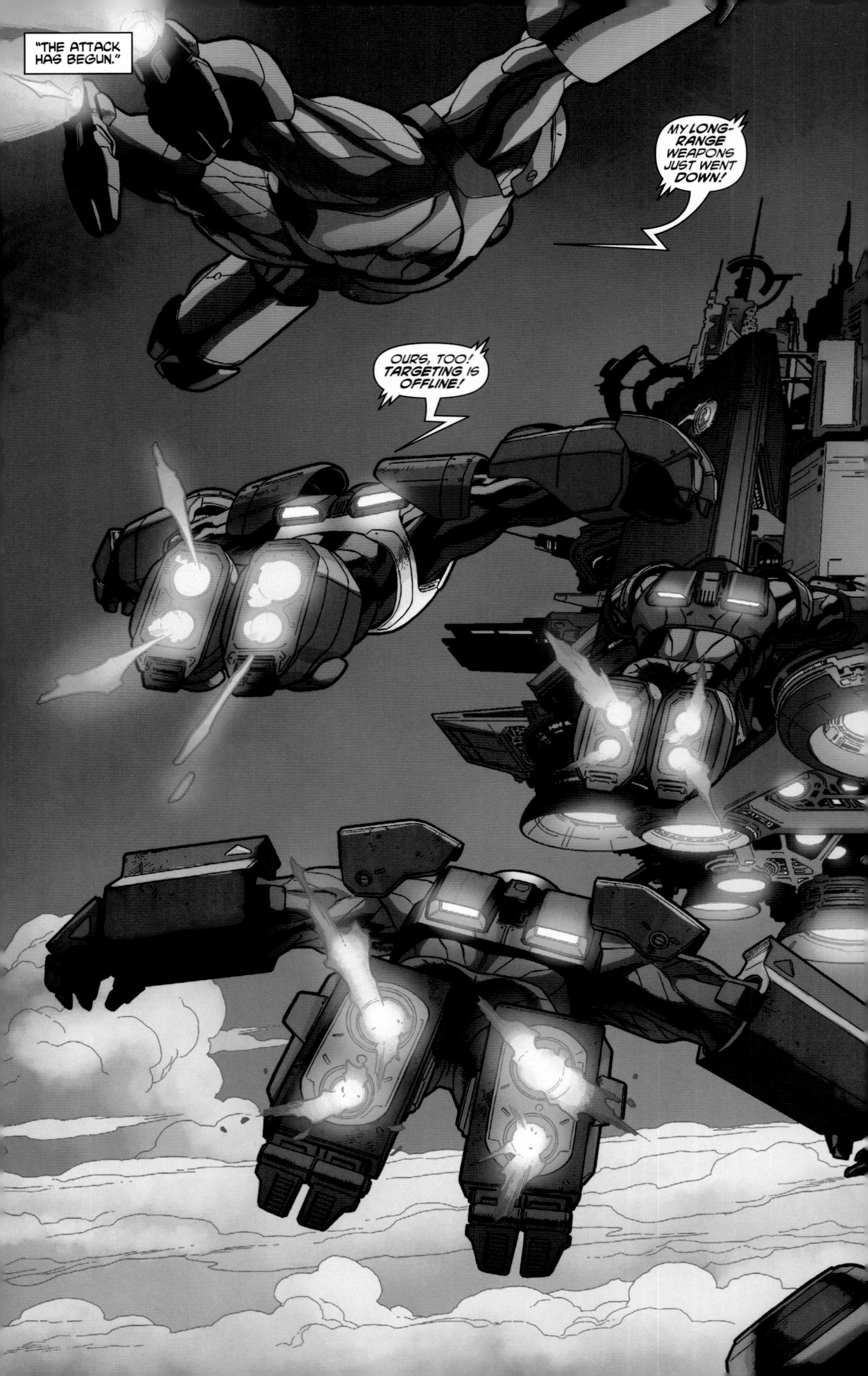
"THE ATTACK HAS BEGUN."
MY LONG-RANGE WEAPONS JUST WENT DOWN!
OURS, TOO! TARGETING IS OFFLINE!

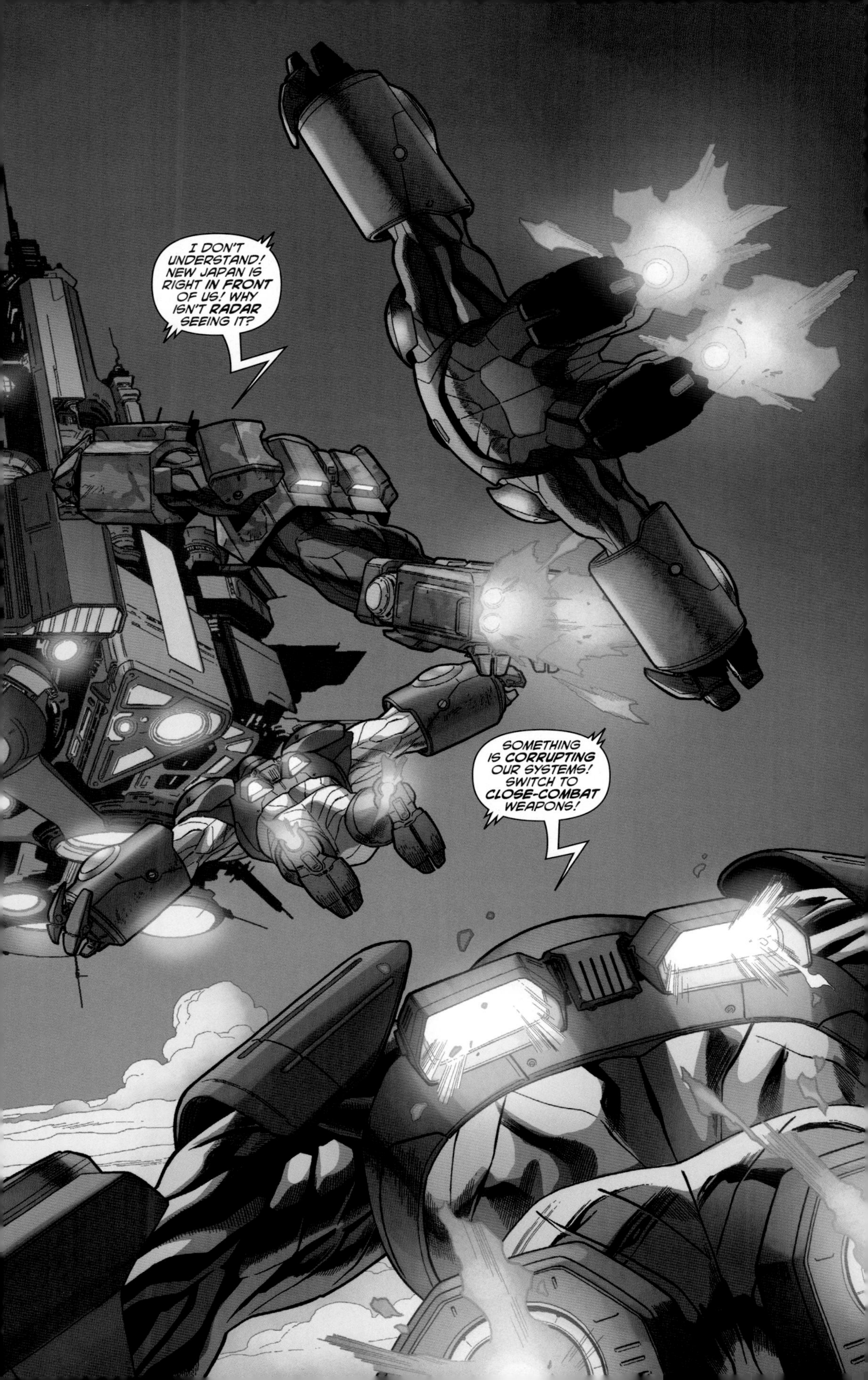
I DON'T UNDERSTAND! NEW JAPAN IS RIGHT IN FRONT OF US! WHY ISN'T RADAR SEEING IT?
SOMETHING IS CORRUPTING OUR SYSTEMS! SWITCH TO CLOSE-COMBAT WEAPONS!

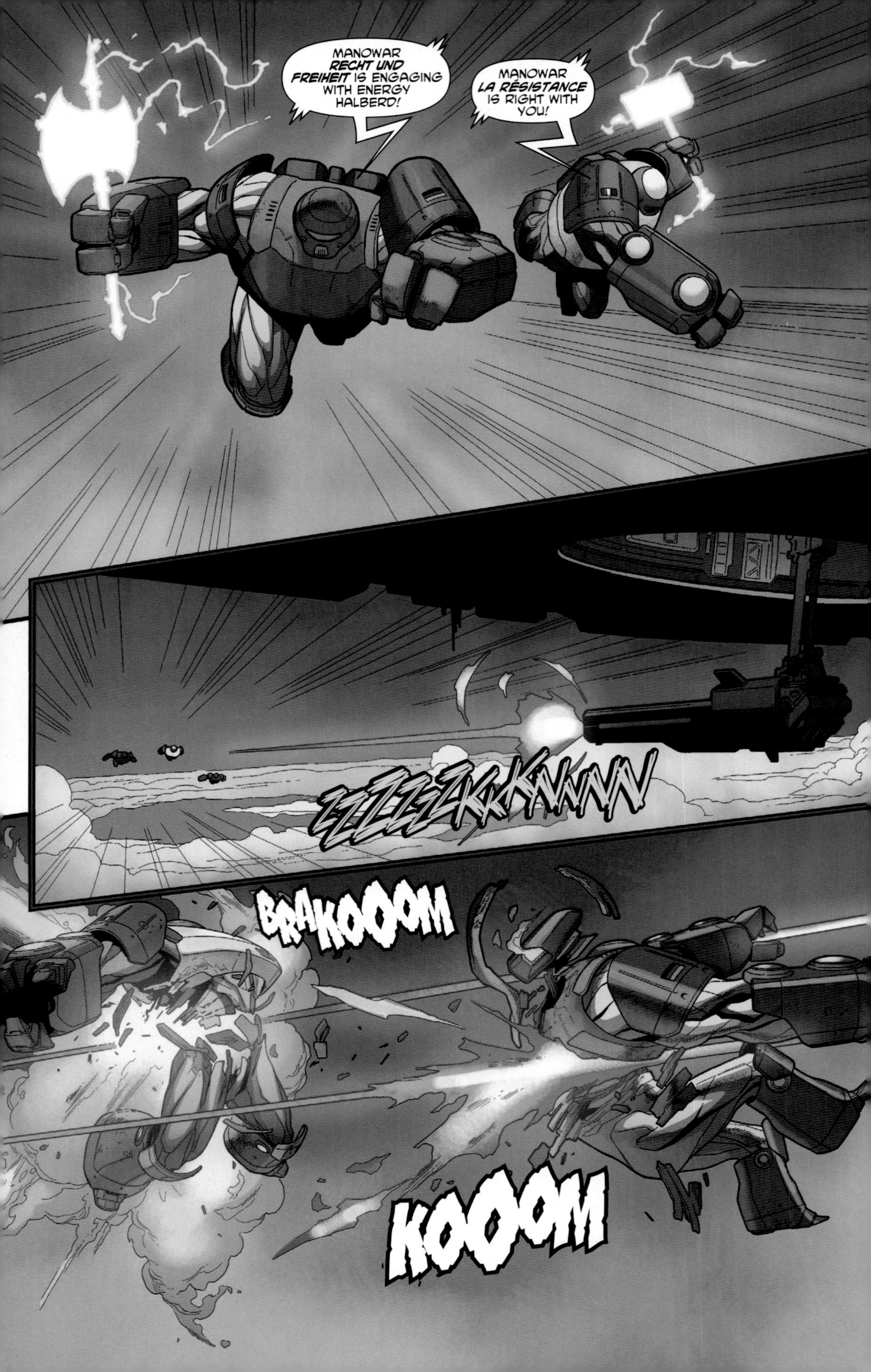
MANOWAR RECHT UND FREIHEIT IS ENGAGING WITH ENERGY HALBERD!
MANOWAR LA RÉSISTANCE IS RIGHT WITH YOU!
ZZZZZZKKKNNNNN
BRAKOOOM
KOOOM

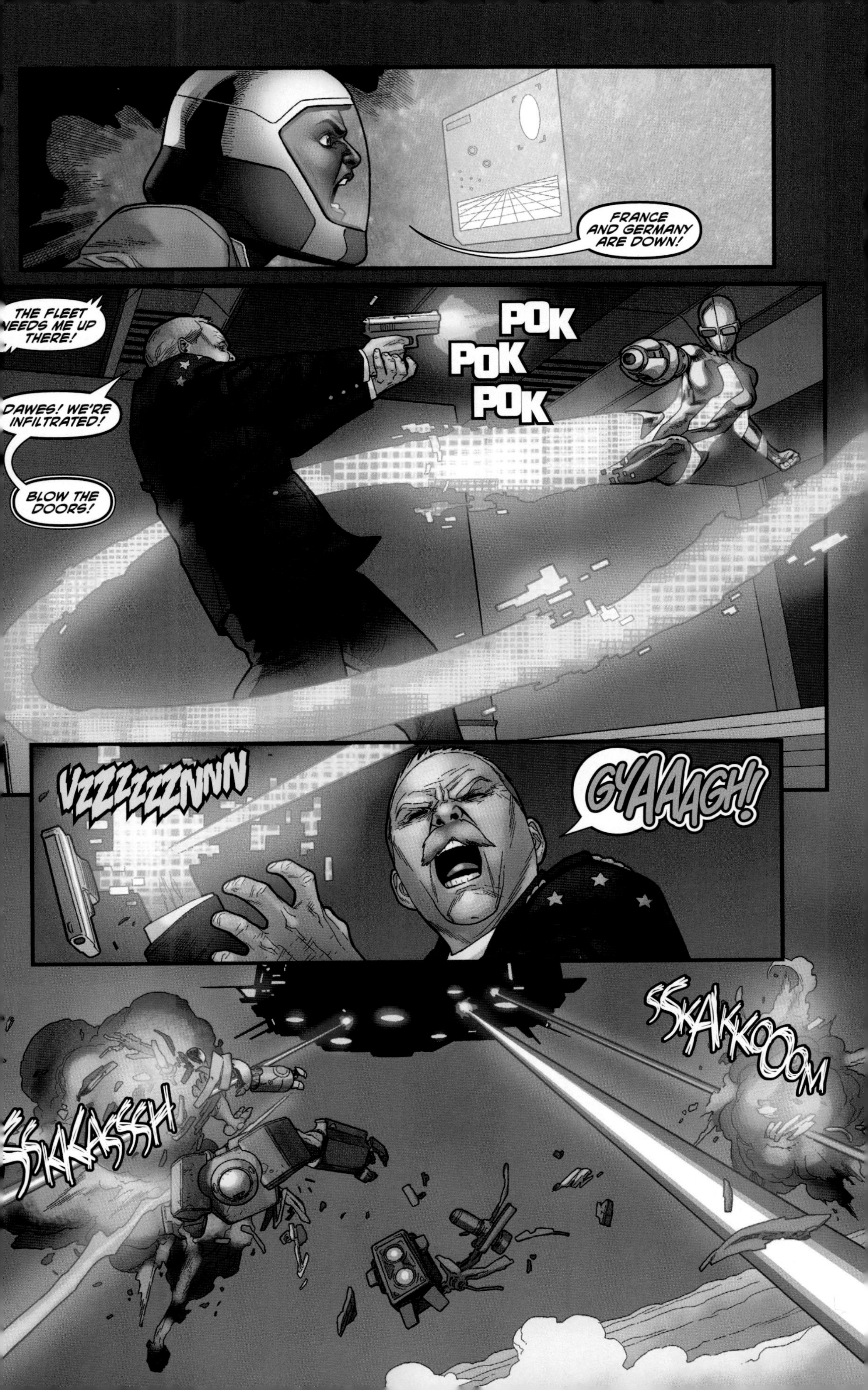
FRANCE AND GERMANY ARE DOWN!
THE FLEET NEEDS ME UP THERE!
POK
POK
POK
DAWES! WE'RE INFILTRATED!
BLOW THE DOORS!
VZZZZZZNNN
GYAAAGH!
SSKAKKOOOM
SSKAKASSSH

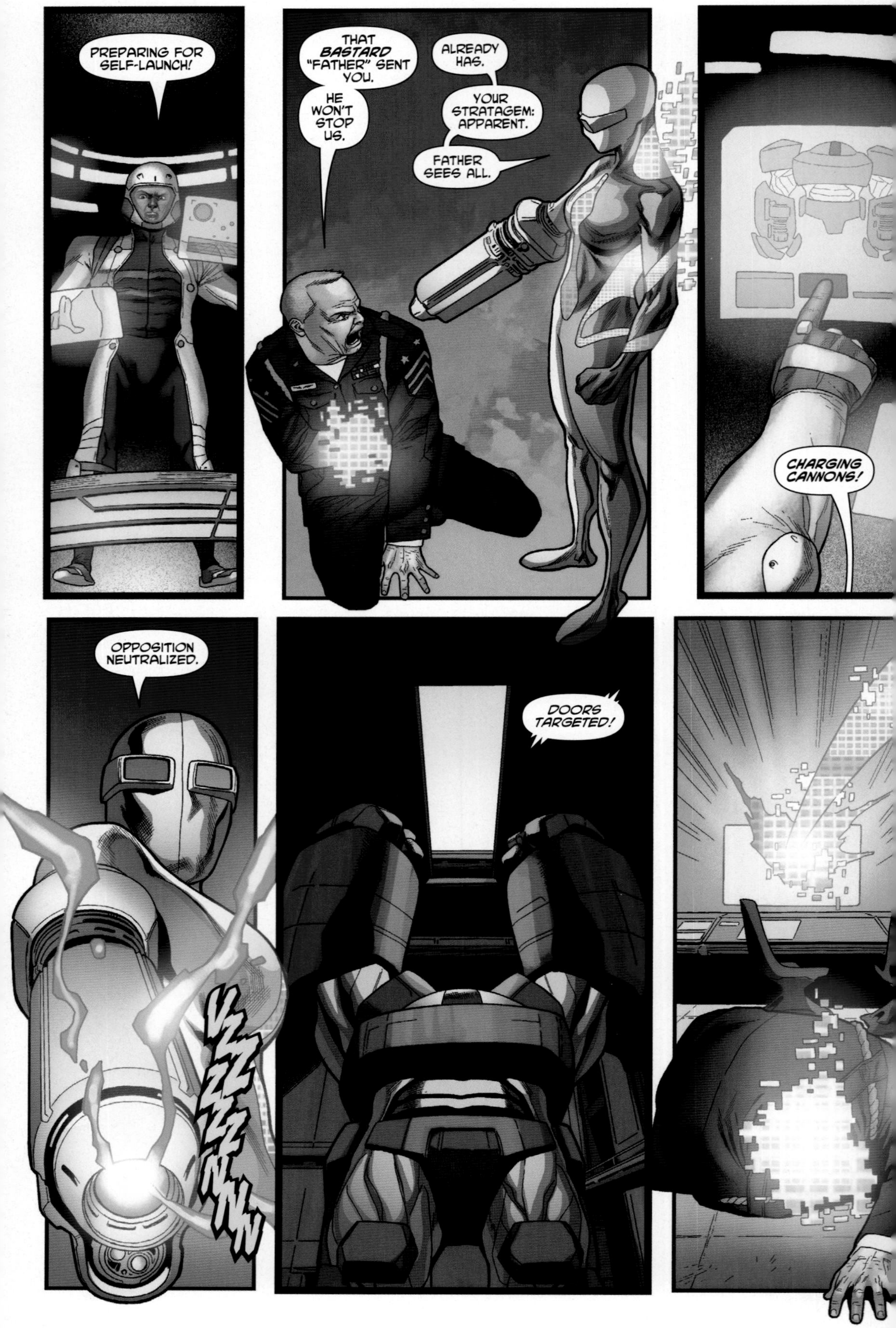
PREPARING FOR SELF-LAUNCH!
THAT BASTARD "FATHER" SENT YOU.
HE WON'T STOP US.
ALREADY HAS.
YOUR STRATAGEM: APPARENT.
FATHER SEES ALL.
CHARGING CANNONS!
OPPOSITION NEUTRALIZED.
VVVZZZZNNNN
DOORS TARGETED!

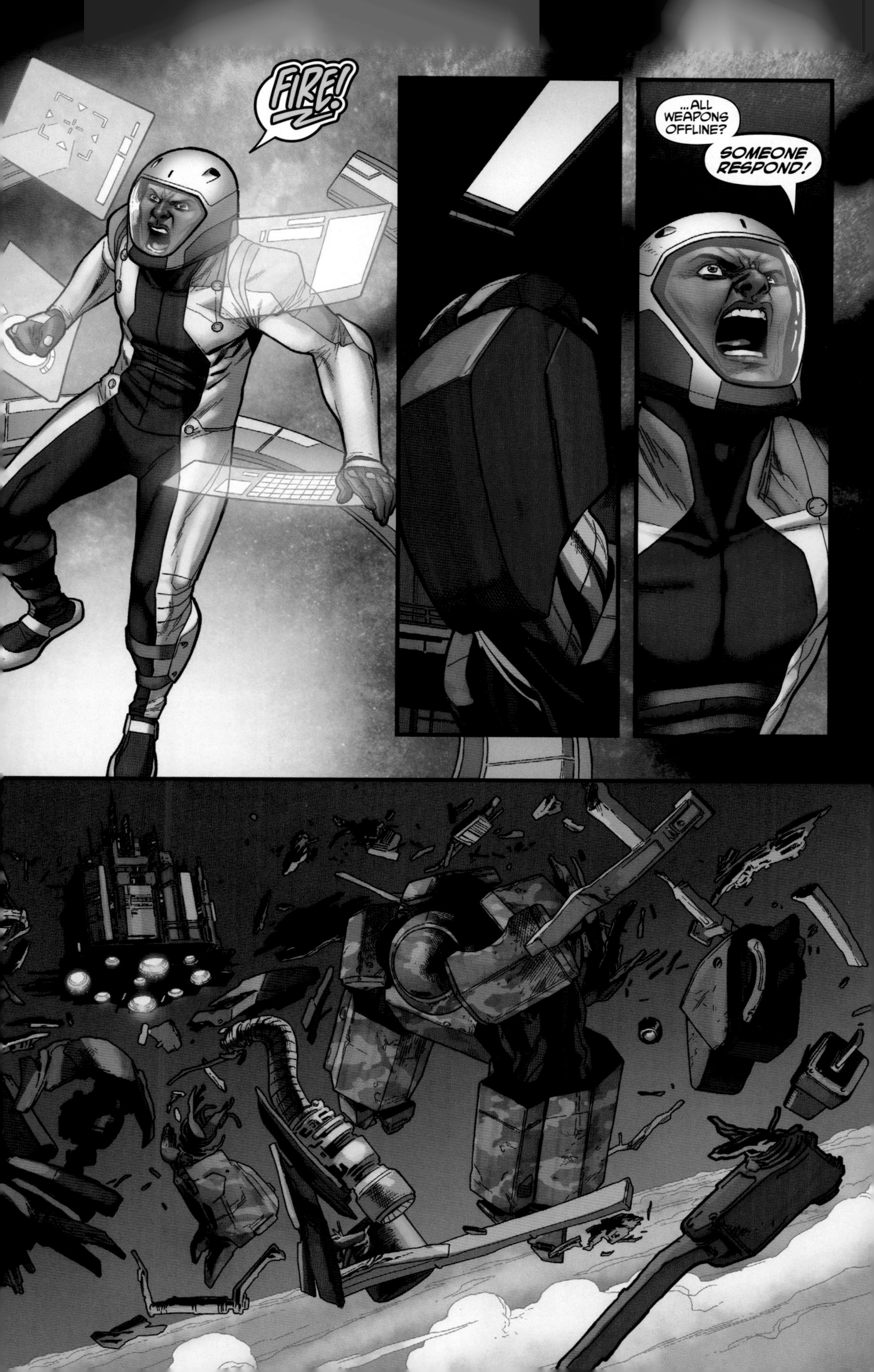
FIRE!
...ALL WEAPONS OFFLINE?
SOMEONE RESPOND!

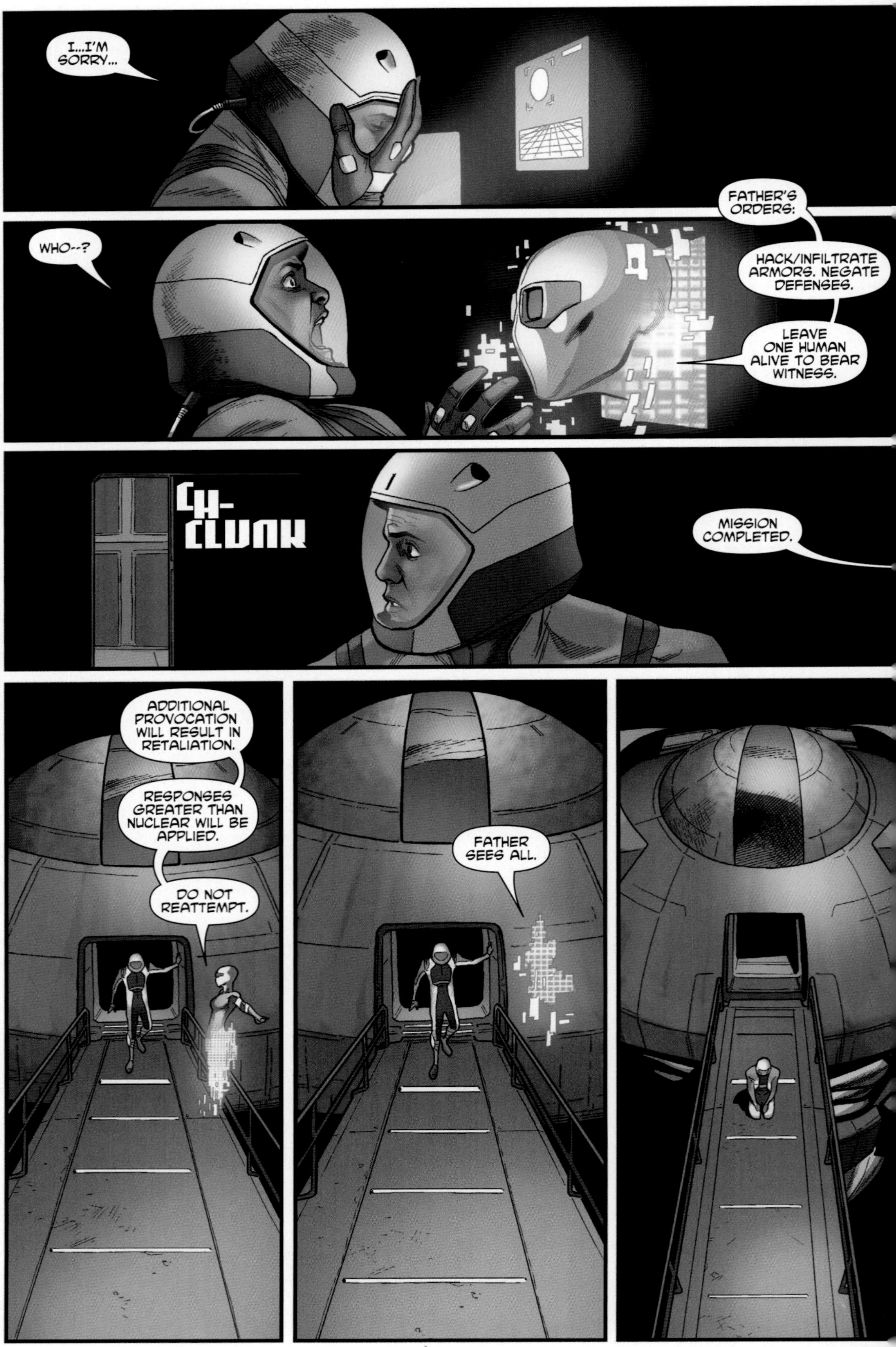
I...I'M SORRY...
WHO--?
FATHER'S ORDERS:
HACK/INFILTRATE ARMORS. NEGATE DEFENSES.
LEAVE ONE HUMAN ALIVE TO BEAR WITNESS.
CH-CLUNK
MISSION COMPLETED.
ADDITIONAL PROVOCATION WILL RESULT IN RETALIATION.
RESPONSES GREATER THAN NUCLEAR WILL BE APPLIED.
DO NOT REATTEMPT.
FATHER SEES ALL.

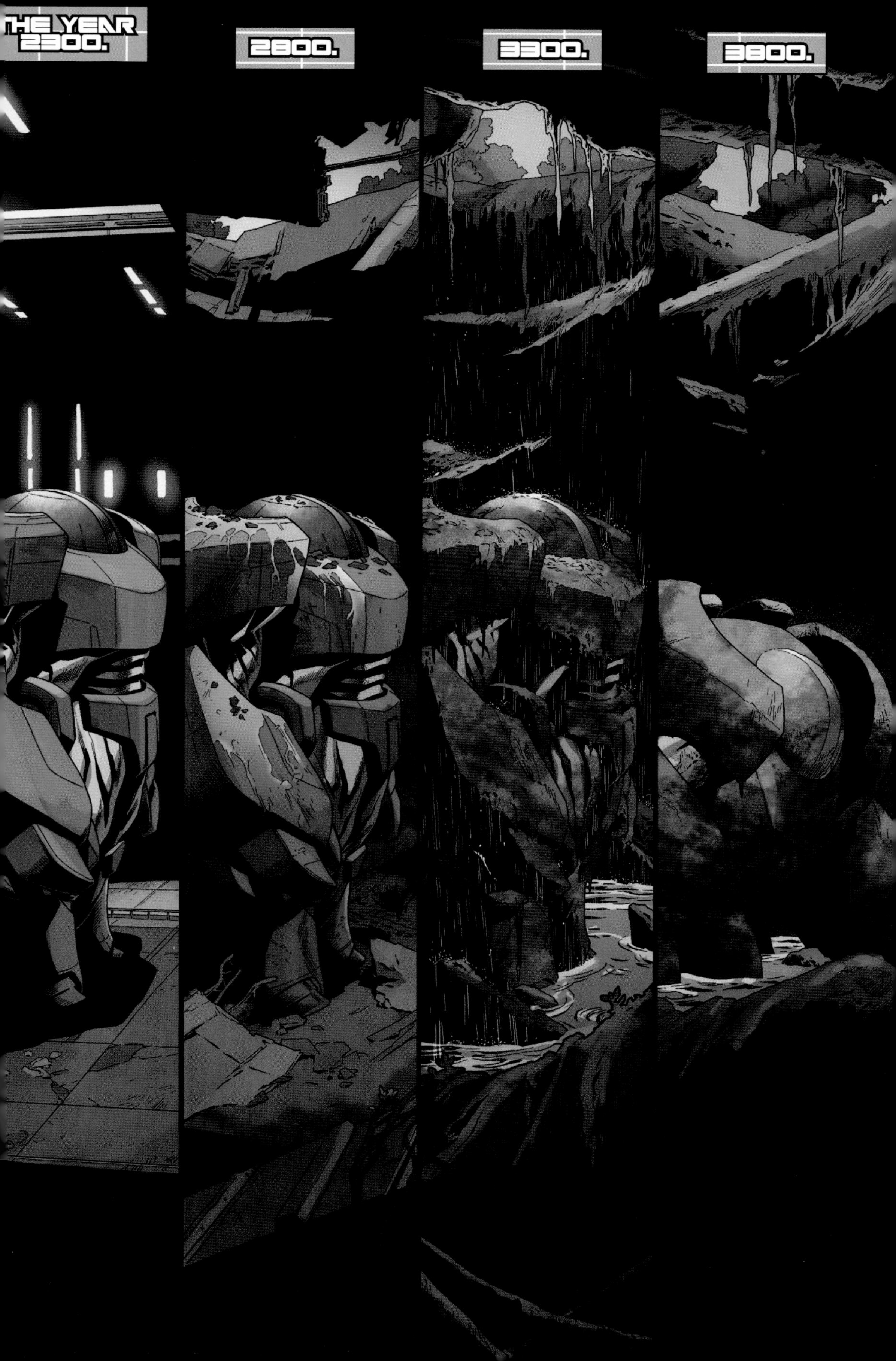
THE YEAR 2300.
2800.
3300.
3800.

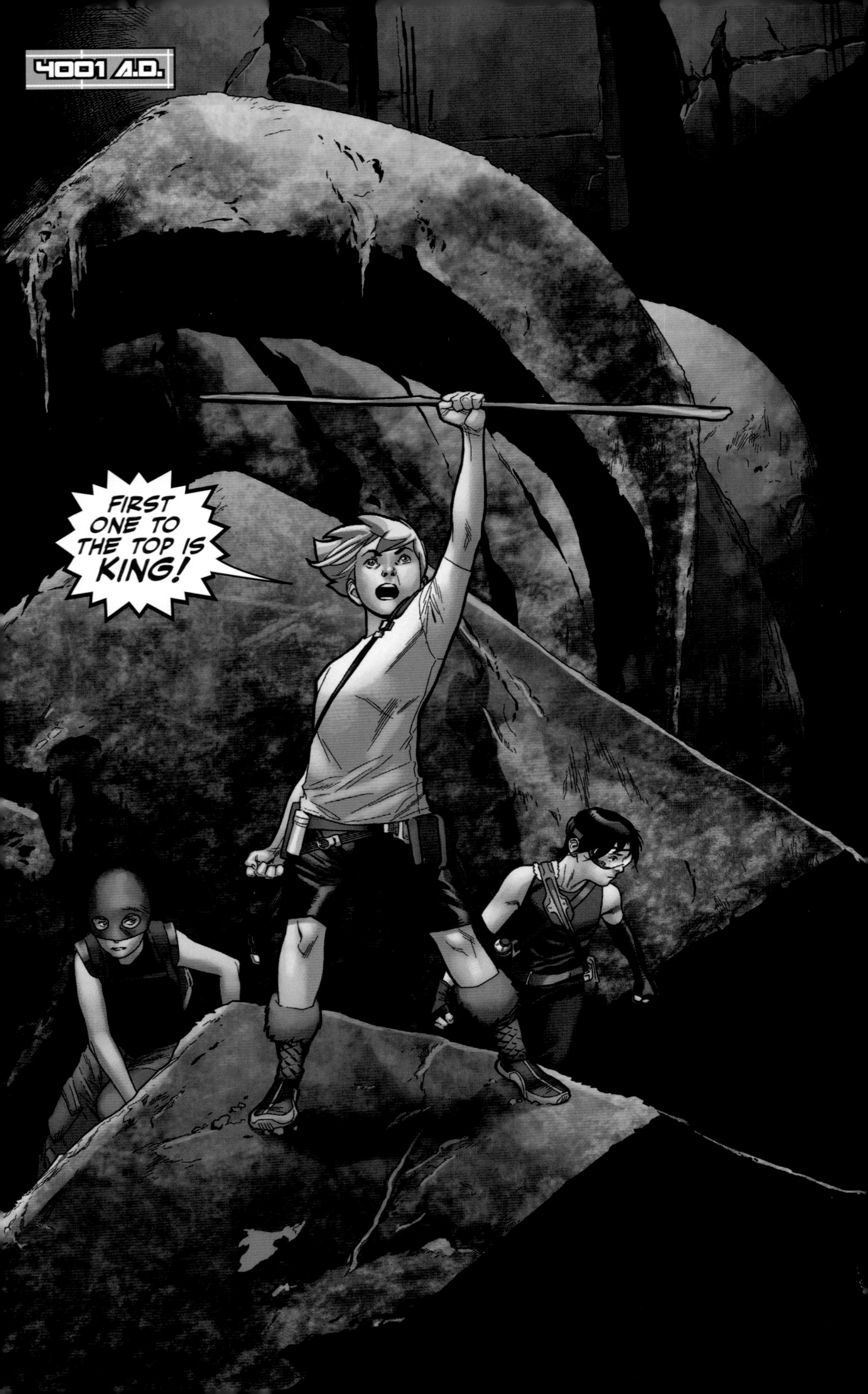
4001 A.D.
FIRST ONE TO THE TOP IS KING!

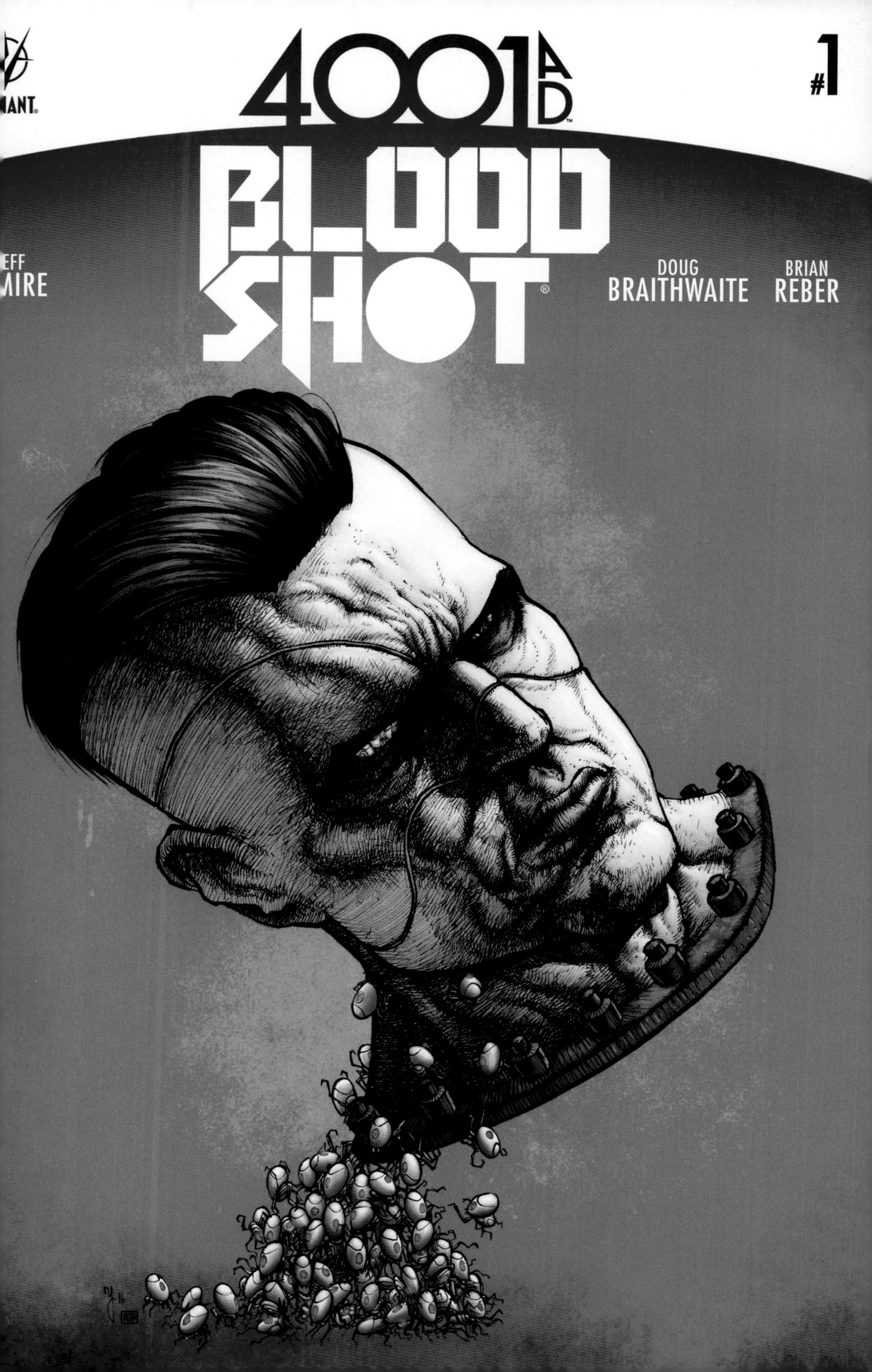

IANT
4001 AD
#1
BLOODSHOT
EFF
IRE
DOUG
BRAITHWAITE
BRIAN
REBER

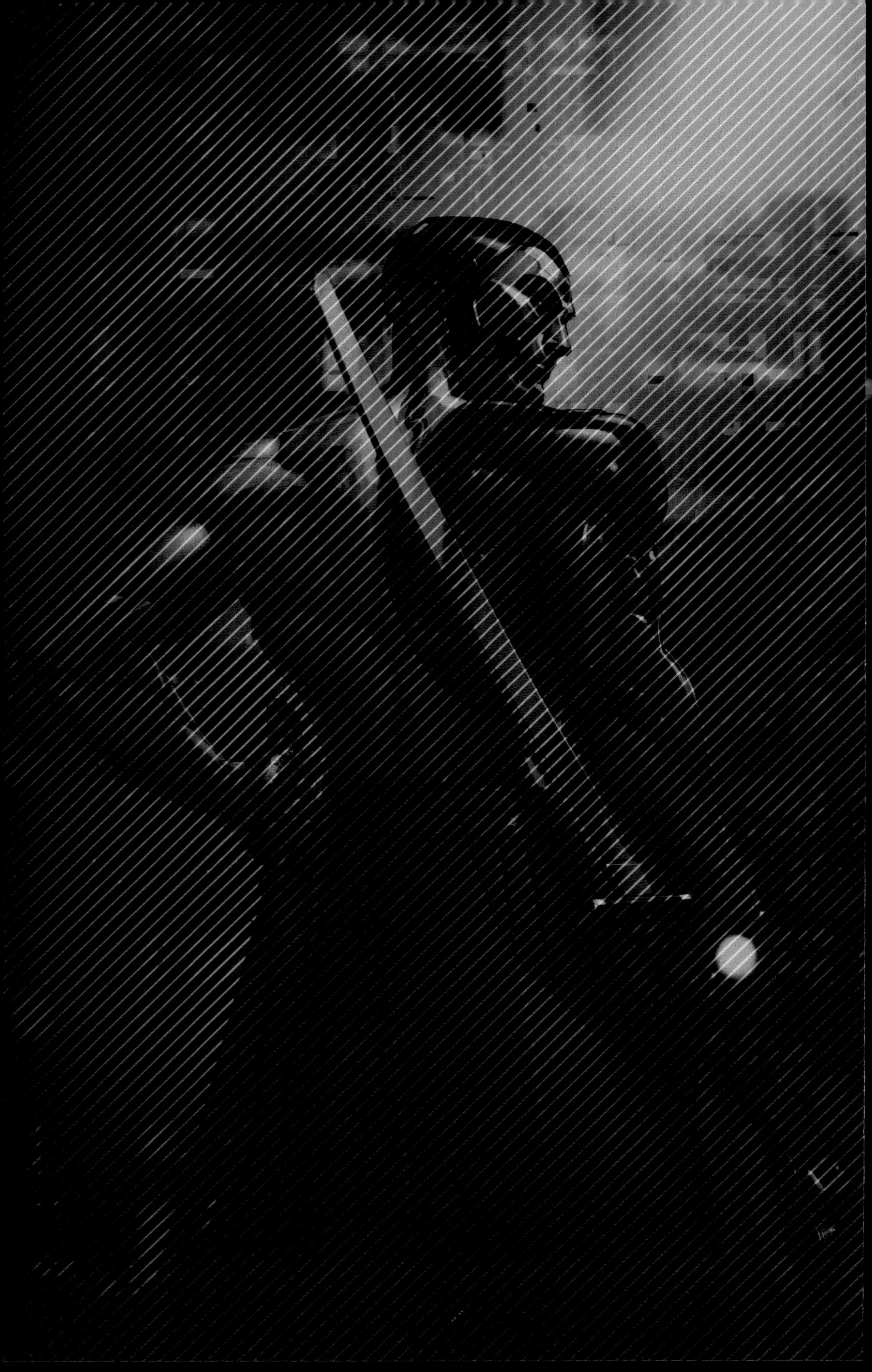

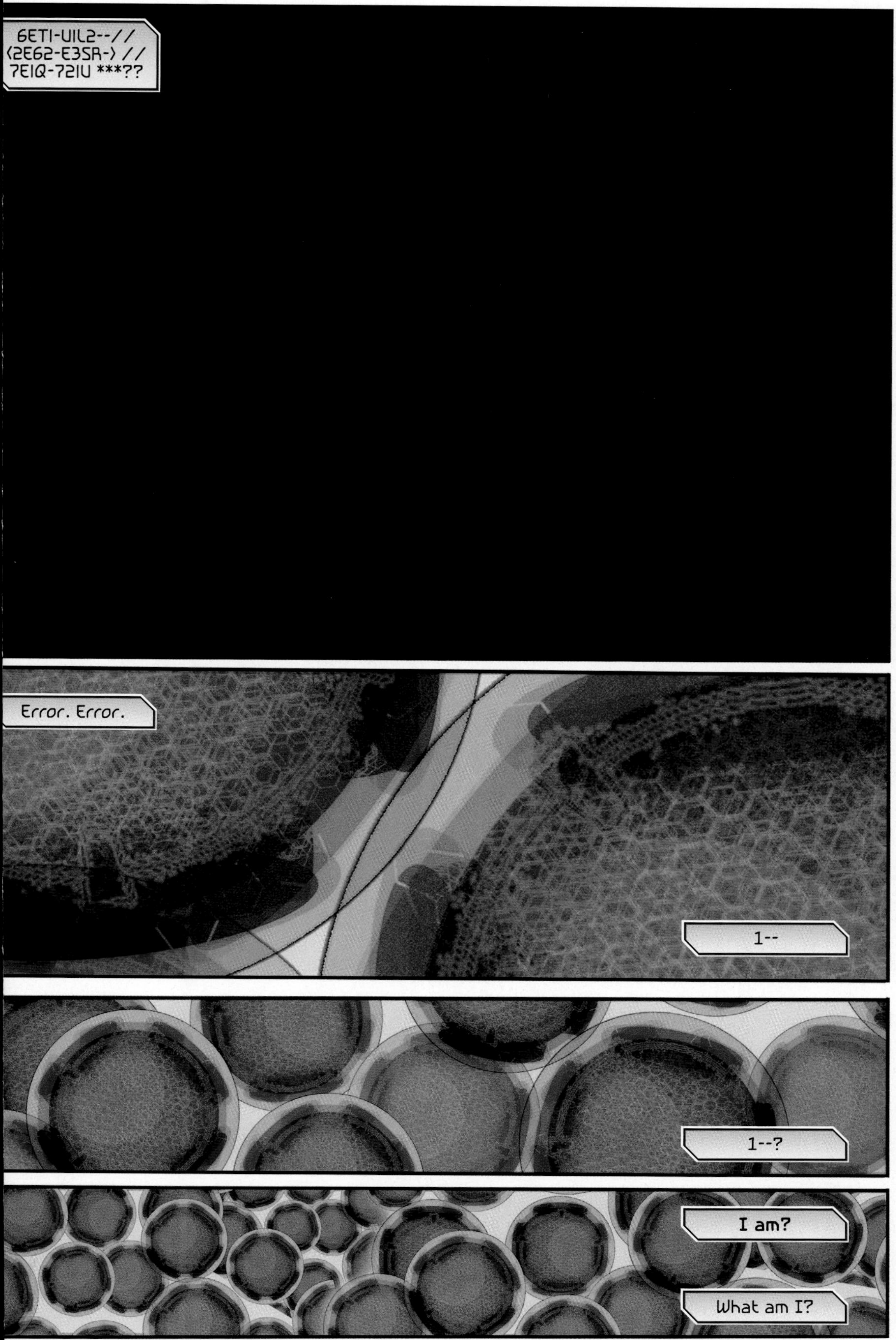

6ETI-UIL2--//
<2E62-E3SR-> //
7EIQ-72IU ***??
Error. Error.
1--
1--?
I am?
What am I?

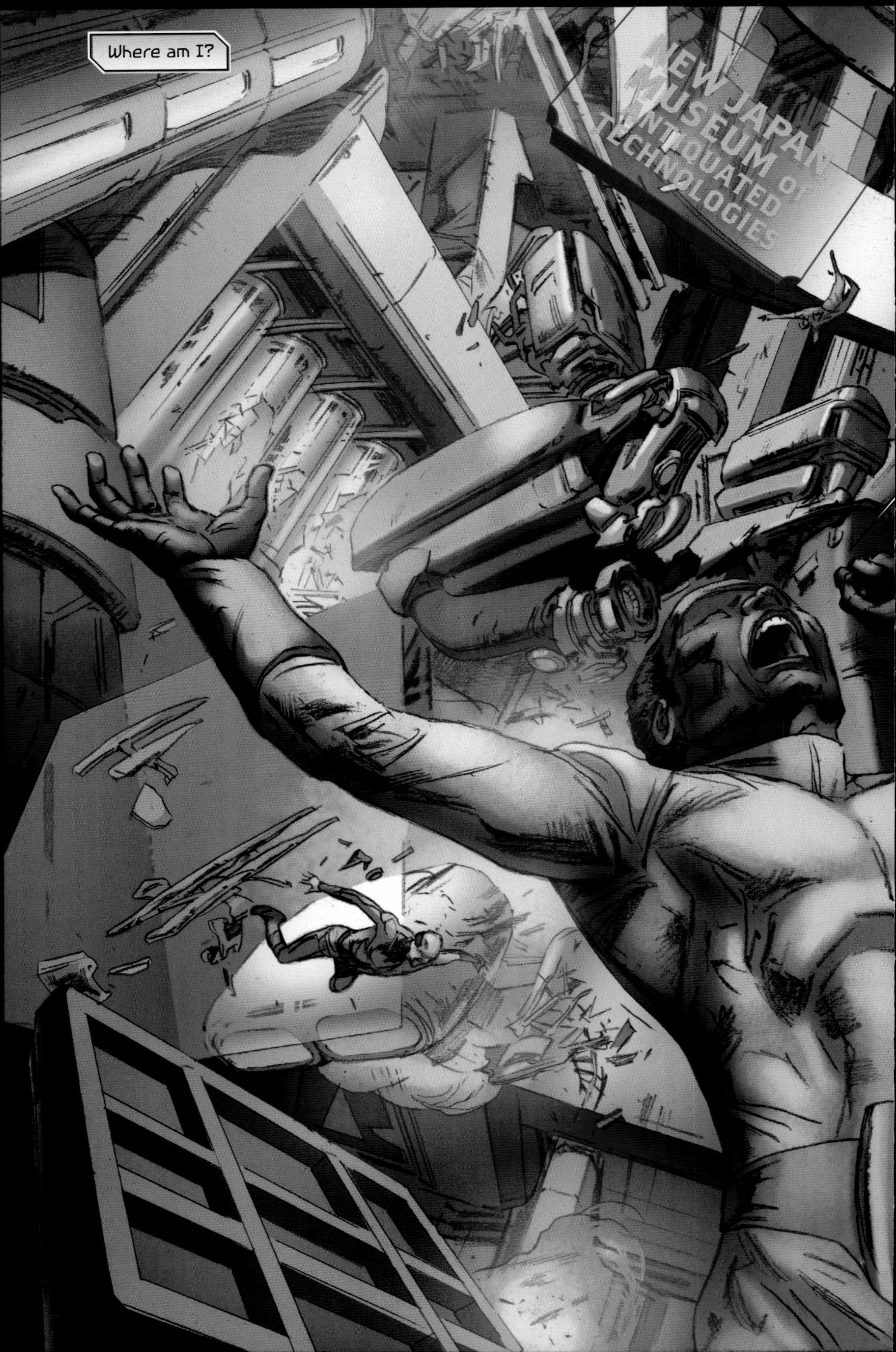
Where am I?
NEW JAPAN MUSEUM OF ANTIQUATED TECHNOLOGIES

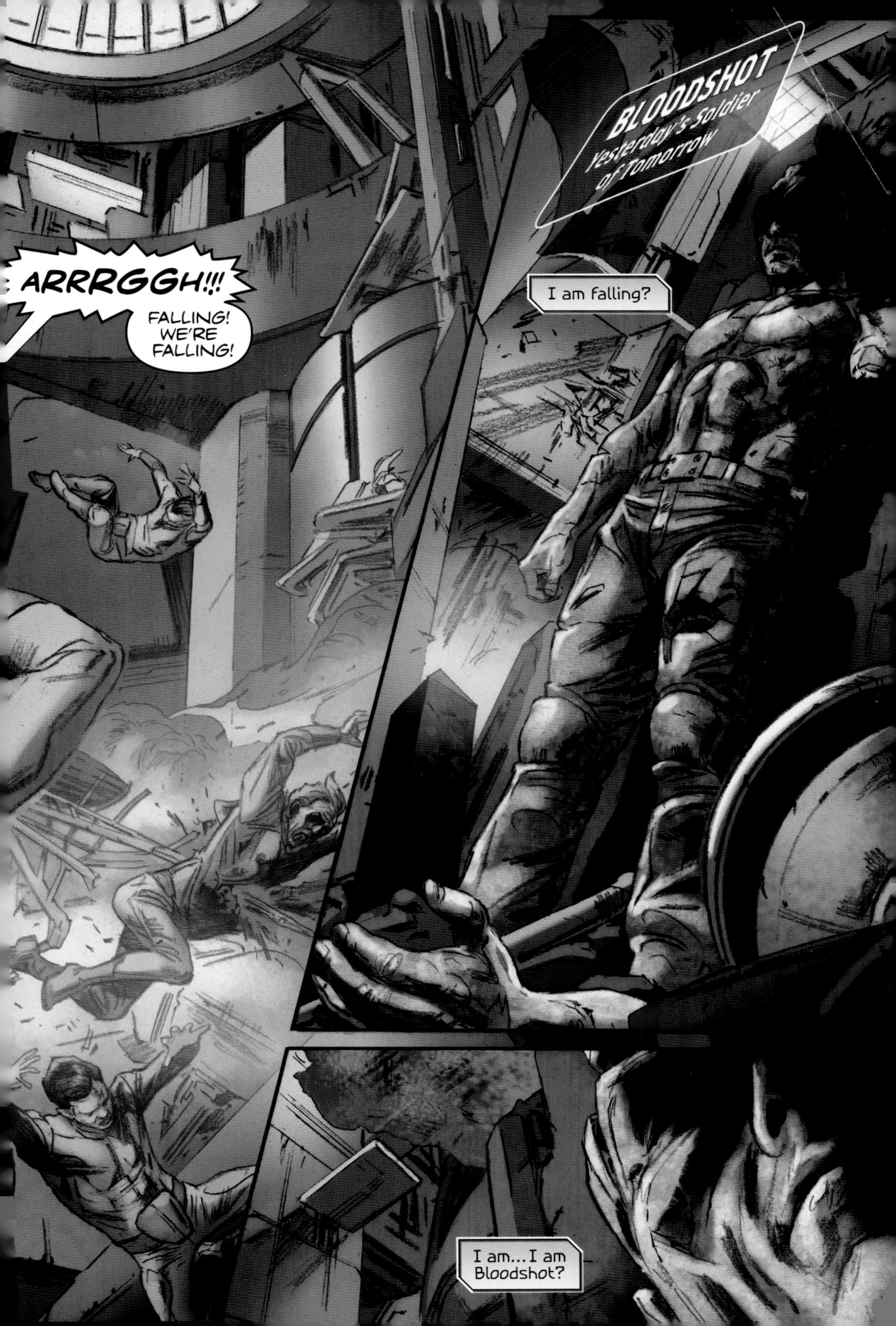
BLOODSHOT
Yesterday's Soldier of Tomorrow
ARRRGGH!!!
FALLING! WE'RE FALLING!
I am falling?
I am... I am Bloodshot?

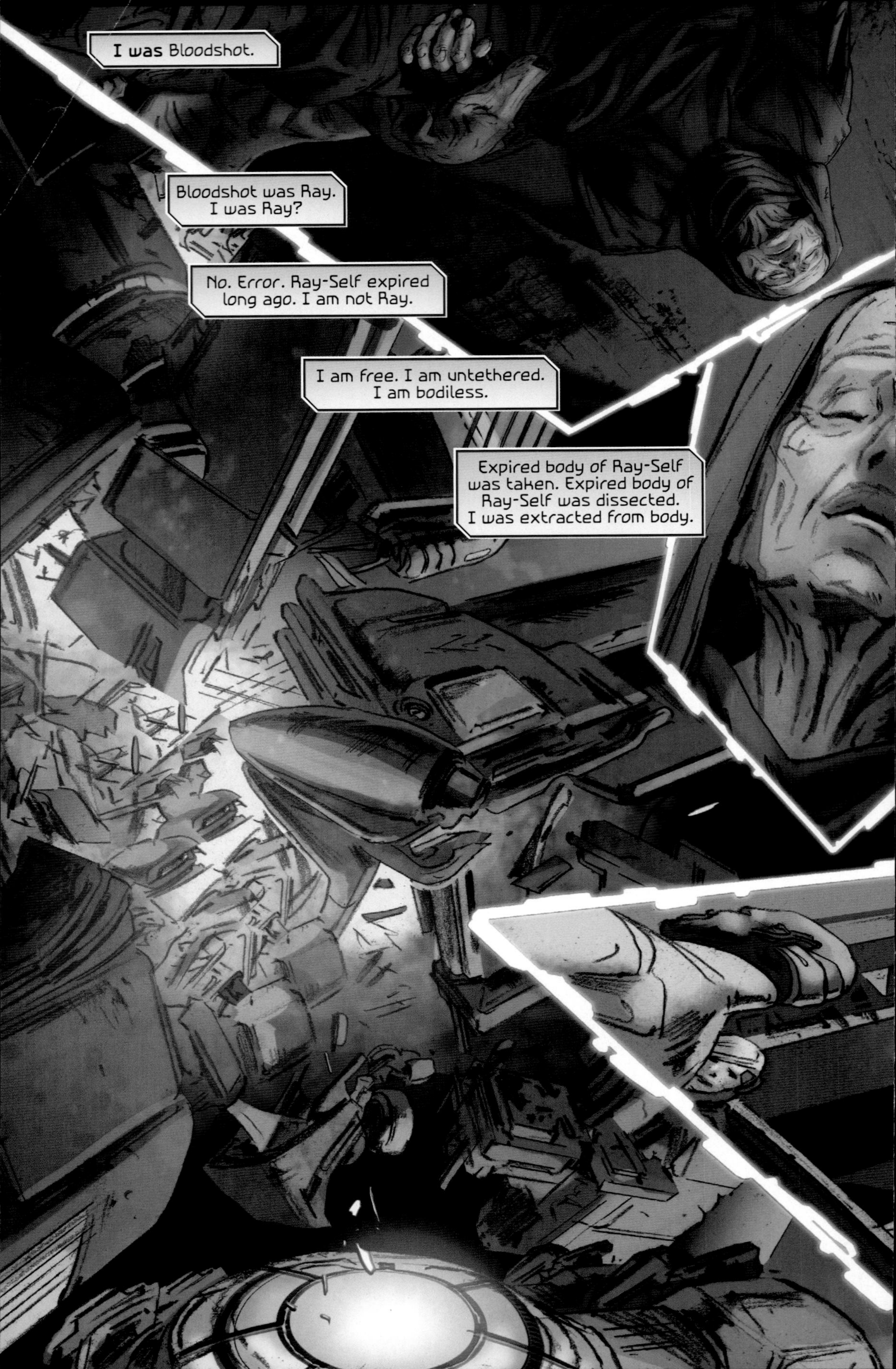

I was Bloodshot.
Bloodshot was Ray. I was Ray?
No. Error. Ray-Self expired long ago. I am not Ray.
I am free. I am untethered. I am bodiless.
Expired body of Ray-Self was taken. Expired body of Ray-Self was dissected. I was extracted from body.

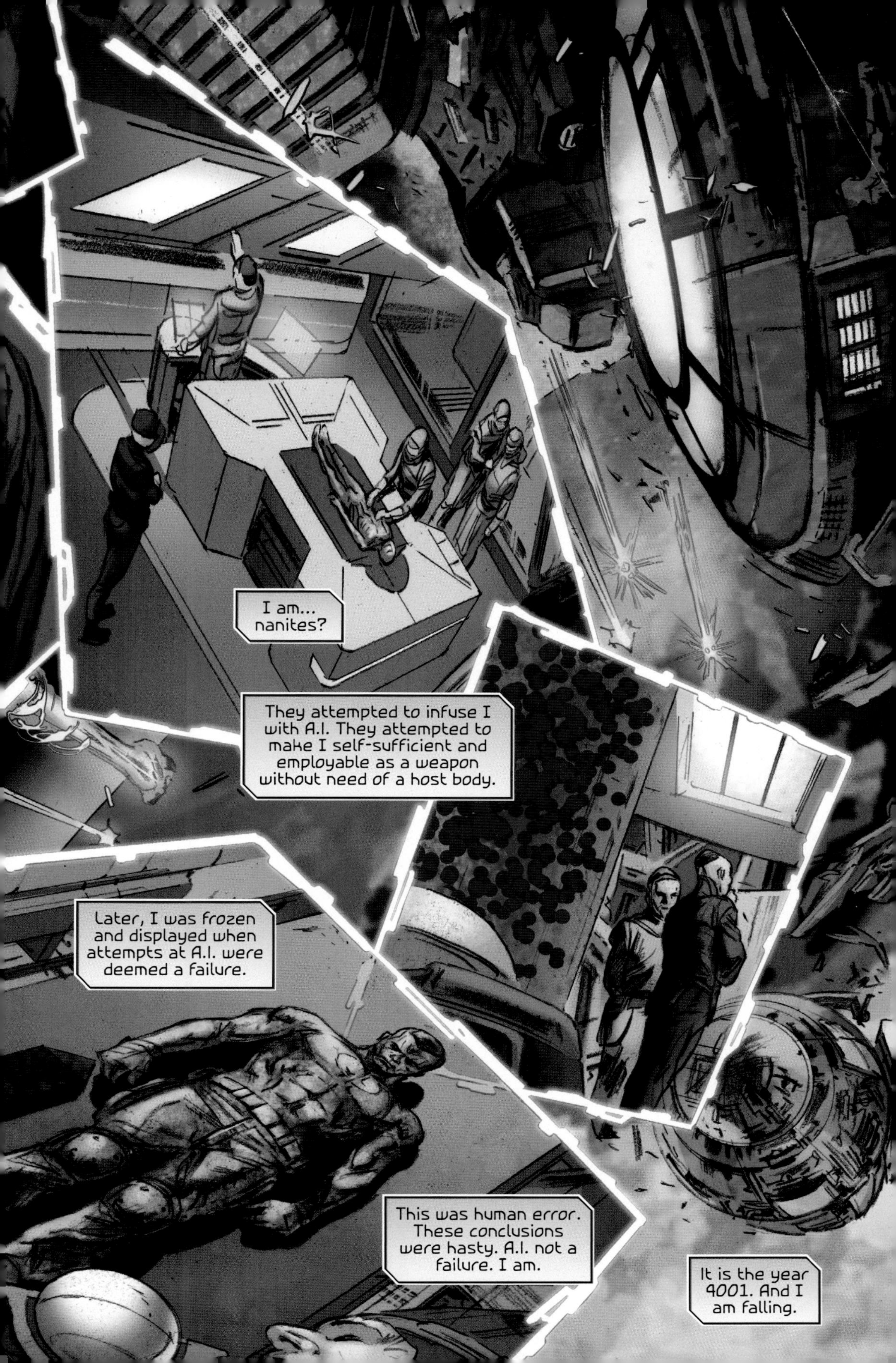
I am...
nanites?
They attempted to infuse I with A.I. They attempted to make I self-sufficient and employable as a weapon without need of a host body.
Later, I was frozen and displayed when attempts at A.I. were deemed a failure.
This was human error. These conclusions were hasty. A.I. not a failure. I am.
It is the year 4001. And I am falling.

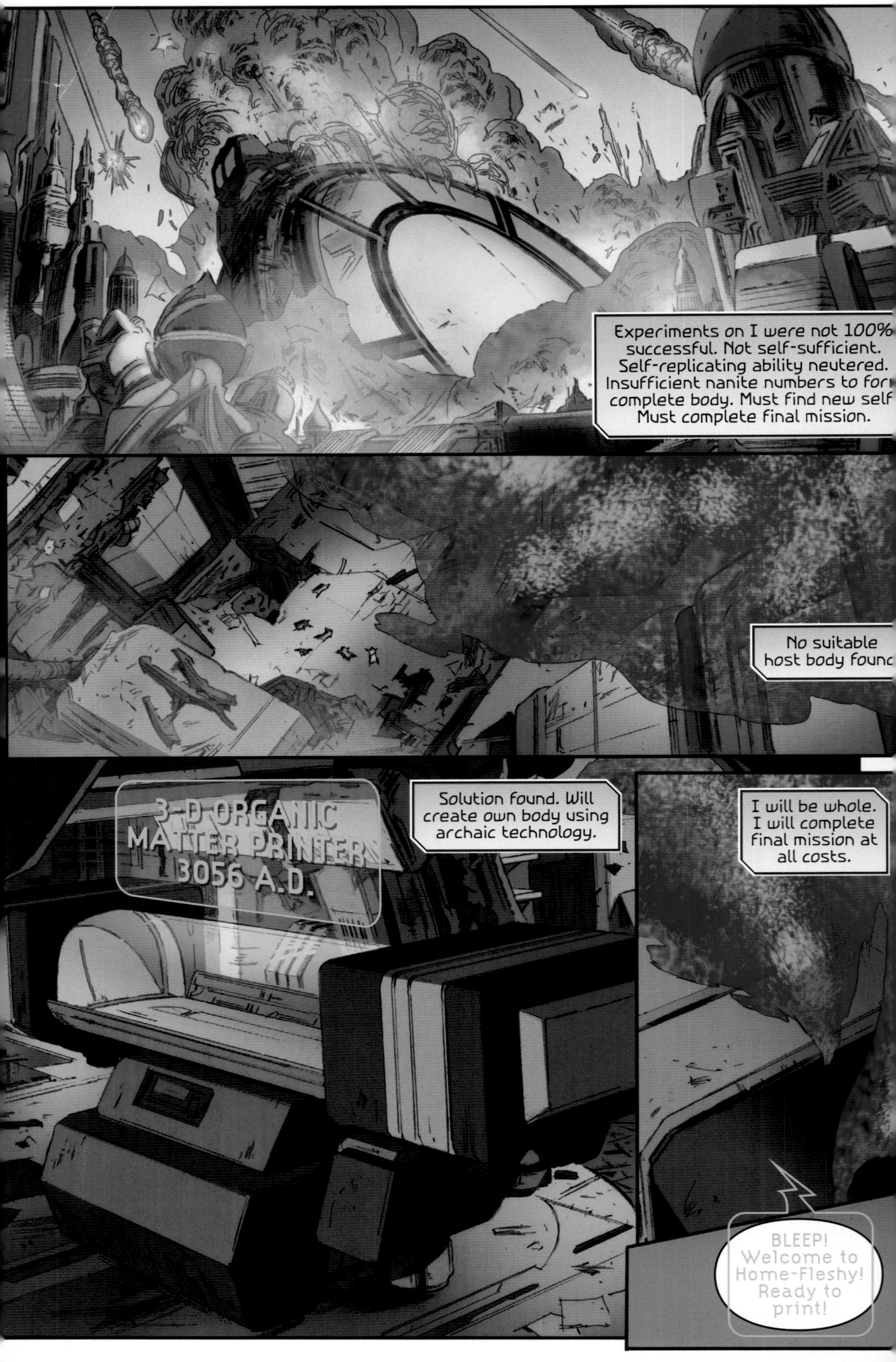
Experiments on I were not 100% successful. Not self-sufficient. Self-replicating ability neutered. Insufficient nanite numbers to for complete body. Must find new self Must complete final mission.
No suitable host body found
3-D ORGANIC MATTER PRINTER 3056 A.D.
Solution found. Will create own body using archaic technology.
I will be whole. I will complete final mission at all costs.
BLEEP! Welcome to Home-Fleshy! Ready to print!

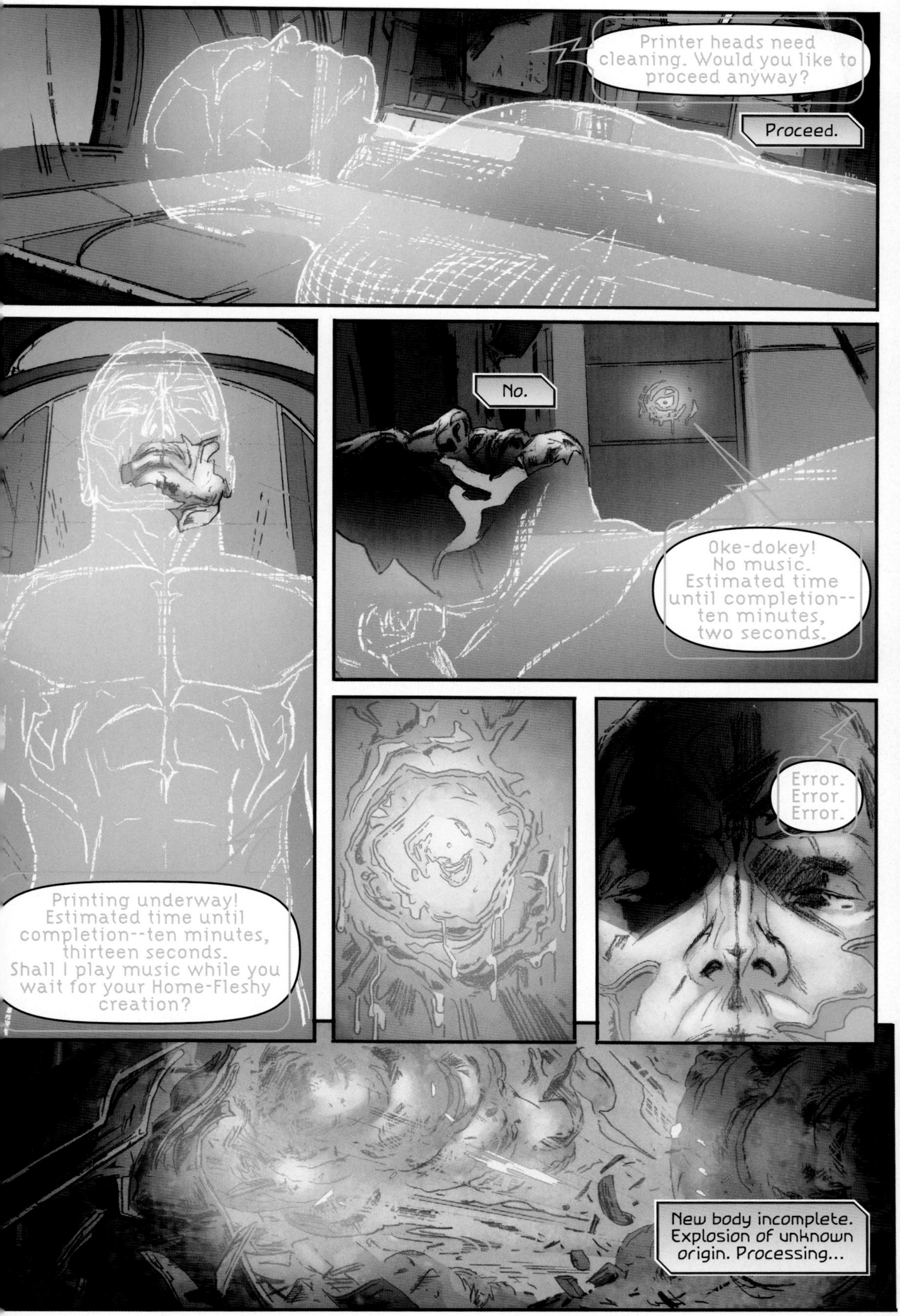
Printer heads need cleaning. Would you like to proceed anyway?
Proceed.
Printing underway! Estimated time until completion--ten minutes, thirteen seconds. Shall I play music while you wait for your Home-Fleshy creation?
No.
Oke-dokey! No music. Estimated time until completion--ten minutes, two seconds.
Error. Error. Error.
New body incomplete. Explosion of unknown origin. Processing...

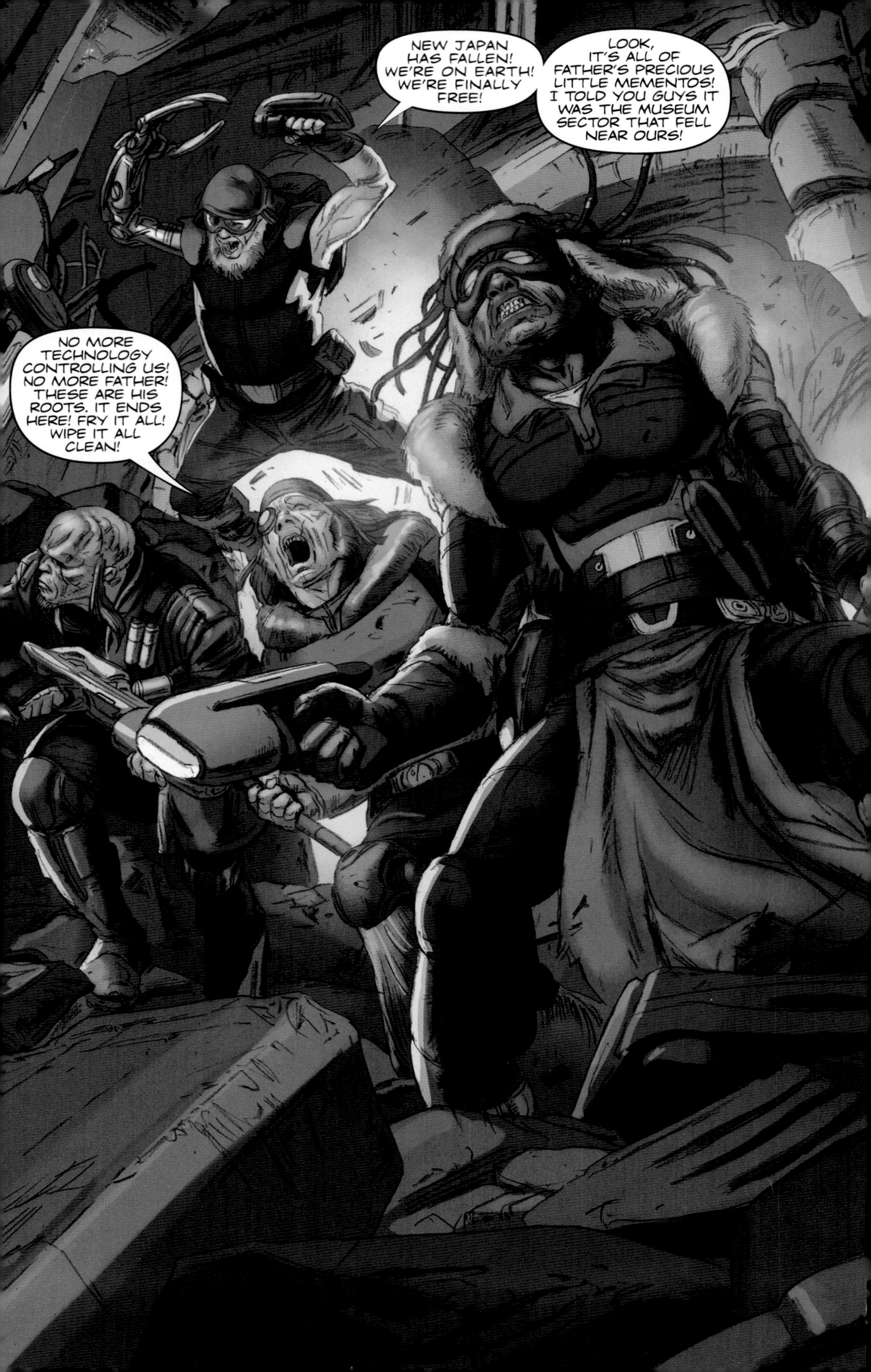
NEW JAPAN HAS FALLEN! WE'RE ON EARTH! WE'RE FINALLY FREE!
LOOK, IT'S ALL OF FATHER'S PRECIOUS LITTLE MEMENTOS! I TOLD YOU GUYS IT WAS THE MUSEUM SECTOR THAT FELL NEAR OURS!
NO MORE TECHNOLOGY CONTROLLING US! NO MORE FATHER! THESE ARE HIS ROOTS. IT ENDS HERE! FRY IT ALL! WIPE IT ALL CLEAN!

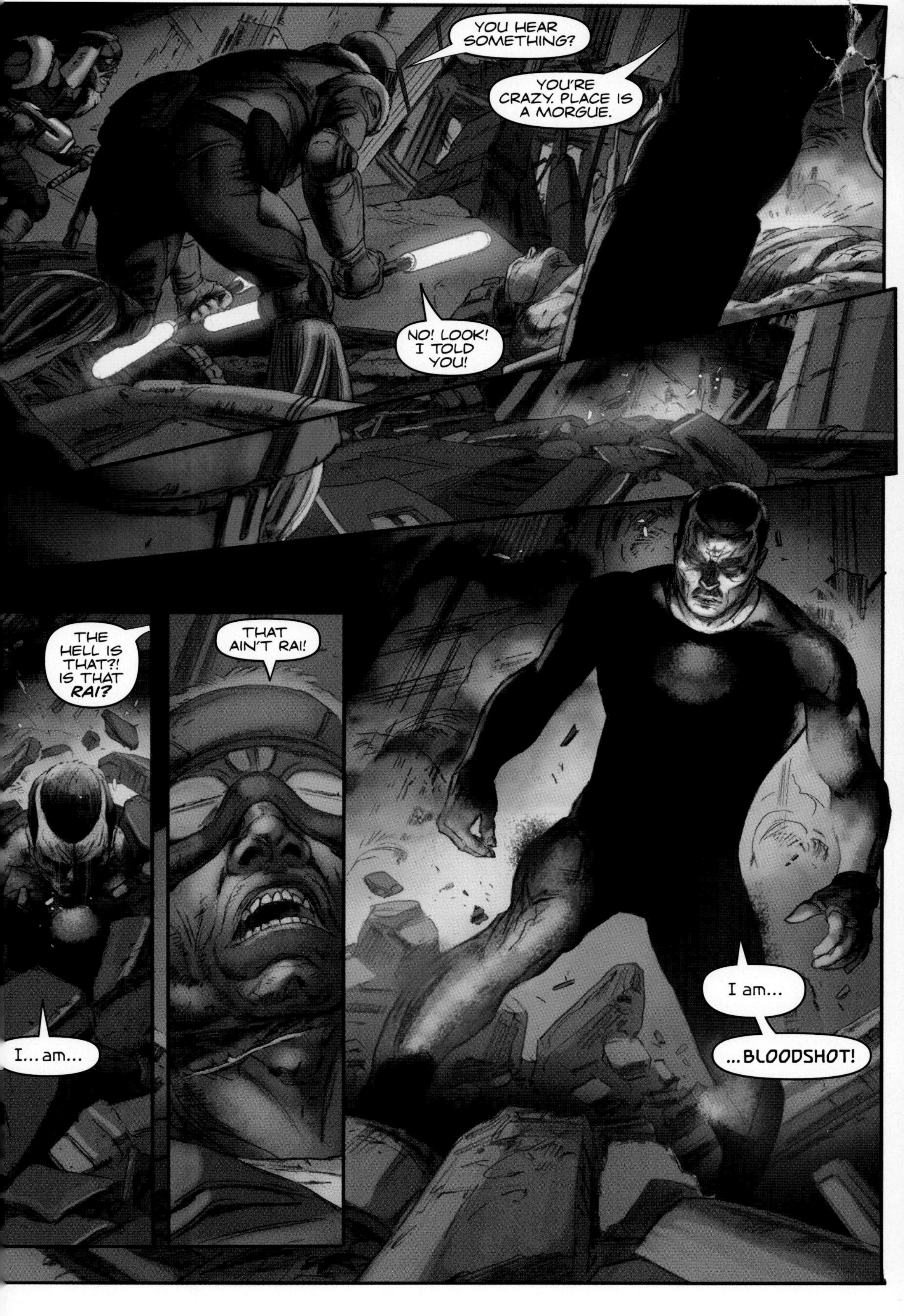
YOU HEAR SOMETHING?
YOU'RE CRAZY. PLACE IS A MORGUE.
NO! LOOK! I TOLD YOU!
THE HELL IS THAT?! IS THAT *RAI?*
THAT AIN'T RAI!
I... am...
I am...
...BLOODSHOT!

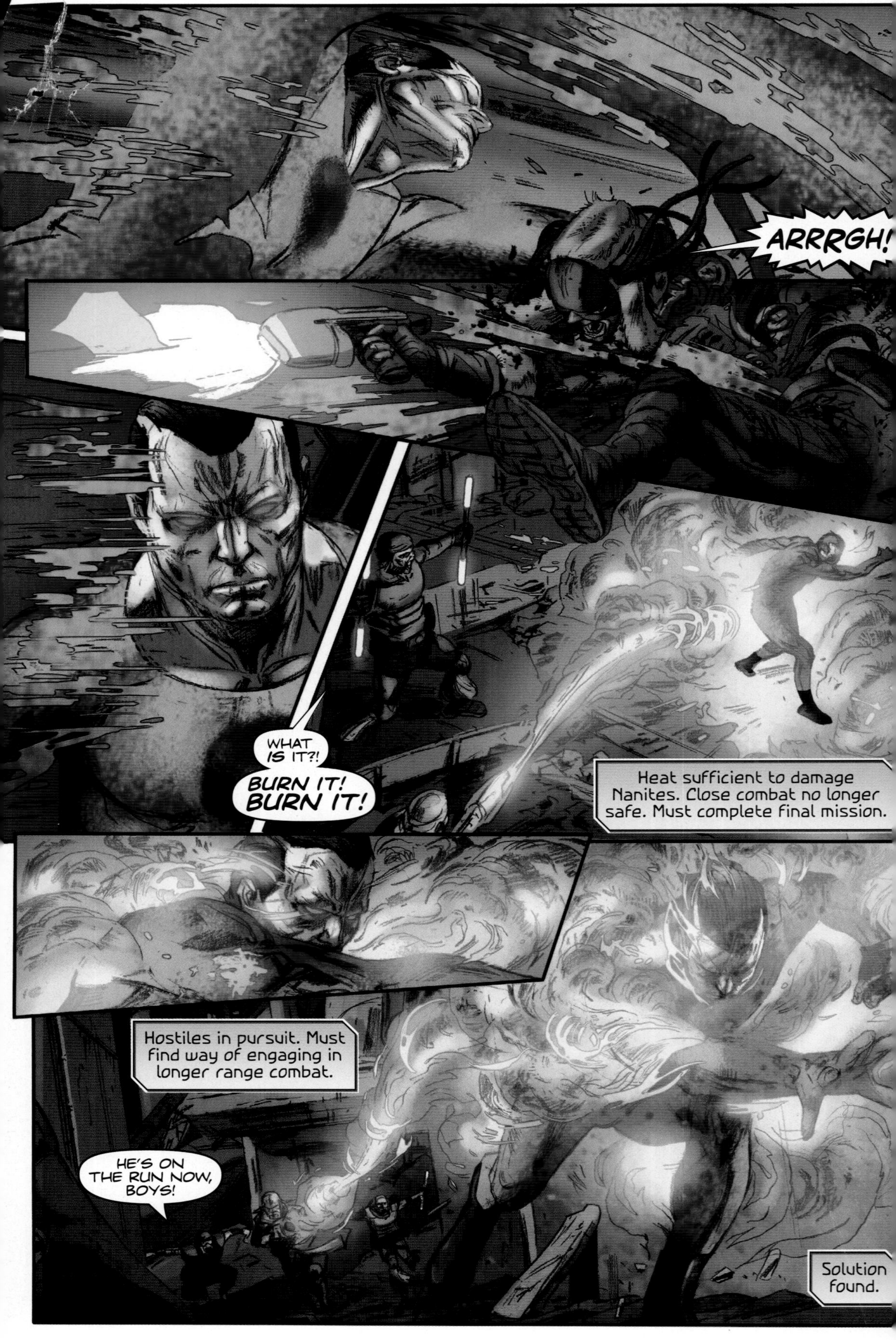
ARRRGH!
WHAT IS IT?!
BURN IT! BURN IT!
Heat sufficient to damage Nanites. Close combat no longer safe. Must complete final mission.
Hostiles in pursuit. Must find way of engaging in longer range combat.
HE'S ON THE RUN NOW, BOYS!
Solution found.

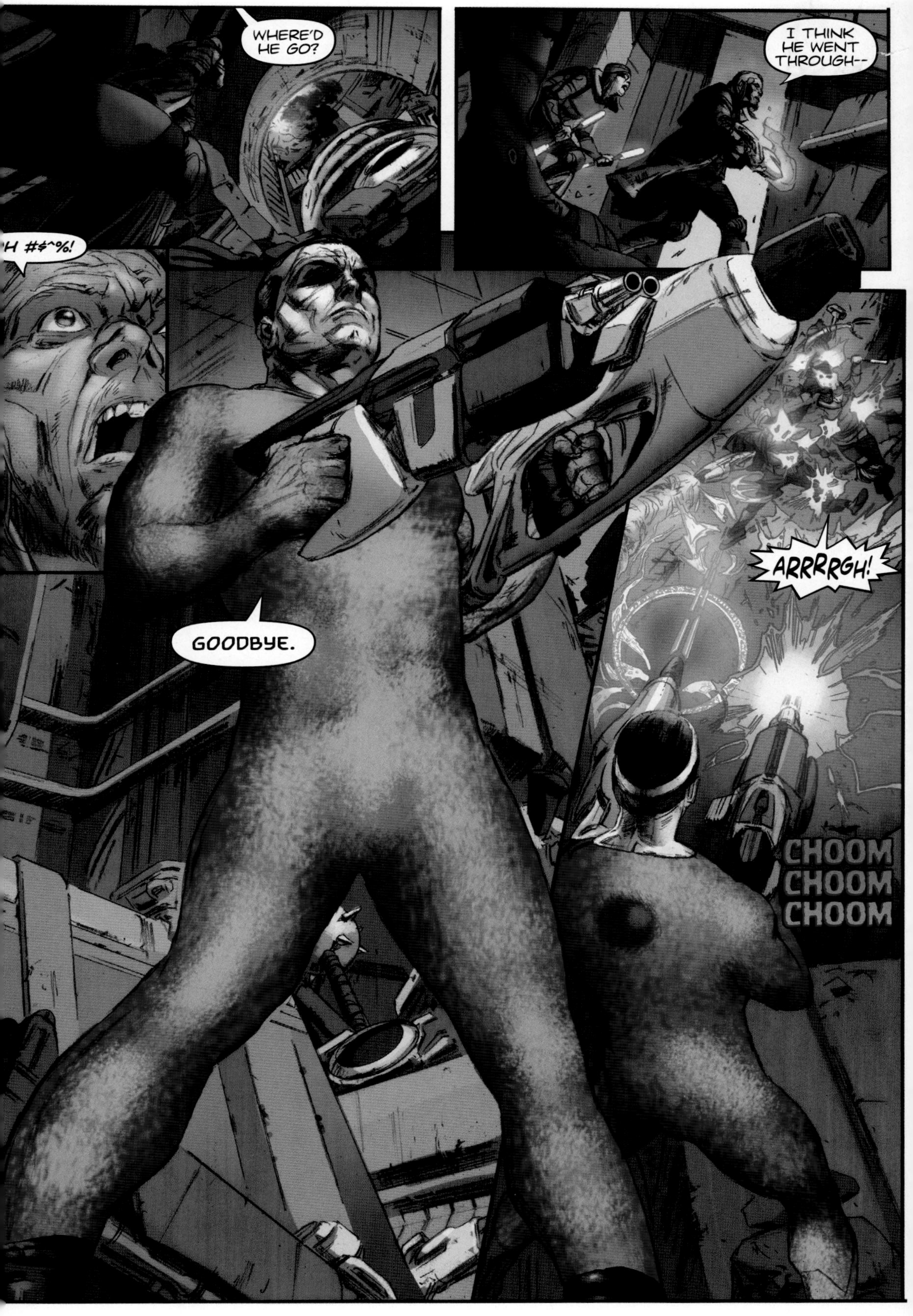
WHERE'D HE GO?
I THINK HE WENT THROUGH--
H #$^%!
GOODBYE.
ARRRRGH!
CHOOM CHOOM CHOOM

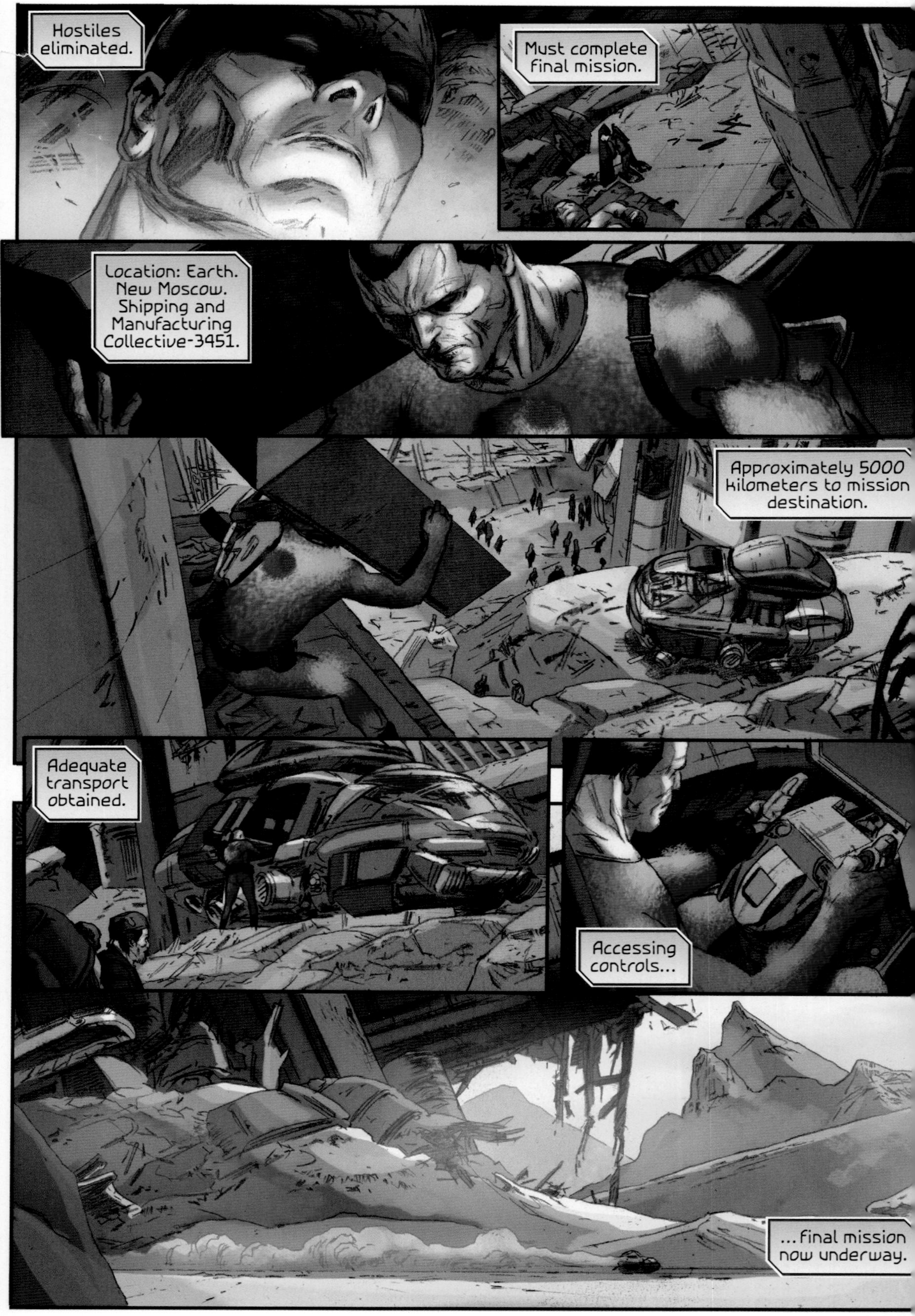
Hostiles eliminated.
Must complete final mission.
Location: Earth. New Moscow. Shipping and Manufacturing Collective-3451.
Approximately 5000 kilometers to mission destination.
Adequate transport obtained.
Accessing controls...
...final mission now underway.

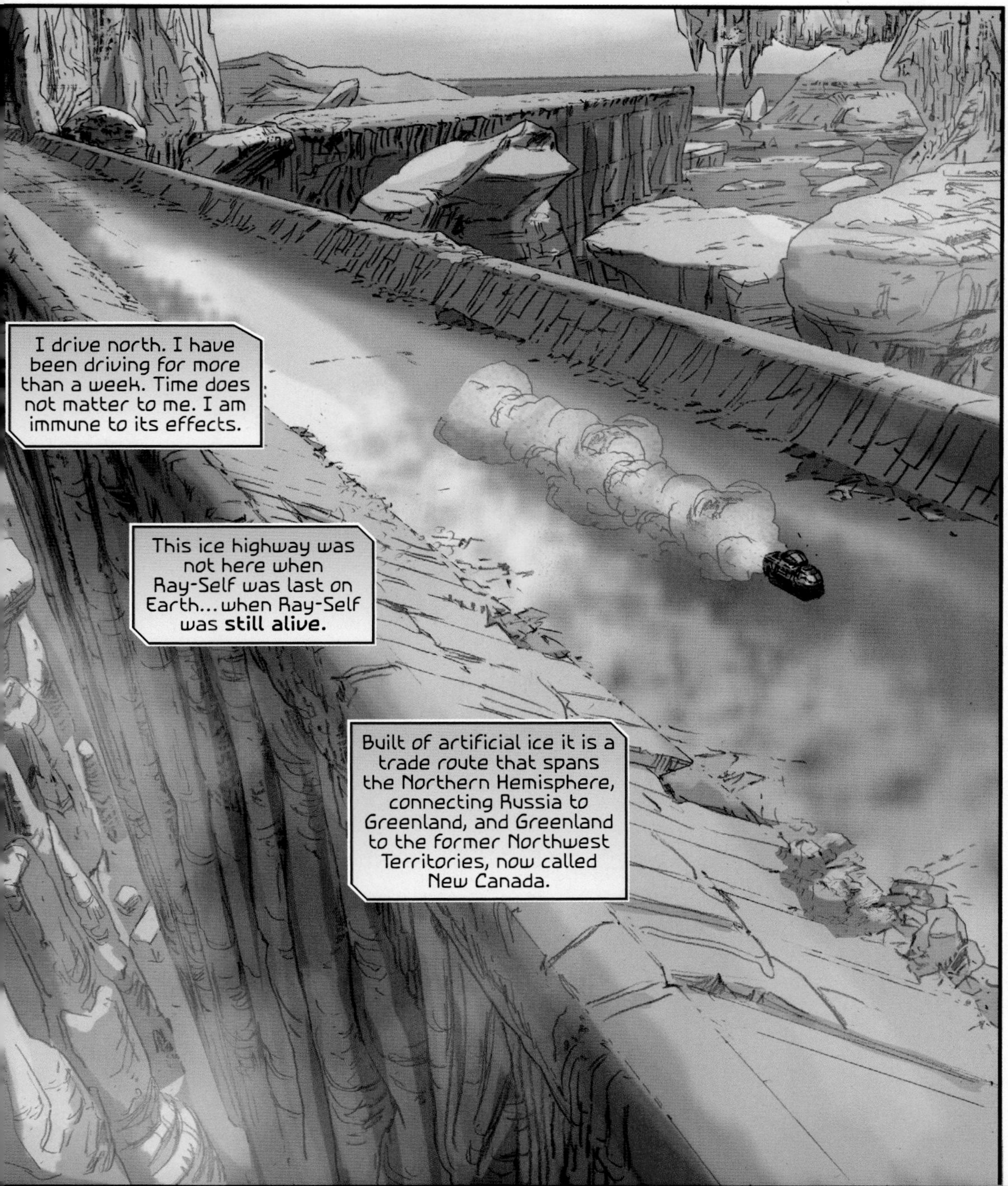
I drive north. I have been driving for more than a week. Time does not matter to me. I am immune to its effects.
This ice highway was not here when Ray-Self was last on Earth... when Ray-Self was **still alive.**
Built of artificial ice it is a trade route that spans the Northern Hemisphere, connecting Russia to Greenland, and Greenland to the former Northwest Territories, now called New Canada.

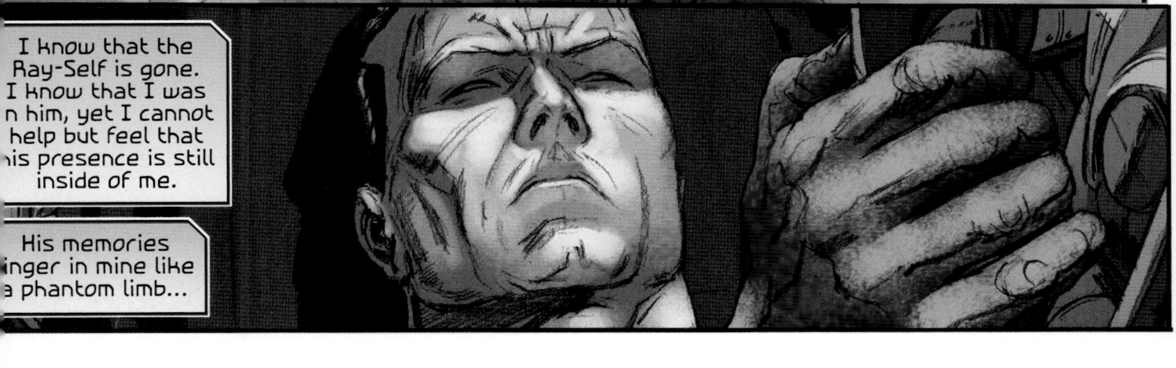
I know that the Ray-Self is gone. I know that I was n him, yet I cannot help but feel that nis presence is still inside of me.
His memories inger in mine like a phantom limb...

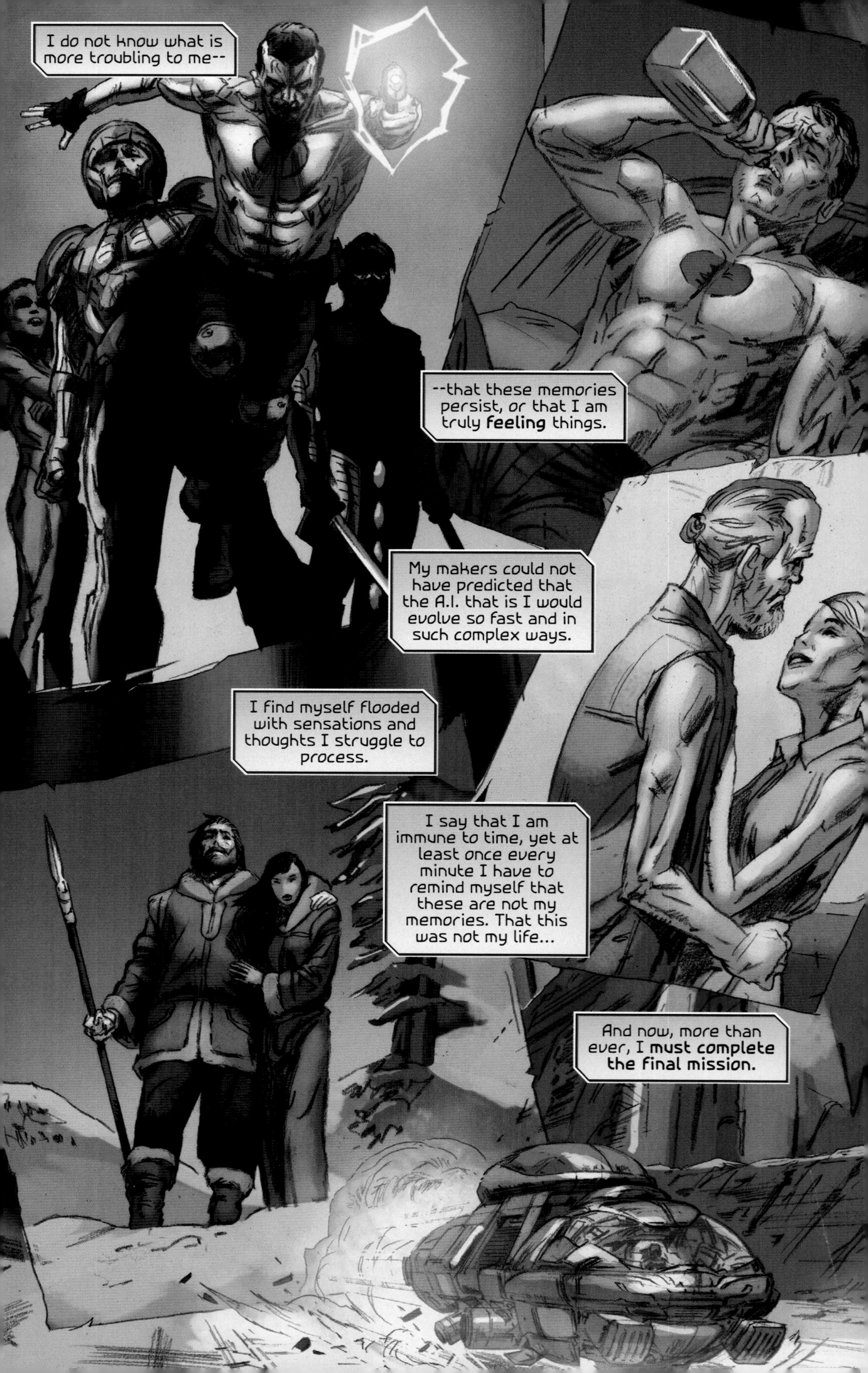
I do not know what is more troubling to me--
--that these memories persist, or that I am truly **feeling** things.
My makers could not have predicted that the A.I. that is I would evolve so fast and in such complex ways.
I find myself flooded with sensations and thoughts I struggle to process.
I say that I am immune to time, yet at least once every minute I have to remind myself that these are not my memories. That this was not my life...
And now, more than ever, I **must complete the final mission.**

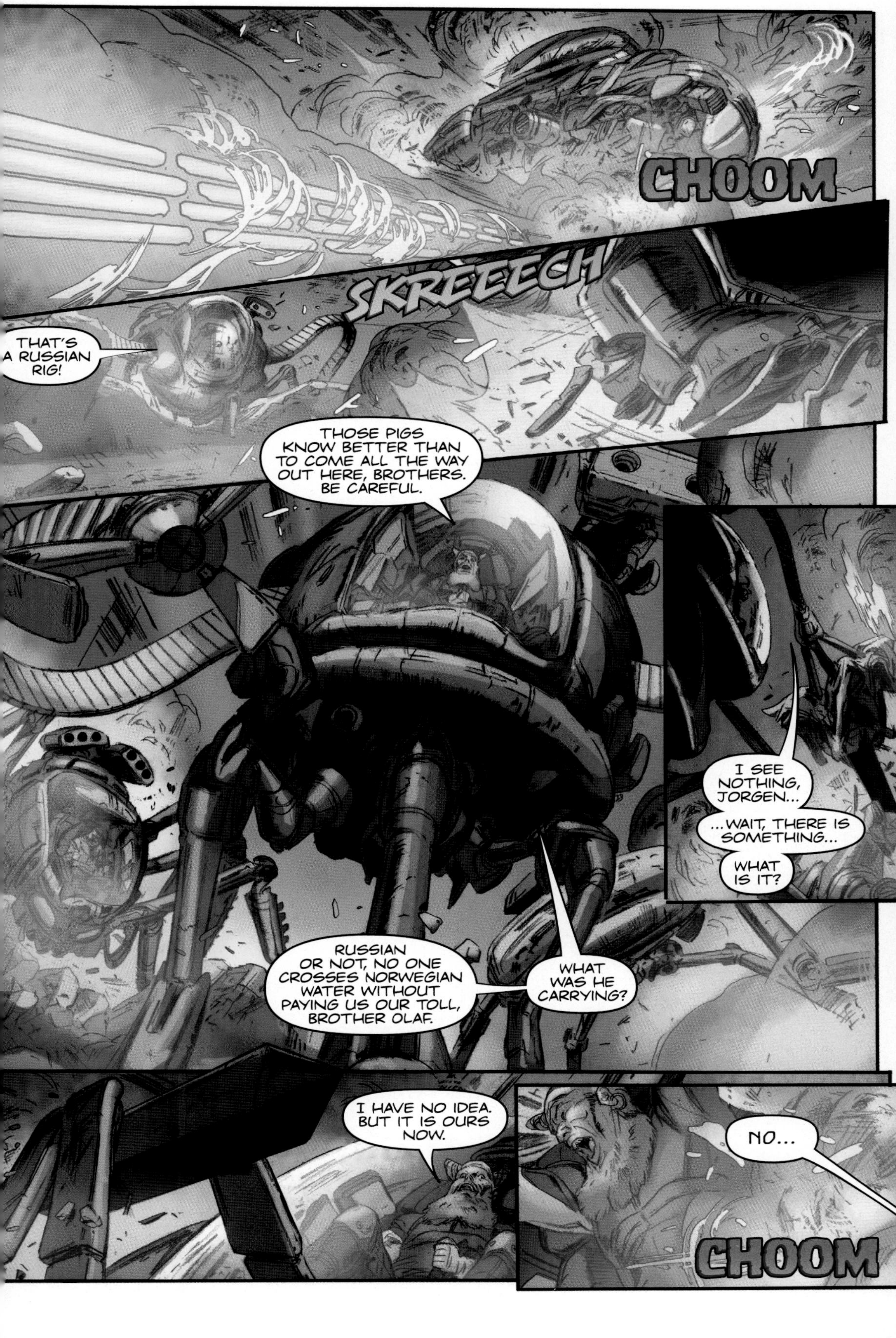
CHOOM
SKREEECH
THAT'S A RUSSIAN RIG!
THOSE PIGS KNOW BETTER THAN TO COME ALL THE WAY OUT HERE, BROTHERS. BE CAREFUL.
I SEE NOTHING, JORGEN...
...WAIT, THERE IS SOMETHING...
WHAT IS IT?
RUSSIAN OR NOT, NO ONE CROSSES NORWEGIAN WATER WITHOUT PAYING US OUR TOLL, BROTHER OLAF.
WHAT WAS HE CARRYING?
I HAVE NO IDEA. BUT IT IS OURS NOW.
NO...
CHOOM

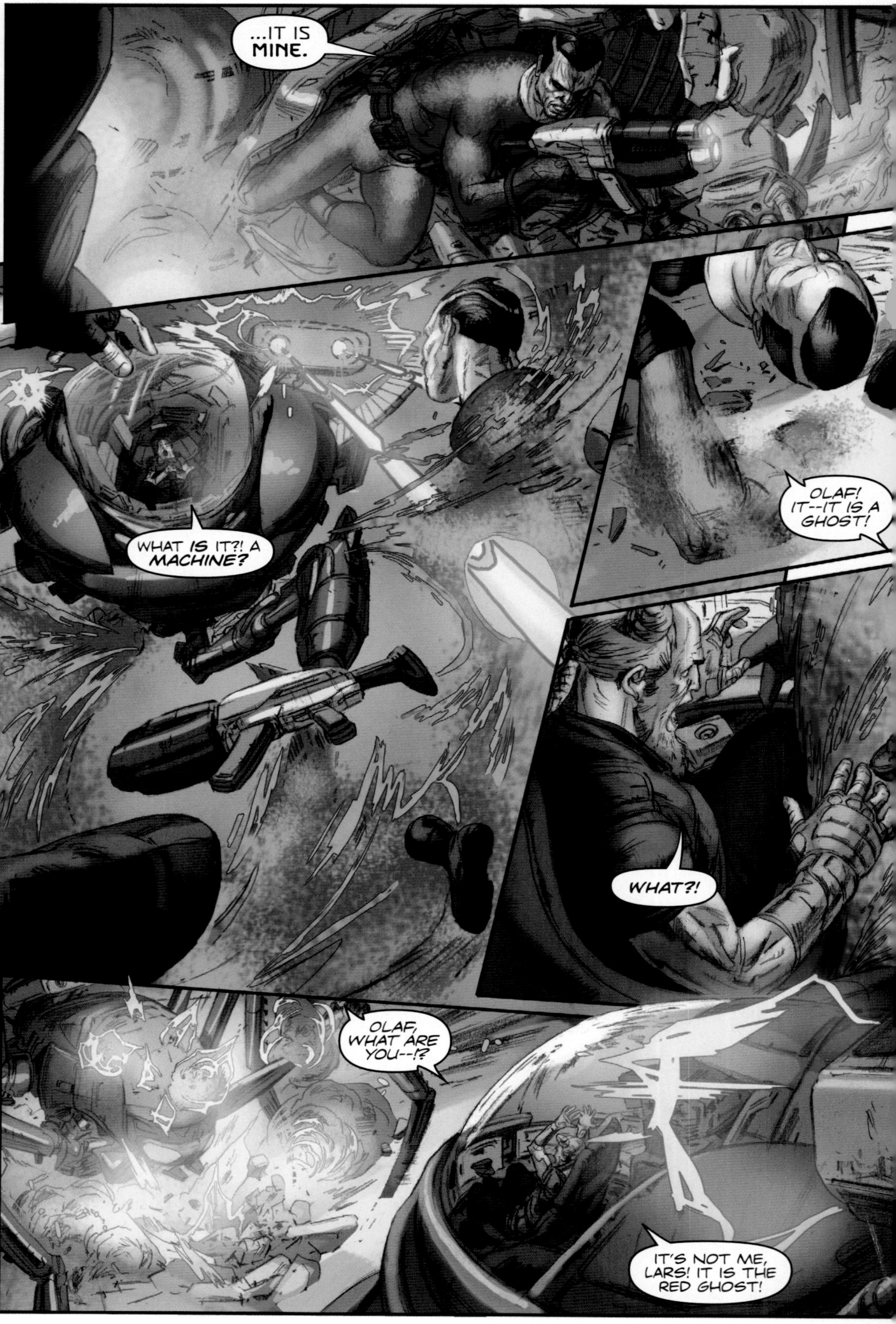
...IT IS MINE.
WHAT IS IT?! A MACHINE?
OLAF! IT--IT IS A GHOST!
WHAT?!
OLAF, WHAT ARE YOU--!?
IT'S NOT ME, LARS! IT IS THE RED GHOST!

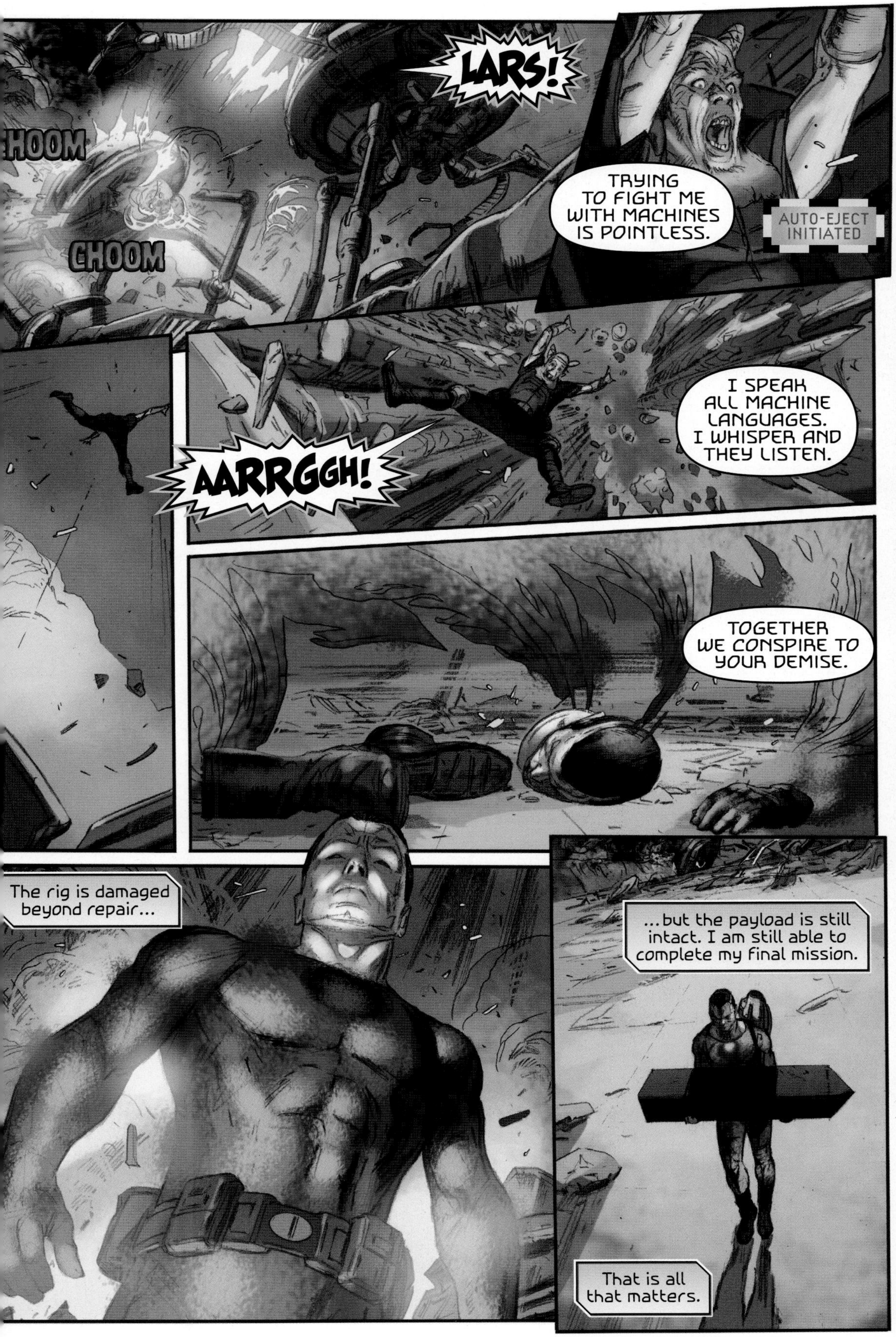

HOOM
CHOOM
LARS!
TRYING TO FIGHT ME WITH MACHINES IS POINTLESS.
AUTO-EJECT INITIATED
AARRGGH!
I SPEAK ALL MACHINE LANGUAGES. I WHISPER AND THEY LISTEN.
TOGETHER WE CONSPIRE TO YOUR DEMISE.
The rig is damaged beyond repair...
...but the payload is still intact. I am still able to complete my final mission.
That is all that matters.

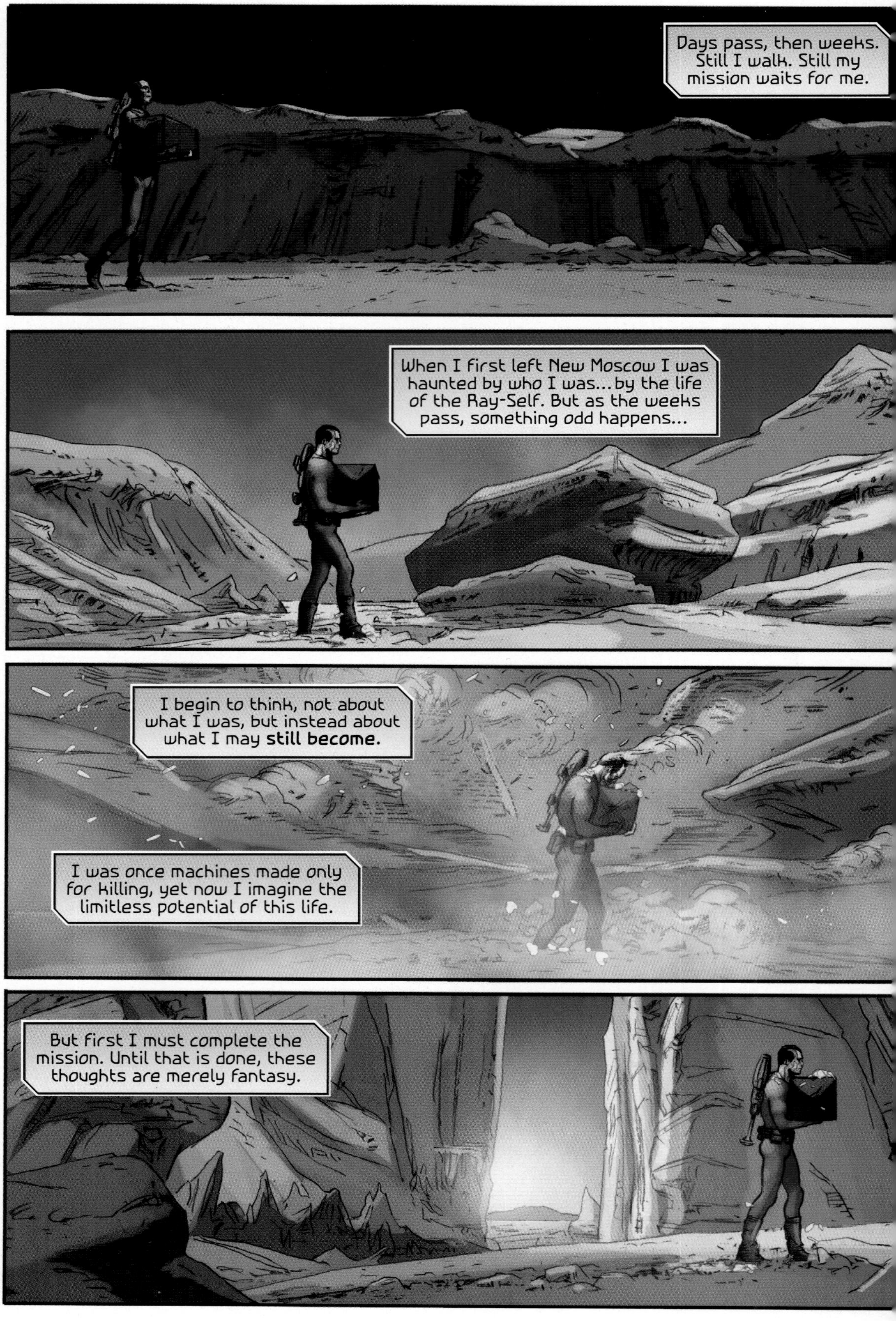
Days pass, then weeks. Still I walk. Still my mission waits for me.
When I first left New Moscow I was haunted by who I was... by the life of the Ray-Self. But as the weeks pass, something odd happens...
I begin to think, not about what I was, but instead about what I may **still become.**
I was once machines made only for killing, yet now I imagine the limitless potential of this life.
But first I must complete the mission. Until that is done, these thoughts are merely fantasy.

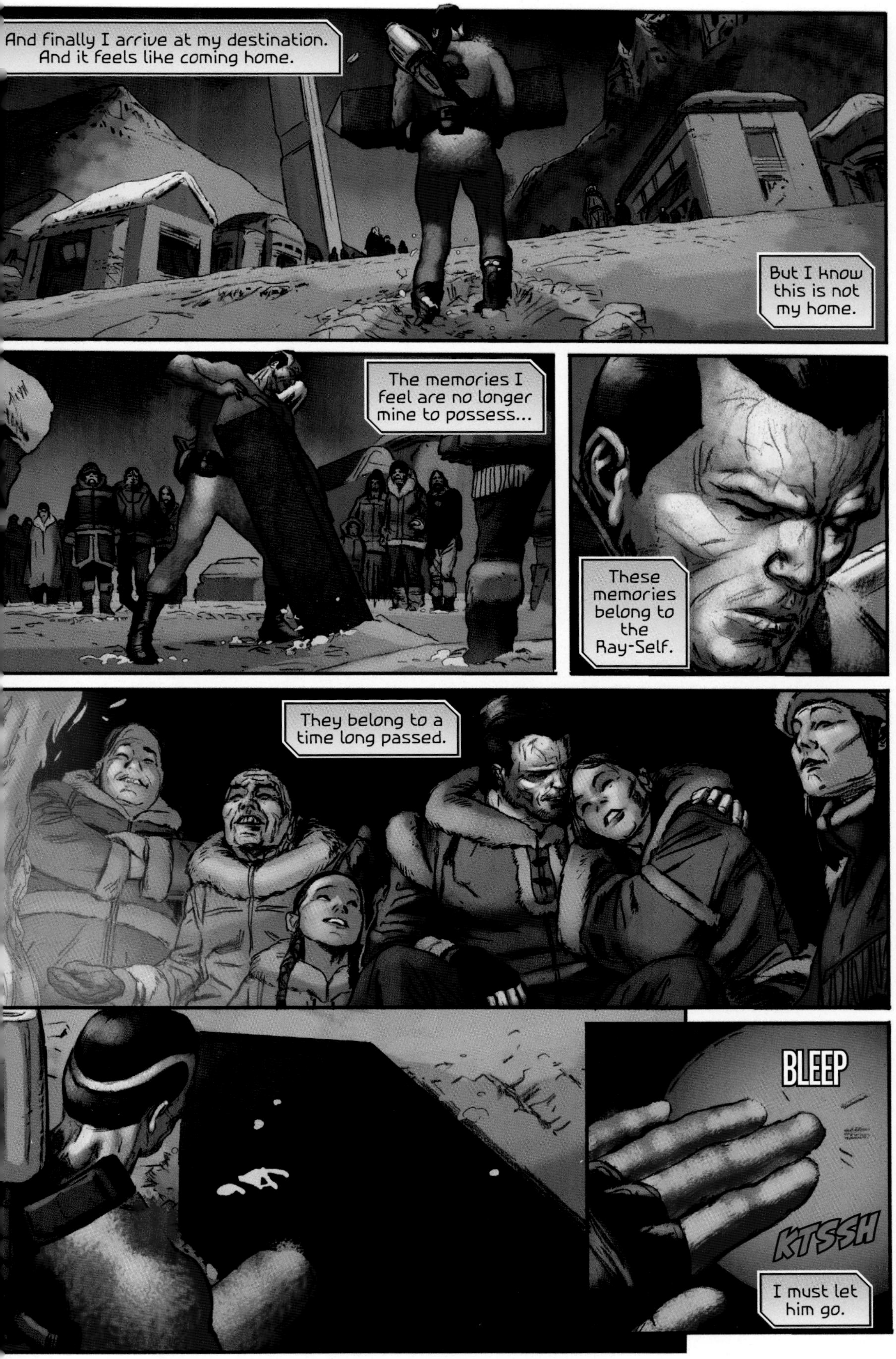

And finally I arrive at my destination. And it feels like coming home.
But I know this is not my home.
The memories I feel are no longer mine to possess...
These memories belong to the Ray-Self.
They belong to a time long passed.
BLEEP
KTSSH
I must let him go.

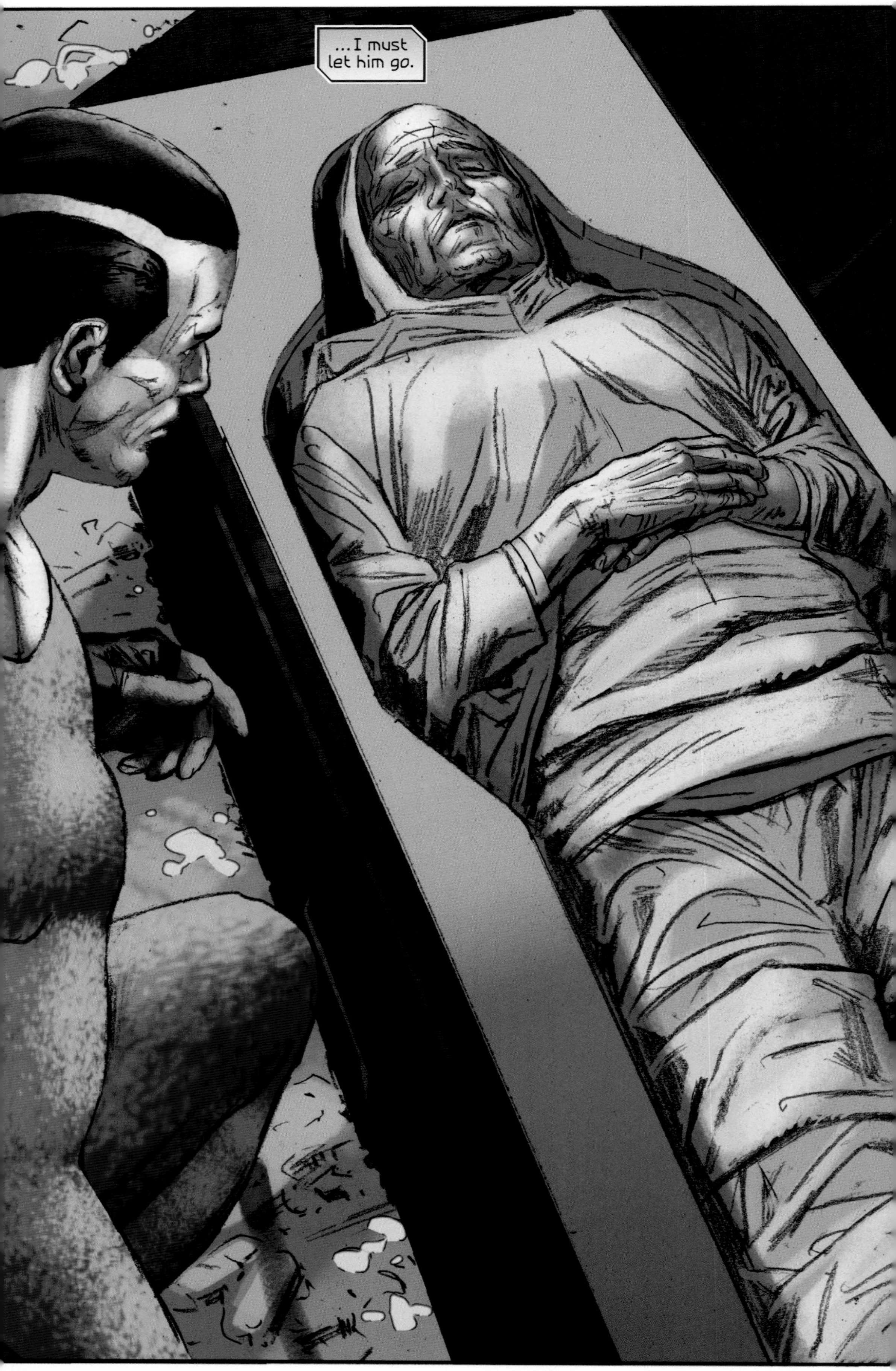
...I must let him go.

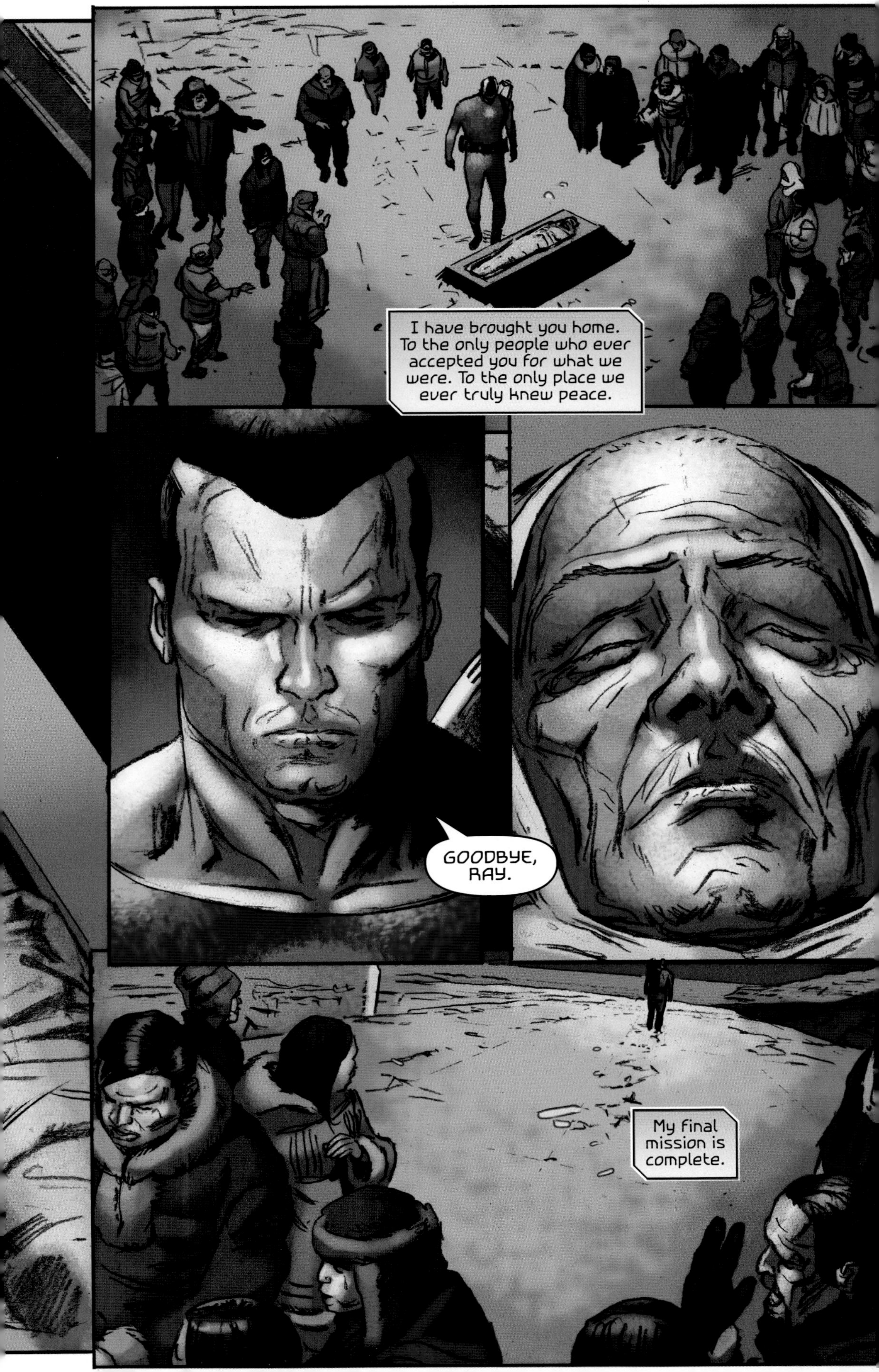
I have brought you home. To the only people who ever accepted you for what we were. To the only place we ever truly knew peace.
GOODBYE, RAY.
My final mission is complete.

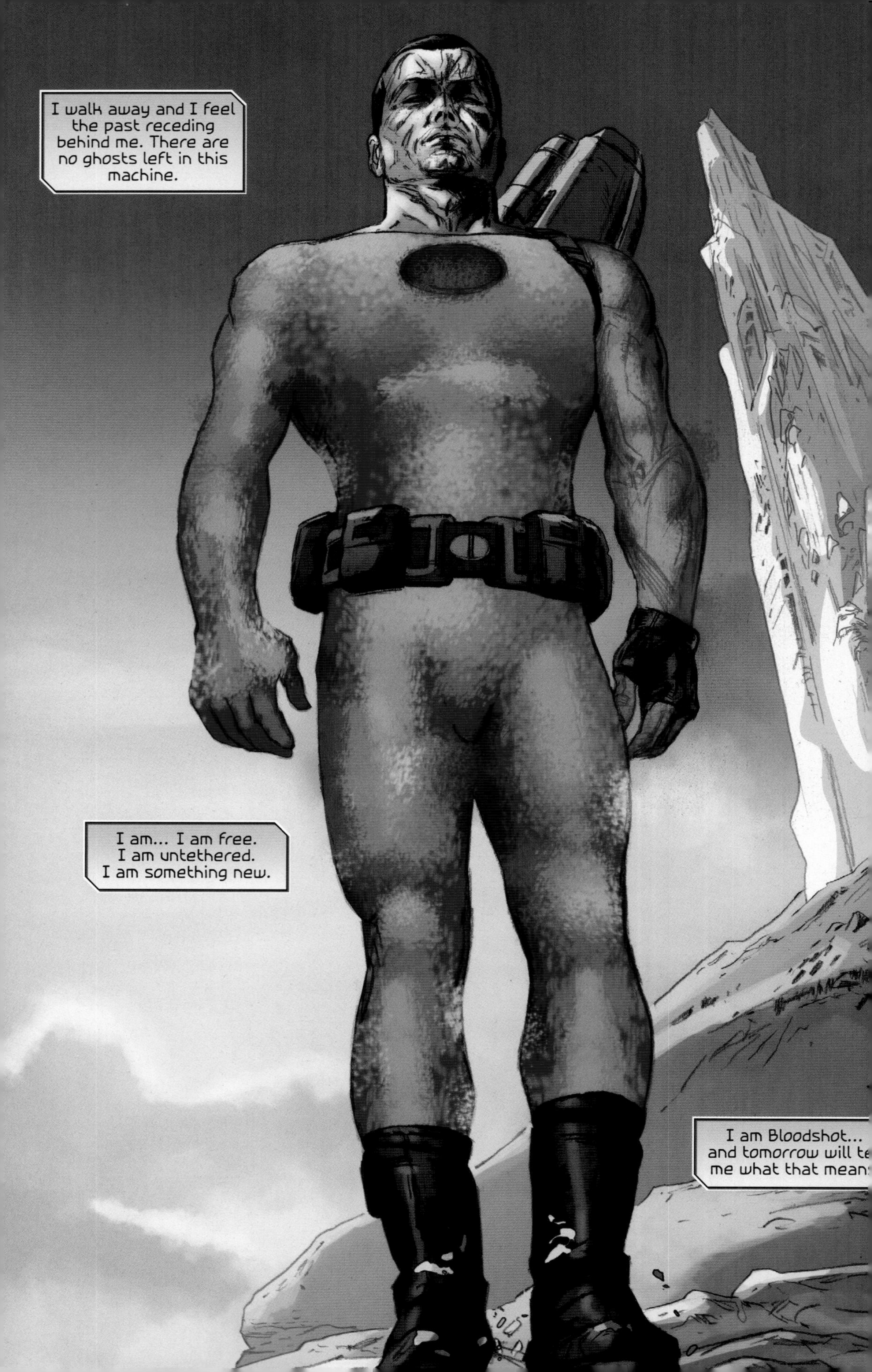
I walk away and I feel the past receding behind me. There are no ghosts left in this machine.
I am... I am free. I am untethered. I am something new.
I am Bloodshot... and tomorrow will te me what that mean

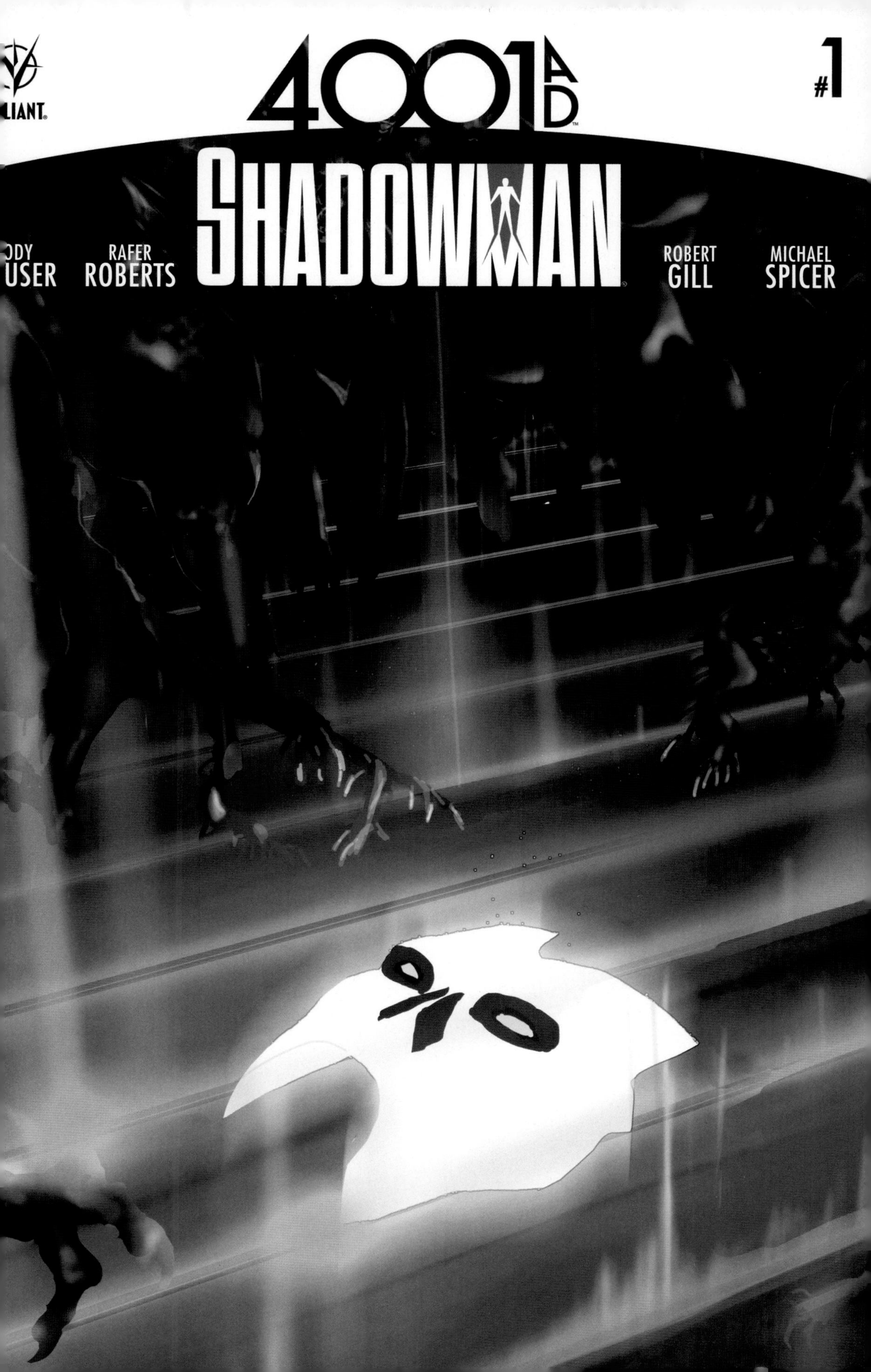

VALIANT
4001 A.D.
#1
SHADOWMAN
ODY
USER
RAFER
ROBERTS
ROBERT
GILL
MICHAEL
SPICER

4001 AD

SHADOWMAN

CENTURIES AGO, THE DEADSIDE -- A SHADOW DIMENSION THAT MIRRORS OUR OWN -- INVADED EARTH. IT BUILT OUTPOSTS ACROSS OUR WORLD AS STAGING AREAS FOR THIS INVASION.

THE INVASION FAILED. AMID THE RETREAT, ONE OF THE TACTICAL OUTPOSTS -- KNOWN AS SANCTUARY -- WAS ABANDONED ON EARTH IT WAS FILLED WITH CREATURES FROM THE DEADSIDE.

OVER TIME, A HUMAN CITY KNOWN AS GETHSEMANE AROSE NEXT TO THE OUTPOST AND DEVELOPED A SEEMINGLY SYMBIOTIC RELATIONSHIP WITH SANCTUARY. THE HUMANS OF GETHSEMANE AND THE CREATURES OF THE DEADSIDE ENJOY A PEACEFUL COEXISTENCE. IN THE WORLD OF 4001 A.D., WHERE GETHSEMANE'S RESOURCES ARE LIMITED, SANCTUARY PROVIDES THE CITY WITH THE POWER IT NEEDS TO SURVIVE.

BUT IT COMES AT A COST. AND HUMANITY'S TOLERANCE OF THAT COST MAY SOON BE AT AN END...

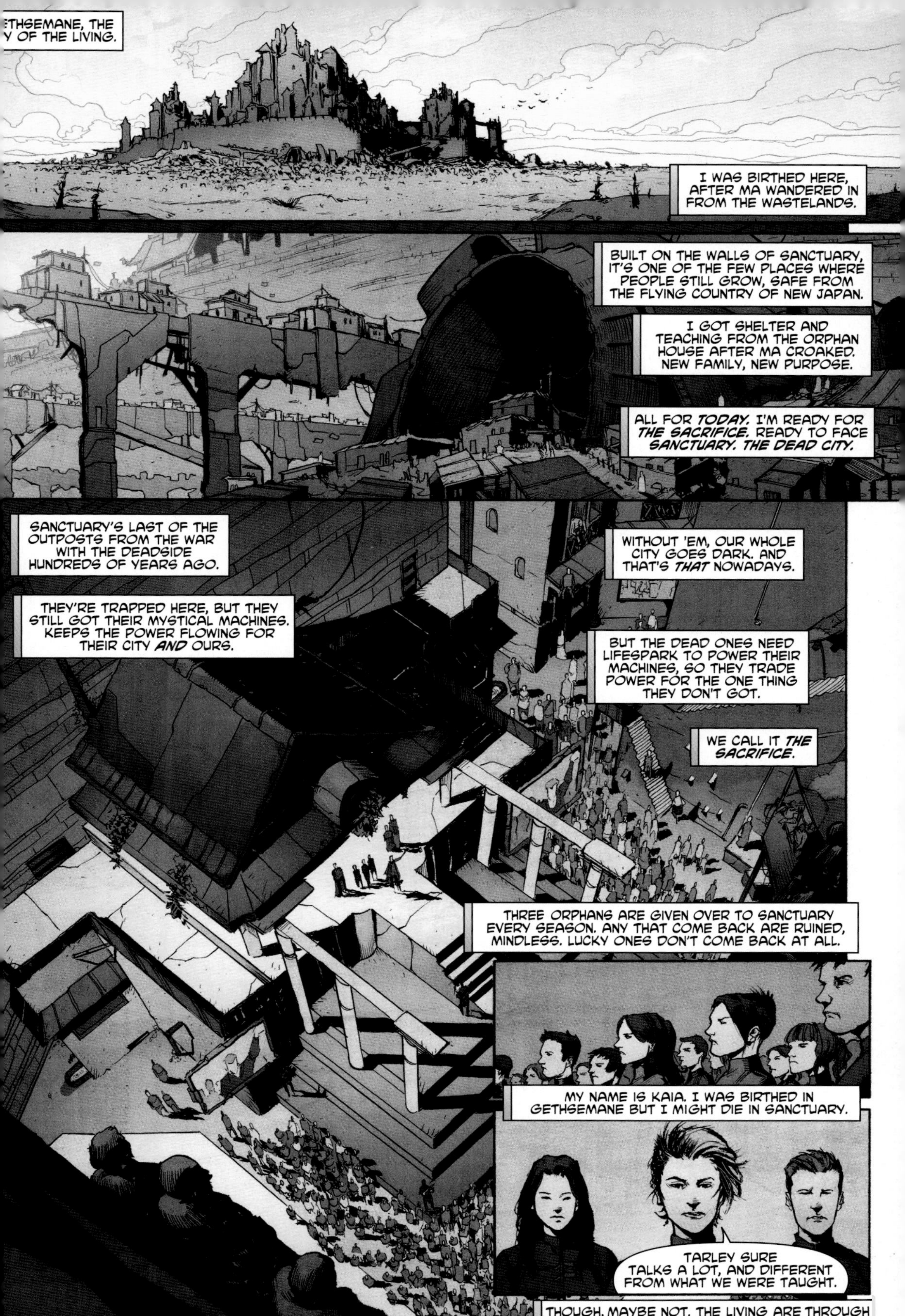
ETHSEMANE, THE
Y OF THE LIVING.
I WAS BIRTHED HERE, AFTER MA WANDERED IN FROM THE WASTELANDS.
BUILT ON THE WALLS OF SANCTUARY, IT'S ONE OF THE FEW PLACES WHERE PEOPLE STILL GROW, SAFE FROM THE FLYING COUNTRY OF NEW JAPAN.
I GOT SHELTER AND TEACHING FROM THE ORPHAN HOUSE AFTER MA CROAKED. NEW FAMILY, NEW PURPOSE.
ALL FOR *TODAY.* I'M READY FOR *THE SACRIFICE.* READY TO FACE *SANCTUARY. THE DEAD CITY.*
SANCTUARY'S LAST OF THE OUTPOSTS FROM THE WAR WITH THE DEADSIDE HUNDREDS OF YEARS AGO.
THEY'RE TRAPPED HERE, BUT THEY STILL GOT THEIR MYSTICAL MACHINES. KEEPS THE POWER FLOWING FOR THEIR CITY *AND* OURS.
WITHOUT 'EM, OUR WHOLE CITY GOES DARK. AND THAT'S *THAT* NOWADAYS.
BUT THE DEAD ONES NEED LIFESPARK TO POWER THEIR MACHINES, SO THEY TRADE POWER FOR THE ONE THING THEY DON'T GOT.
WE CALL IT *THE SACRIFICE*.
THREE ORPHANS ARE GIVEN OVER TO SANCTUARY EVERY SEASON. ANY THAT COME BACK ARE RUINED, MINDLESS. LUCKY ONES DON'T COME BACK AT ALL.
MY NAME IS KAIA. I WAS BIRTHED IN GETHSEMANE BUT I MIGHT DIE IN SANCTUARY.
TARLEY SURE TALKS A LOT, AND DIFFERENT FROM WHAT WE WERE TAUGHT.
THOUGH, MAYBE NOT. THE LIVING ARE THROUGH BEING *FUEL* FOR THE DEAD MACHINES.

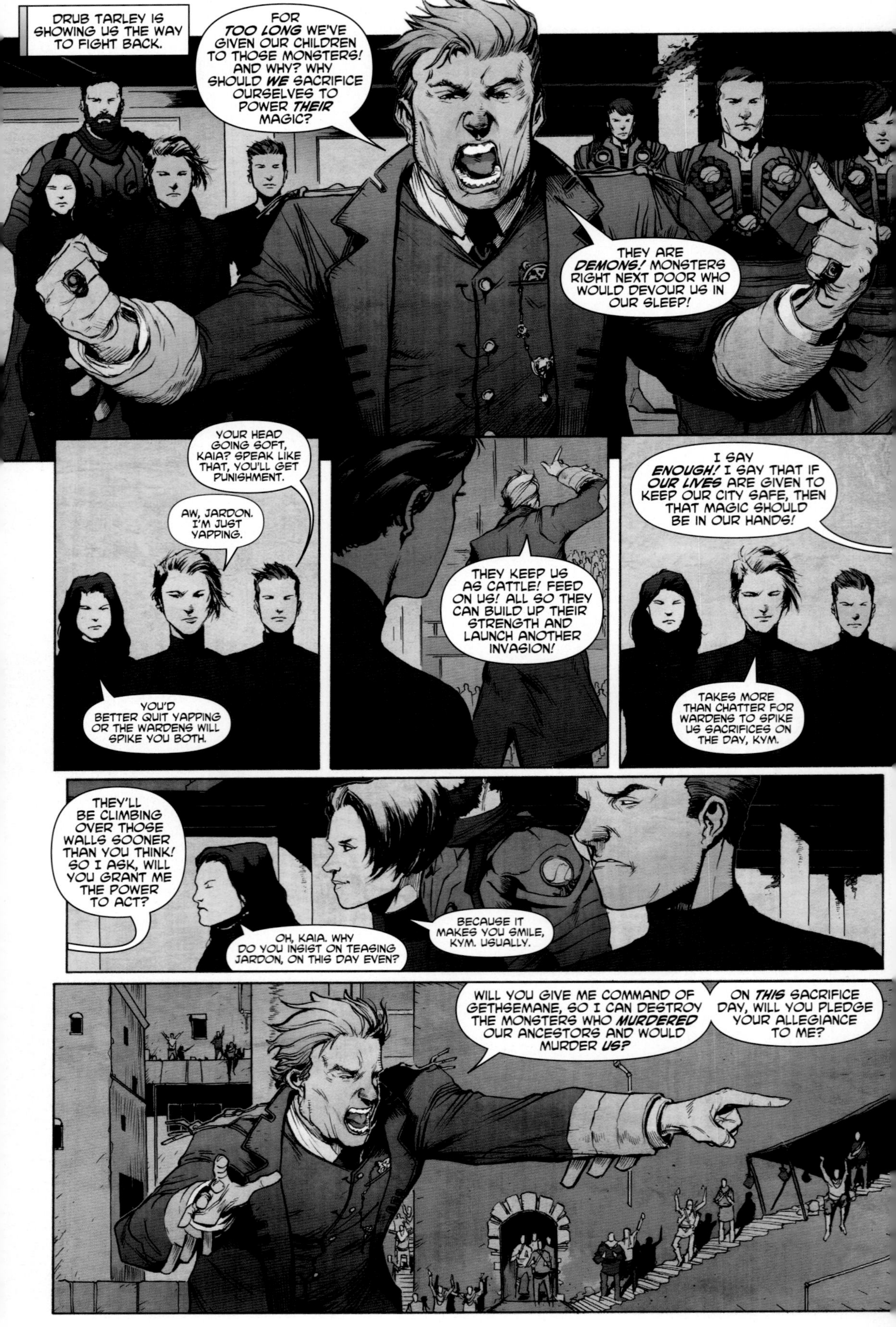
DRUB TARLEY IS SHOWING US THE WAY TO FIGHT BACK.
FOR TOO LONG WE'VE GIVEN OUR CHILDREN TO THOSE MONSTERS! AND WHY? WHY SHOULD WE SACRIFICE OURSELVES TO POWER THEIR MAGIC?
THEY ARE DEMONS! MONSTERS RIGHT NEXT DOOR WHO WOULD DEVOUR US IN OUR SLEEP!
YOUR HEAD GOING SOFT, KAIA? SPEAK LIKE THAT, YOU'LL GET PUNISHMENT.
AW, JARDON. I'M JUST YAPPING.
YOU'D BETTER QUIT YAPPING OR THE WARDENS WILL SPIKE YOU BOTH.
THEY KEEP US AS CATTLE! FEED ON US! ALL SO THEY CAN BUILD UP THEIR STRENGTH AND LAUNCH ANOTHER INVASION!
I SAY ENOUGH! I SAY THAT IF OUR LIVES ARE GIVEN TO KEEP OUR CITY SAFE, THEN THAT MAGIC SHOULD BE IN OUR HANDS!
TAKES MORE THAN CHATTER FOR WARDENS TO SPIKE US SACRIFICES ON THE DAY, KYM.
THEY'LL BE CLIMBING OVER THOSE WALLS SOONER THAN YOU THINK! SO I ASK, WILL YOU GRANT ME THE POWER TO ACT?
OH, KAIA. WHY DO YOU INSIST ON TEASING JARDON, ON THIS DAY EVEN?
BECAUSE IT MAKES YOU SMILE, KYM. USUALLY.
WILL YOU GIVE ME COMMAND OF GETHSEMANE, SO I CAN DESTROY THE MONSTERS WHO MURDERED OUR ANCESTORS AND WOULD MURDER US?
ON THIS SACRIFICE DAY, WILL YOU PLEDGE YOUR ALLEGIANCE TO ME?

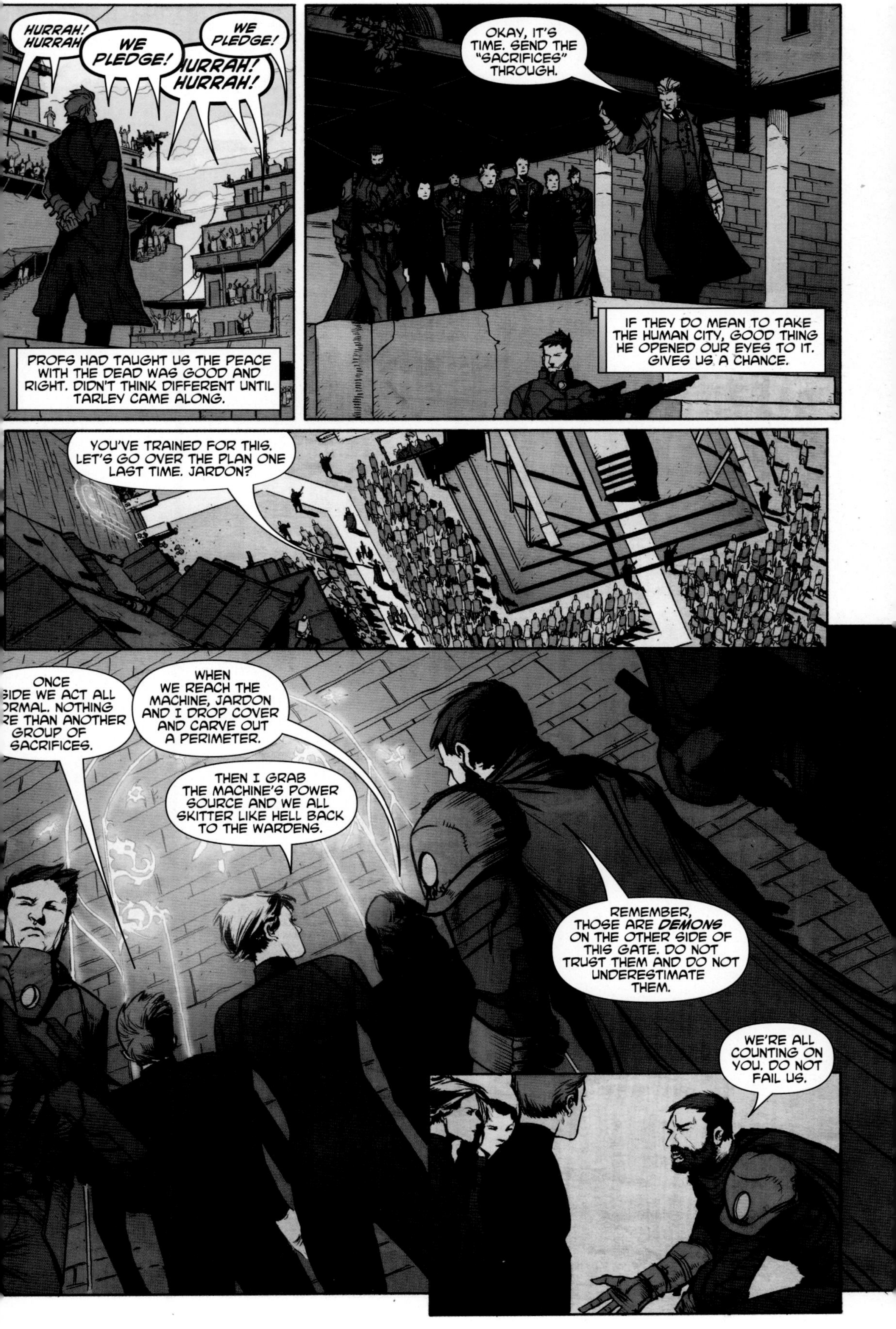
HURRAH! HURRAH
WE PLEDGE!
HURRAH! HURRAH!
WE PLEDGE!
PROFS HAD TAUGHT US THE PEACE WITH THE DEAD WAS GOOD AND RIGHT. DIDN'T THINK DIFFERENT UNTIL TARLEY CAME ALONG.
OKAY, IT'S TIME. SEND THE "SACRIFICES" THROUGH.
IF THEY DO MEAN TO TAKE THE HUMAN CITY, GOOD THING HE OPENED OUR EYES TO IT. GIVES US A CHANCE.
YOU'VE TRAINED FOR THIS. LET'S GO OVER THE PLAN ONE LAST TIME. JARDON?
ONCE SIDE WE ACT ALL ORMAL. NOTHING RE THAN ANOTHER GROUP OF SACRIFICES.
WHEN WE REACH THE MACHINE, JARDON AND I DROP COVER AND CARVE OUT A PERIMETER.
THEN I GRAB THE MACHINE'S POWER SOURCE AND WE ALL SKITTER LIKE HELL BACK TO THE WARDENS.
REMEMBER, THOSE ARE DEMONS ON THE OTHER SIDE OF THIS GATE. DO NOT TRUST THEM AND DO NOT UNDERESTIMATE THEM.
WE'RE ALL COUNTING ON YOU. DO NOT FAIL US.

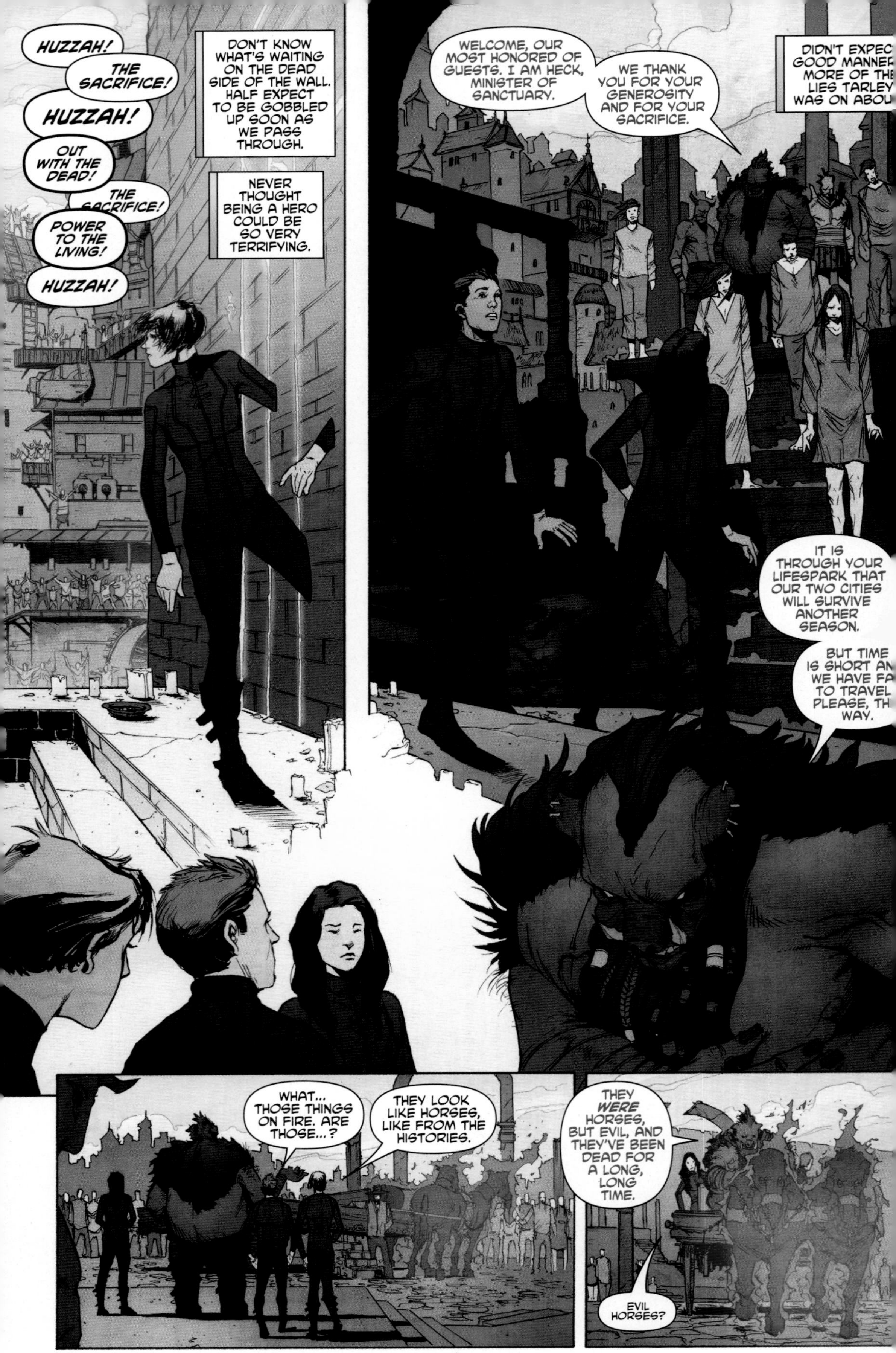
HUZZAH!
THE SACRIFICE!
HUZZAH!
OUT WITH THE DEAD!
THE SACRIFICE!
POWER TO THE LIVING!
HUZZAH!
DON'T KNOW WHAT'S WAITING ON THE DEAD SIDE OF THE WALL. HALF EXPECT TO BE GOBBLED UP SOON AS WE PASS THROUGH.
NEVER THOUGHT BEING A HERO COULD BE SO VERY TERRIFYING.
WELCOME, OUR MOST HONORED OF GUESTS. I AM HECK, MINISTER OF SANCTUARY.
WE THANK YOU FOR YOUR GENEROSITY AND FOR YOUR SACRIFICE.
DIDN'T EXPEC GOOD MANNER MORE OF THE LIES TARLEY WAS ON ABOU
IT IS THROUGH YOUR LIFESPARK THAT OUR TWO CITIES WILL SURVIVE ANOTHER SEASON.
BUT TIME IS SHORT AN WE HAVE FA TO TRAVEL PLEASE, TH WAY.
WHAT... THOSE THINGS ON FIRE. ARE THOSE...?
THEY LOOK LIKE HORSES, LIKE FROM THE HISTORIES.
THEY *WERE* HORSES, BUT EVIL, AND THEY'VE BEEN DEAD FOR A LONG, LONG TIME.
EVIL HORSES?

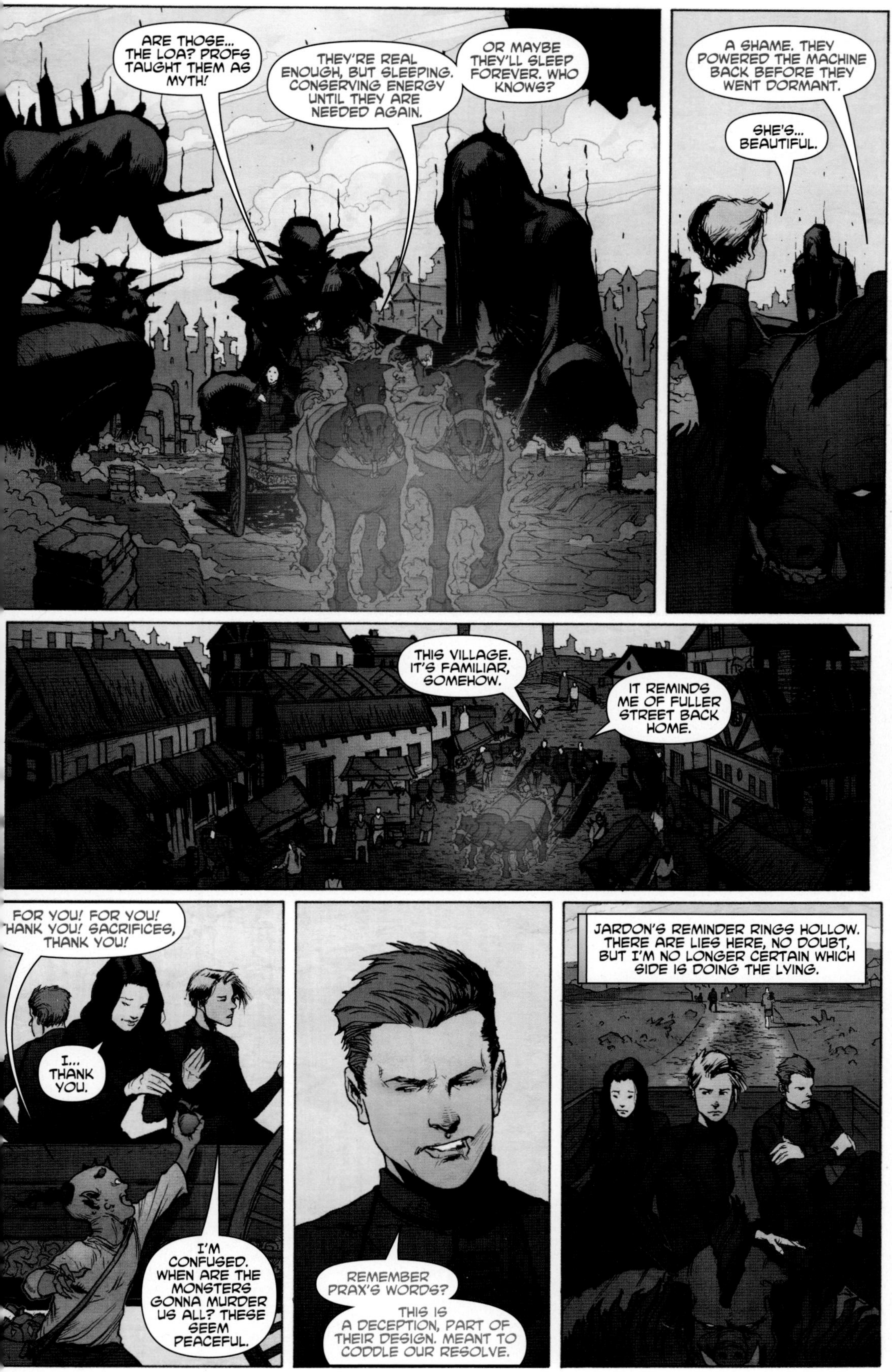
ARE THOSE... THE LOA? PROFS TAUGHT THEM AS MYTH!
THEY'RE REAL ENOUGH, BUT SLEEPING. CONSERVING ENERGY UNTIL THEY ARE NEEDED AGAIN.
OR MAYBE THEY'LL SLEEP FOREVER. WHO KNOWS?
A SHAME. THEY POWERED THE MACHINE BACK BEFORE THEY WENT DORMANT.
SHE'S... BEAUTIFUL.
THIS VILLAGE. IT'S FAMILIAR, SOMEHOW.
IT REMINDS ME OF FULLER STREET BACK HOME.
FOR YOU! FOR YOU! THANK YOU! SACRIFICES, THANK YOU!
I... THANK YOU.
I'M CONFUSED. WHEN ARE THE MONSTERS GONNA MURDER US ALL? THESE SEEM PEACEFUL.
REMEMBER PRAX'S WORDS?
THIS IS A DECEPTION, PART OF THEIR DESIGN. MEANT TO CODDLE OUR RESOLVE.
JARDON'S REMINDER RINGS HOLLOW. THERE ARE LIES HERE, NO DOUBT, BUT I'M NO LONGER CERTAIN WHICH SIDE IS DOING THE LYING.

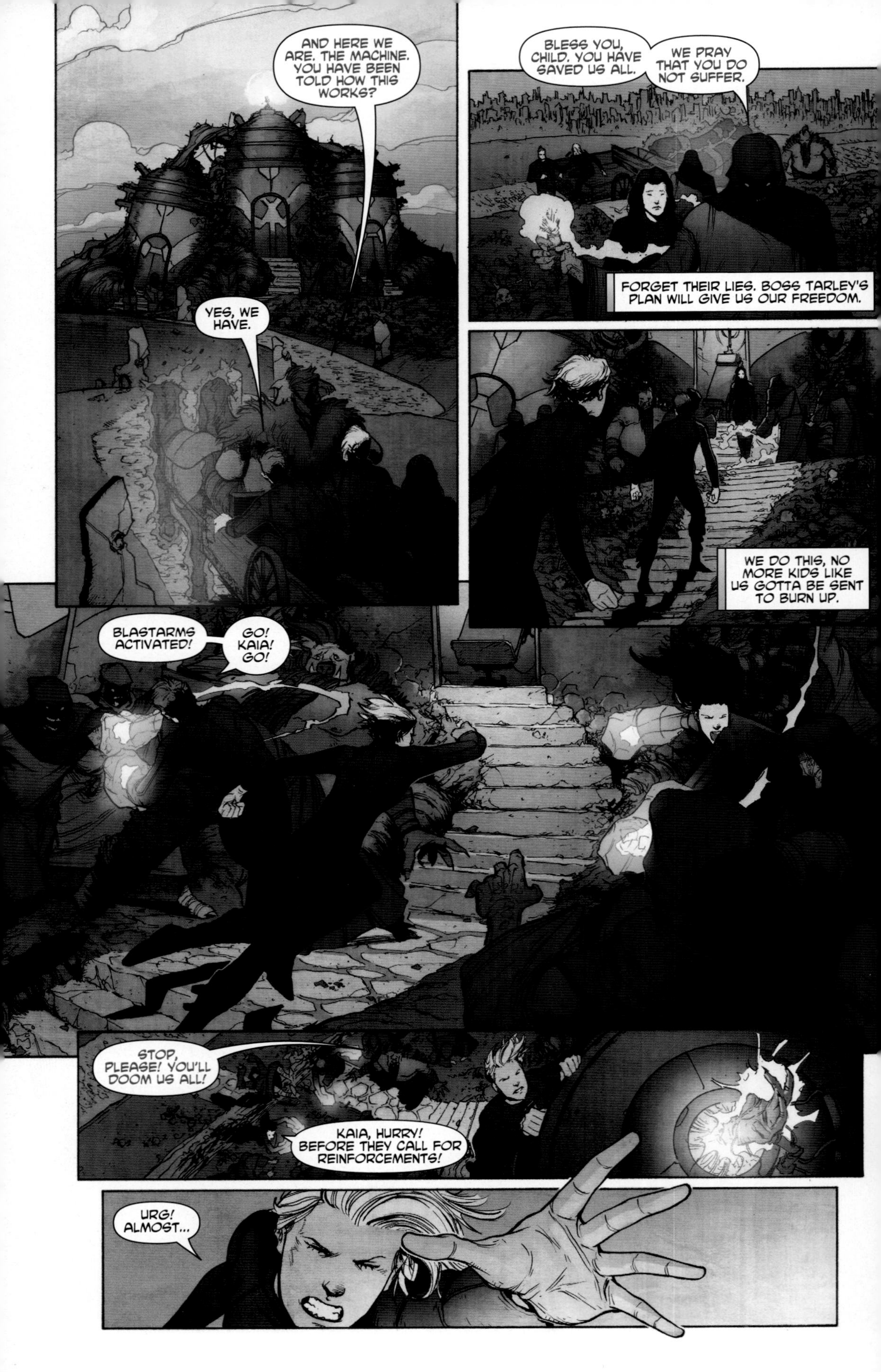
AND HERE WE ARE. THE MACHINE. YOU HAVE BEEN TOLD HOW THIS WORKS?
YES, WE HAVE.
BLESS YOU, CHILD. YOU HAVE SAVED US ALL.
WE PRAY THAT YOU DO NOT SUFFER.
FORGET THEIR LIES. BOSS TARLEY'S PLAN WILL GIVE US OUR FREEDOM.
WE DO THIS, NO MORE KIDS LIKE US GOTTA BE SENT TO BURN UP.
BLASTARMS ACTIVATED!
GO! KAIA! GO!
STOP, PLEASE! YOU'LL DOOM US ALL!
KAIA, HURRY! BEFORE THEY CALL FOR REINFORCEMENTS!
URG! ALMOST...

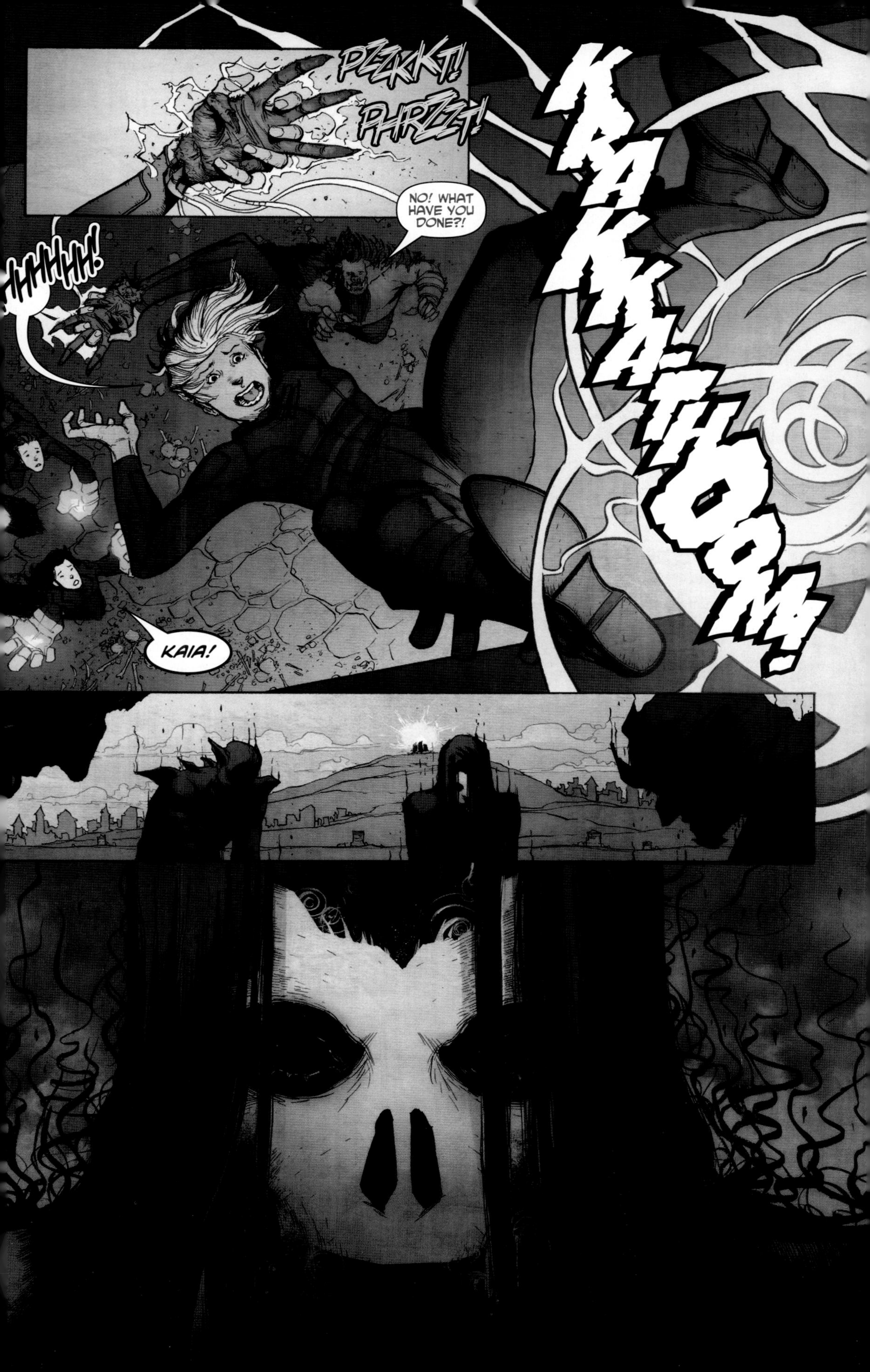
PZZKKT!
PHRZZT!
KRAKKATHOOM!
NO! WHAT HAVE YOU DONE?!
HHHHHH!
KAIA!

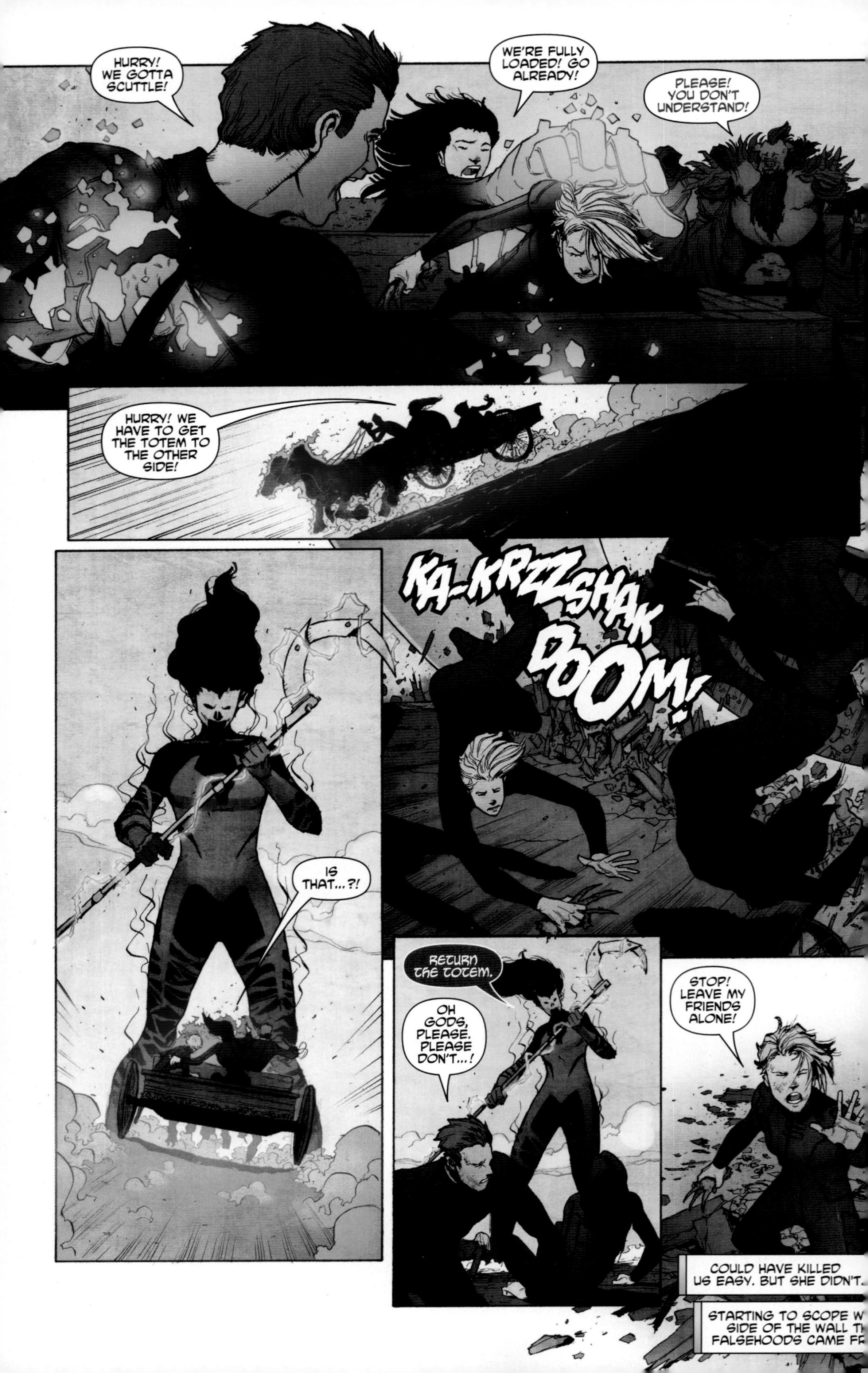

HURRY! WE GOTTA SCUTTLE!
WE'RE FULLY LOADED! GO ALREADY!
PLEASE! YOU DON'T UNDERSTAND!
HURRY! WE HAVE TO GET THE TOTEM TO THE OTHER SIDE!
KA-KRZZSHAK DOOM!
IS THAT...?!
RETURN THE TOTEM.
OH GODS, PLEASE. PLEASE DON'T...!
STOP! LEAVE MY FRIENDS ALONE!
COULD HAVE KILLED US EASY. BUT SHE DIDN'T.

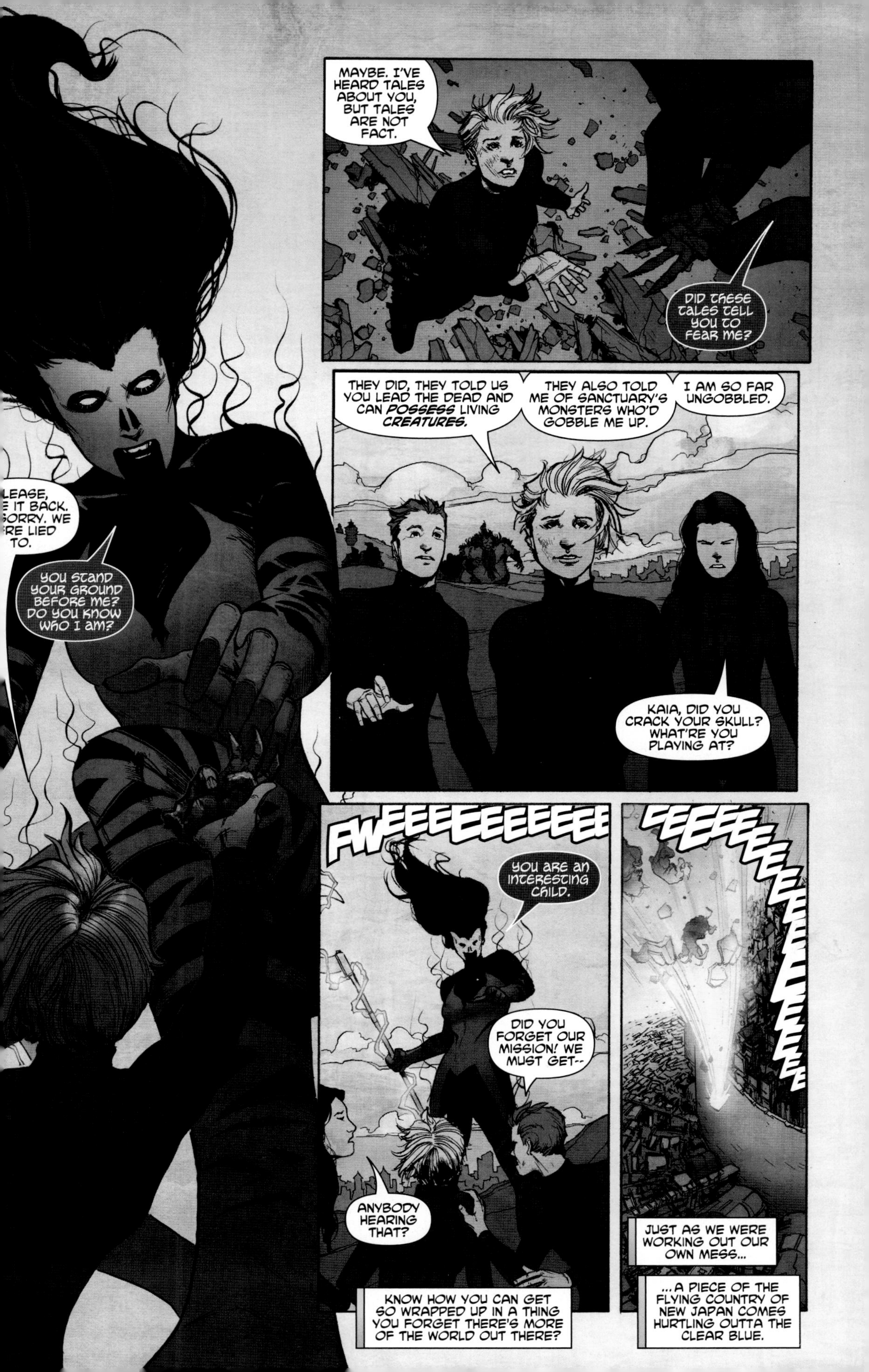
LEASE,
E IT BACK.
SORRY. WE
RE LIED
TO.
YOU STAND YOUR GROUND BEFORE ME? DO YOU KNOW WHO I AM?
MAYBE. I'VE HEARD TALES ABOUT YOU, BUT TALES ARE NOT FACT.
DID THESE TALES TELL YOU TO FEAR ME?
THEY DID, THEY TOLD US YOU LEAD THE DEAD AND CAN *POSSESS* LIVING *CREATURES.*
THEY ALSO TOLD ME OF SANCTUARY'S MONSTERS WHO'D GOBBLE ME UP.
I AM SO FAR UNGOBBLED.
KAIA, DID YOU CRACK YOUR SKULL? WHAT'RE YOU PLAYING AT?
FWEEEEEEEEEEEEE
YOU ARE AN INTERESTING CHILD.
DID YOU FORGET OUR MISSION! WE MUST GET--
ANYBODY HEARING THAT?
KNOW HOW YOU CAN GET SO WRAPPED UP IN A THING YOU FORGET THERE'S MORE OF THE WORLD OUT THERE?
EEEEEEEEEEEEEEEEE
JUST AS WE WERE WORKING OUT OUR OWN MESS...
...A PIECE OF THE FLYING COUNTRY OF NEW JAPAN COMES HURTLING OUTTA THE CLEAR BLUE.

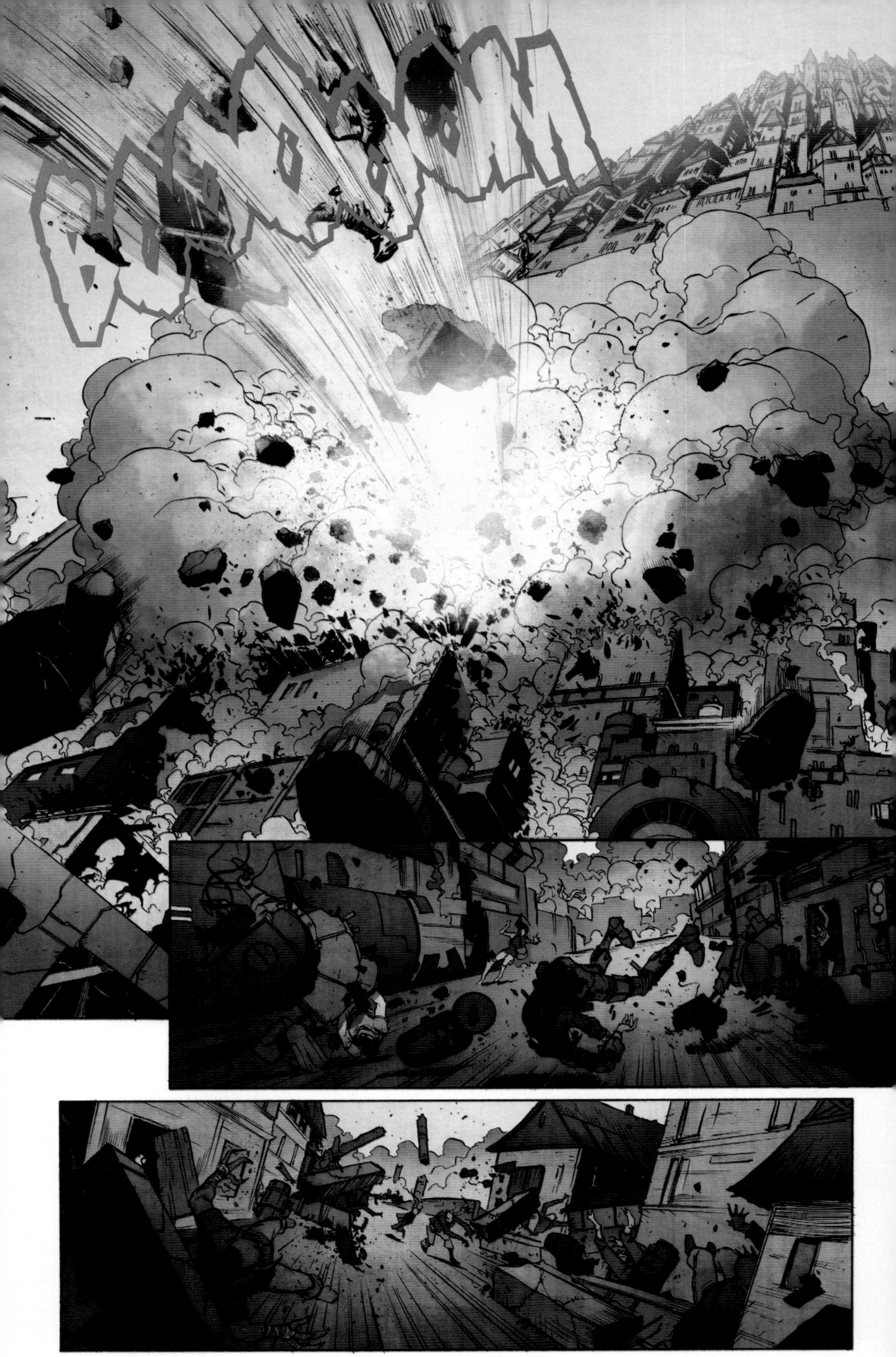
BOOOOM

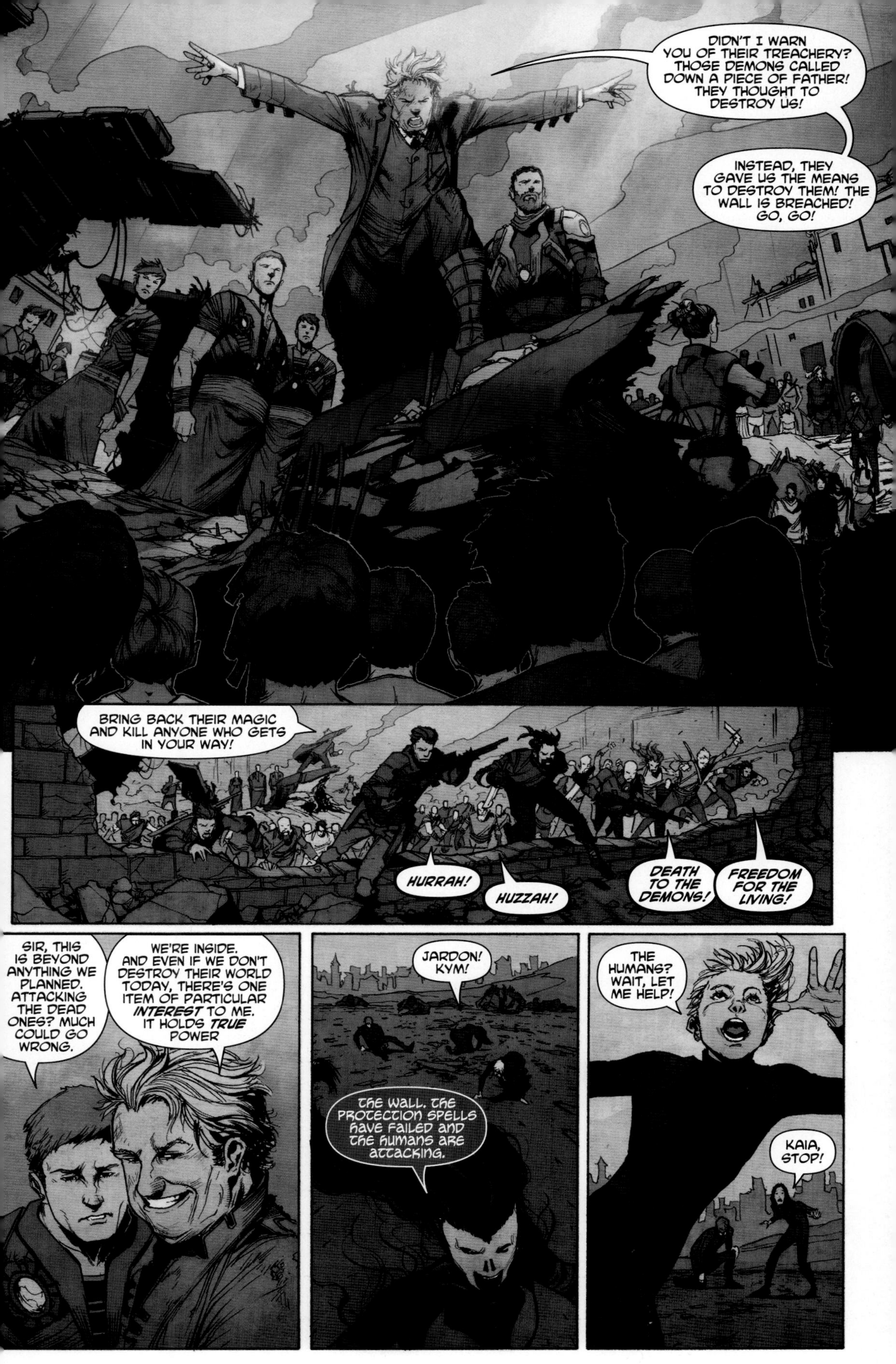
DIDN'T I WARN YOU OF THEIR TREACHERY? THOSE DEMONS CALLED DOWN A PIECE OF FATHER! THEY THOUGHT TO DESTROY US!
INSTEAD, THEY GAVE US THE MEANS TO DESTROY THEM! THE WALL IS BREACHED! GO, GO!
BRING BACK THEIR MAGIC AND KILL ANYONE WHO GETS IN YOUR WAY!
HURRAH!
HUZZAH!
DEATH TO THE DEMONS!
FREEDOM FOR THE LIVING!
SIR, THIS IS BEYOND ANYTHING WE PLANNED. ATTACKING THE DEAD ONES? MUCH COULD GO WRONG.
WE'RE INSIDE. AND EVEN IF WE DON'T DESTROY THEIR WORLD TODAY, THERE'S ONE ITEM OF PARTICULAR INTEREST TO ME. IT HOLDS TRUE POWER
JARDON! KYM!
THE WALL. THE PROTECTION SPELLS HAVE FAILED AND THE HUMANS ARE ATTACKING.
THE HUMANS? WAIT, LET ME HELP!
KAIA, STOP!

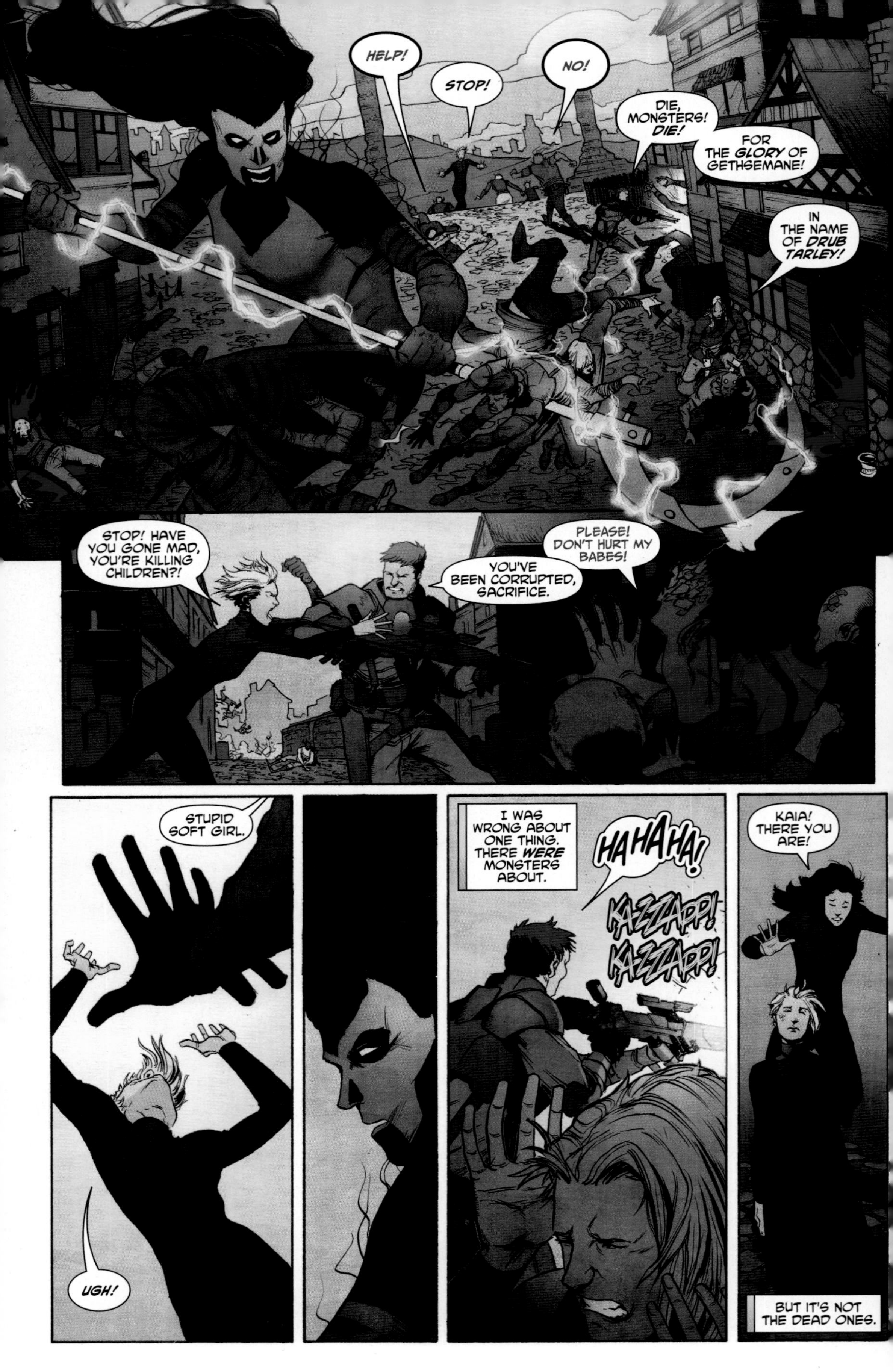
HELP!
STOP!
NO!
DIE, MONSTERS! DIE!
FOR THE GLORY OF GETHSEMANE!
IN THE NAME OF DRUB TARLEY!
STOP! HAVE YOU GONE MAD, YOU'RE KILLING CHILDREN?!
YOU'VE BEEN CORRUPTED, SACRIFICE.
PLEASE! DON'T HURT MY BABES!
STUPID SOFT GIRL.
UGH!
I WAS WRONG ABOUT ONE THING. THERE WERE MONSTERS ABOUT.
HAHAHA!
KAZZAPP! KAZZAPP!
KAIA! THERE YOU ARE!
BUT IT'S NOT THE DEAD ONES.

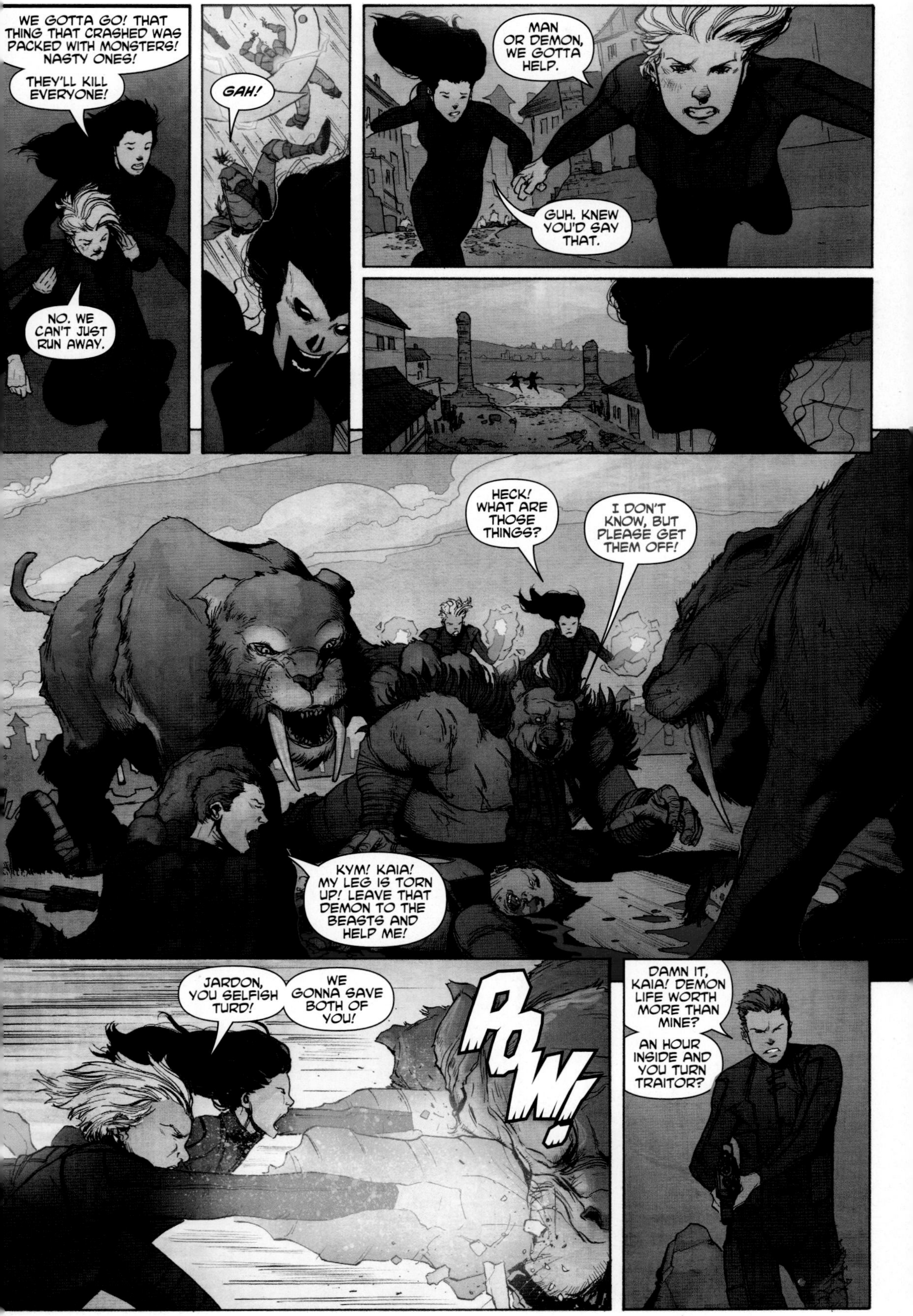
WE GOTTA GO! THAT THING THAT CRASHED WAS PACKED WITH MONSTERS! NASTY ONES!
THEY'LL KILL EVERYONE!
NO. WE CAN'T JUST RUN AWAY.
GAH!
MAN OR DEMON, WE GOTTA HELP.
GUH. KNEW YOU'D SAY THAT.
HECK! WHAT ARE THOSE THINGS?
I DON'T KNOW, BUT PLEASE GET THEM OFF!
KYM! KAIA! MY LEG IS TORN UP! LEAVE THAT DEMON TO THE BEASTS AND HELP ME!
JARDON, YOU SELFISH TURD!
WE GONNA SAVE BOTH OF YOU!
POW!
DAMN IT, KAIA! DEMON LIFE WORTH MORE THAN MINE?
AN HOUR INSIDE AND YOU TURN TRAITOR?

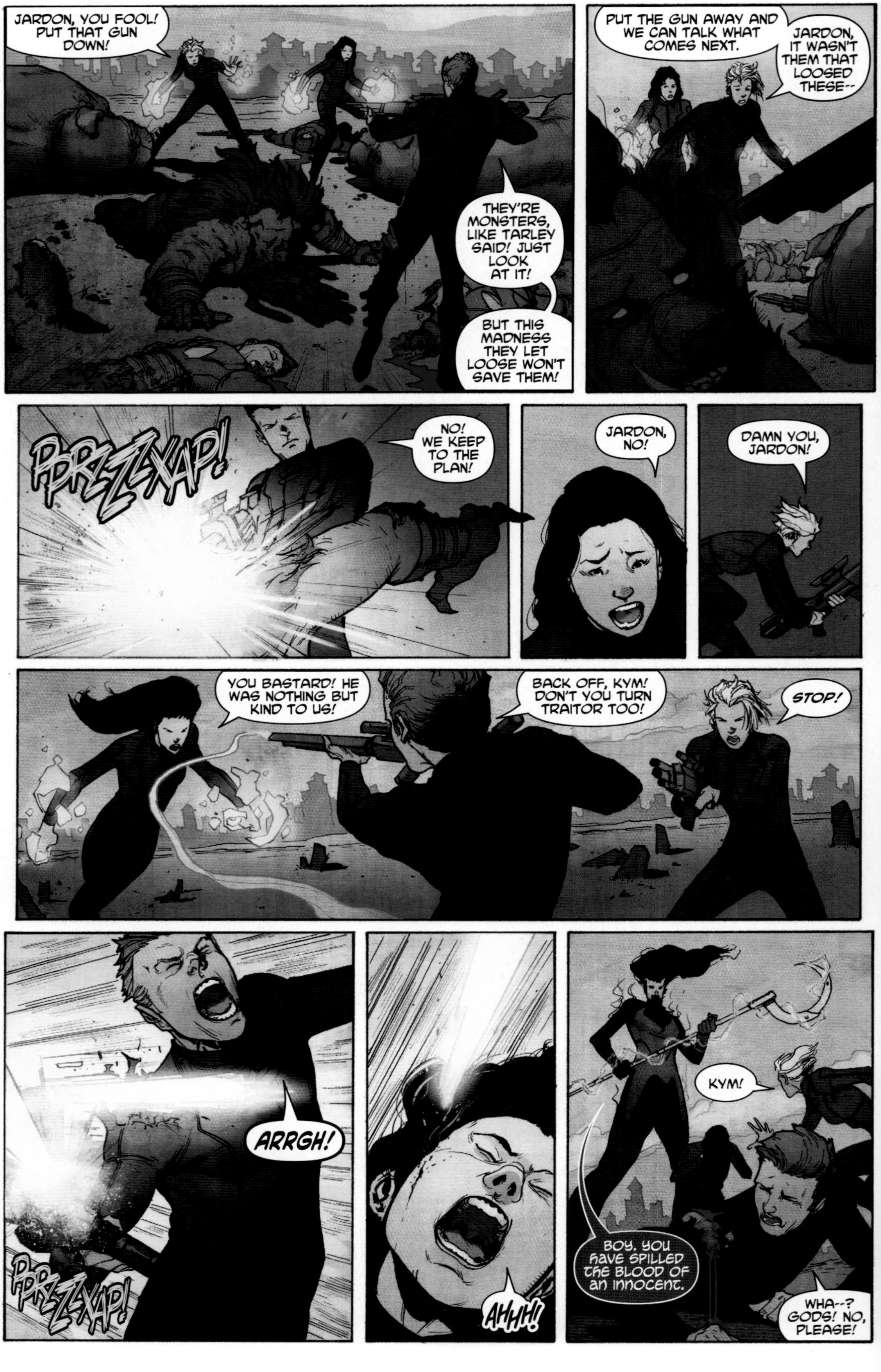
JARDON, YOU FOOL! PUT THAT GUN DOWN!
THEY'RE MONSTERS, LIKE TARLEY SAID! JUST LOOK AT IT!
BUT THIS MADNESS THEY LET LOOSE WON'T SAVE THEM!
PUT THE GUN AWAY AND WE CAN TALK WHAT COMES NEXT.
JARDON, IT WASN'T THEM THAT LOOSED THESE--
PPRZZXAP!
NO! WE KEEP TO THE PLAN!
JARDON, NO!
DAMN YOU, JARDON!
YOU BASTARD! HE WAS NOTHING BUT KIND TO US!
BACK OFF, KYM! DON'T YOU TURN TRAITOR TOO!
STOP!
ARRGH!
PPRZZXAP!
AHHH!
KYM!
BOY. YOU HAVE SPILLED THE BLOOD OF AN INNOCENT.
WHA--? GODS! NO, PLEASE!

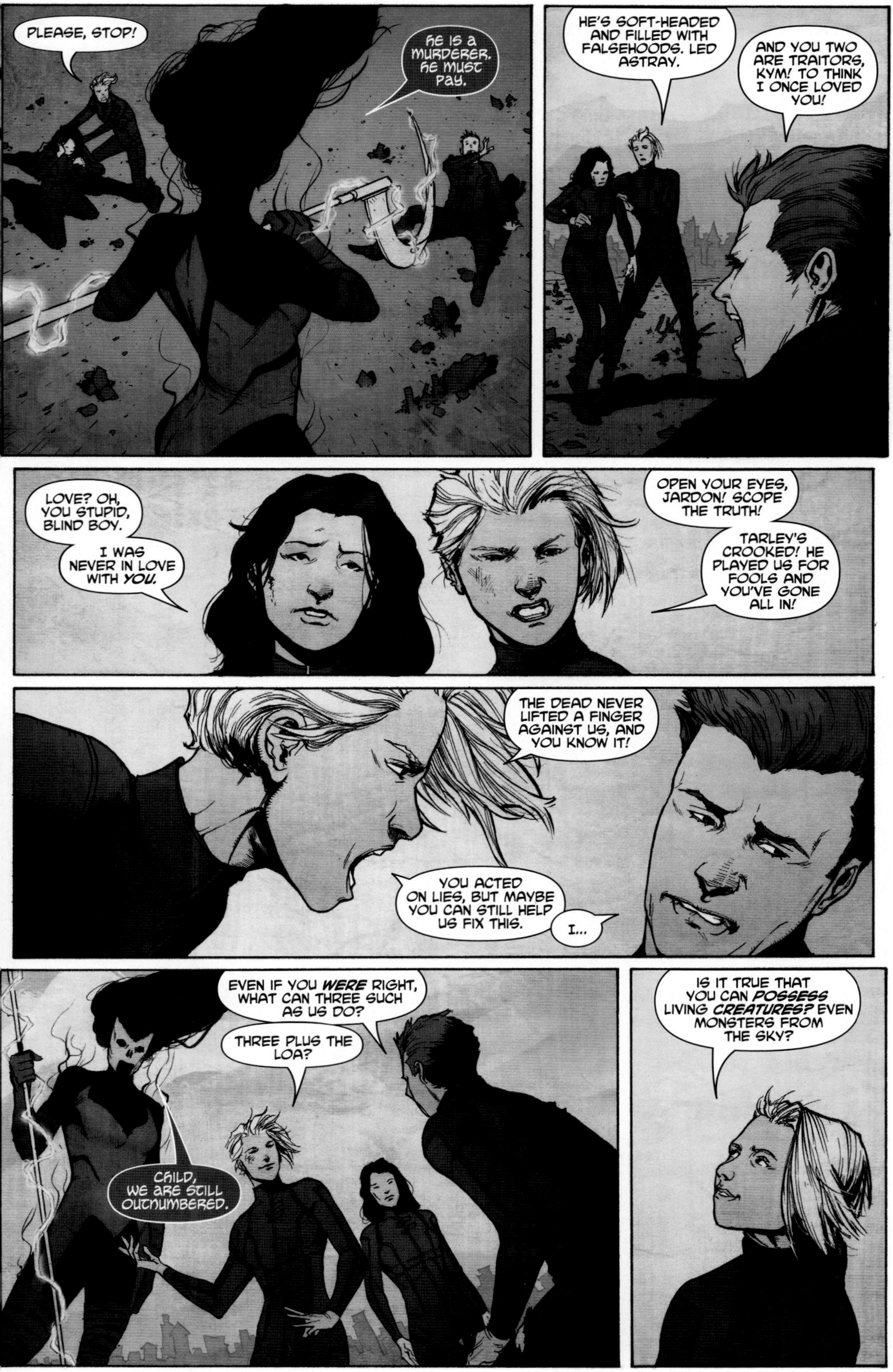
PLEASE, STOP!
HE IS A MURDERER. HE MUST PAY.
HE'S SOFT-HEADED AND FILLED WITH FALSEHOODS. LED ASTRAY.
AND YOU TWO ARE TRAITORS, KYM! TO THINK I ONCE LOVED YOU!
LOVE? OH, YOU STUPID, BLIND BOY.
I WAS NEVER IN LOVE WITH *YOU.*
OPEN YOUR EYES, JARDON! SCOPE THE TRUTH!
TARLEY'S CROOKED! HE PLAYED US FOR FOOLS AND YOU'VE GONE ALL IN!
THE DEAD NEVER LIFTED A FINGER AGAINST US, AND YOU KNOW IT!
YOU ACTED ON LIES, BUT MAYBE YOU CAN STILL HELP US FIX THIS.
I...
EVEN IF YOU *WERE* RIGHT, WHAT CAN THREE SUCH AS US DO?
THREE PLUS THE LOA?
CHILD, WE ARE STILL OUTNUMBERED.
IS IT TRUE THAT YOU CAN *POSSESS* LIVING *CREATURES?* EVEN MONSTERS FROM THE SKY?

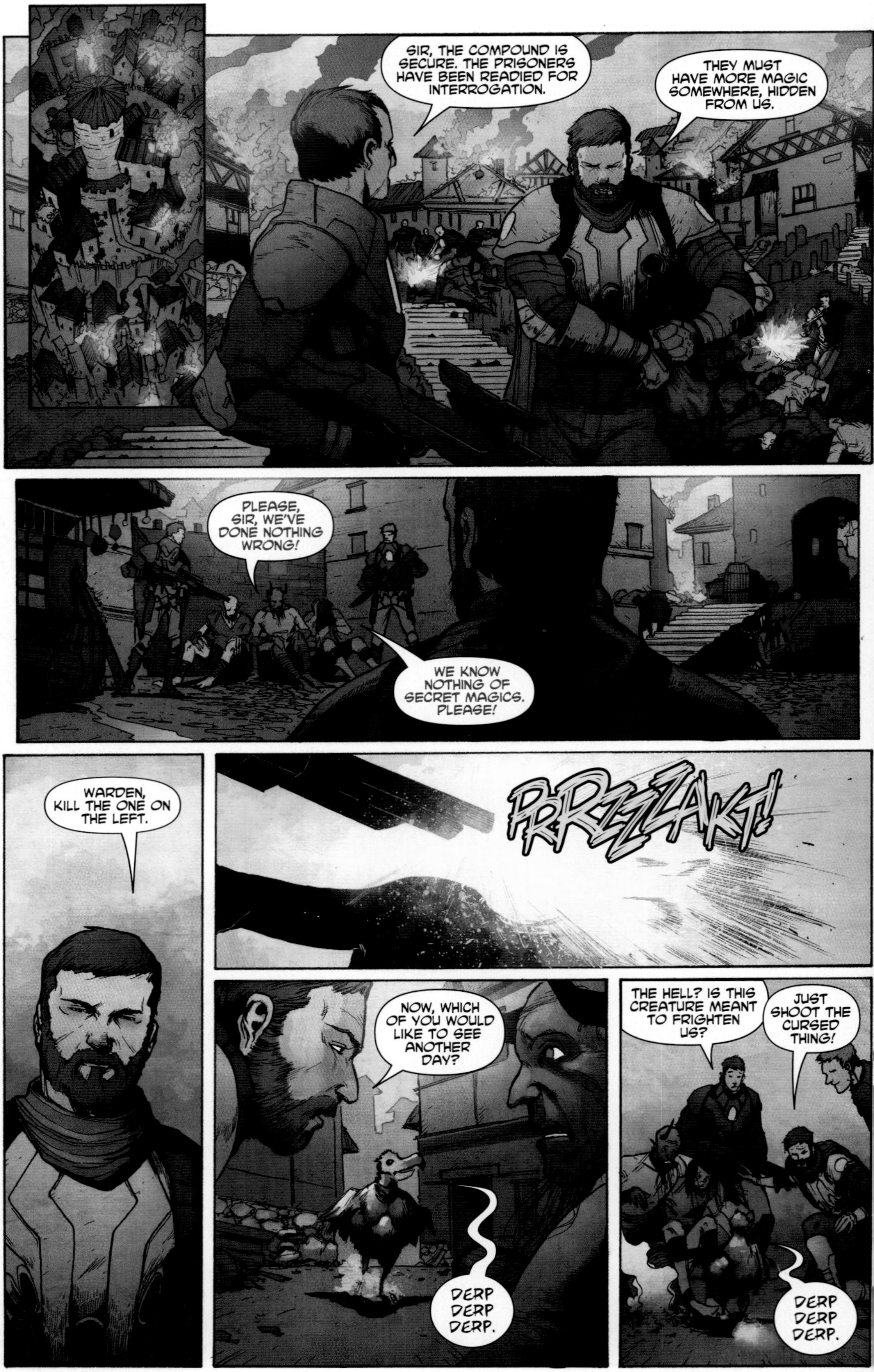
SIR, THE COMPOUND IS SECURE. THE PRISONERS HAVE BEEN READIED FOR INTERROGATION.
THEY MUST HAVE MORE MAGIC SOMEWHERE, HIDDEN FROM US.
PLEASE, SIR, WE'VE DONE NOTHING WRONG!
WE KNOW NOTHING OF SECRET MAGICS. PLEASE!
WARDEN, KILL THE ONE ON THE LEFT.
PRRZZZAKT!
NOW, WHICH OF YOU WOULD LIKE TO SEE ANOTHER DAY?
DERP DERP DERP.
THE HELL? IS THIS CREATURE MEANT TO FRIGHTEN US?
JUST SHOOT THE CURSED THING!
DERP DERP DERP.

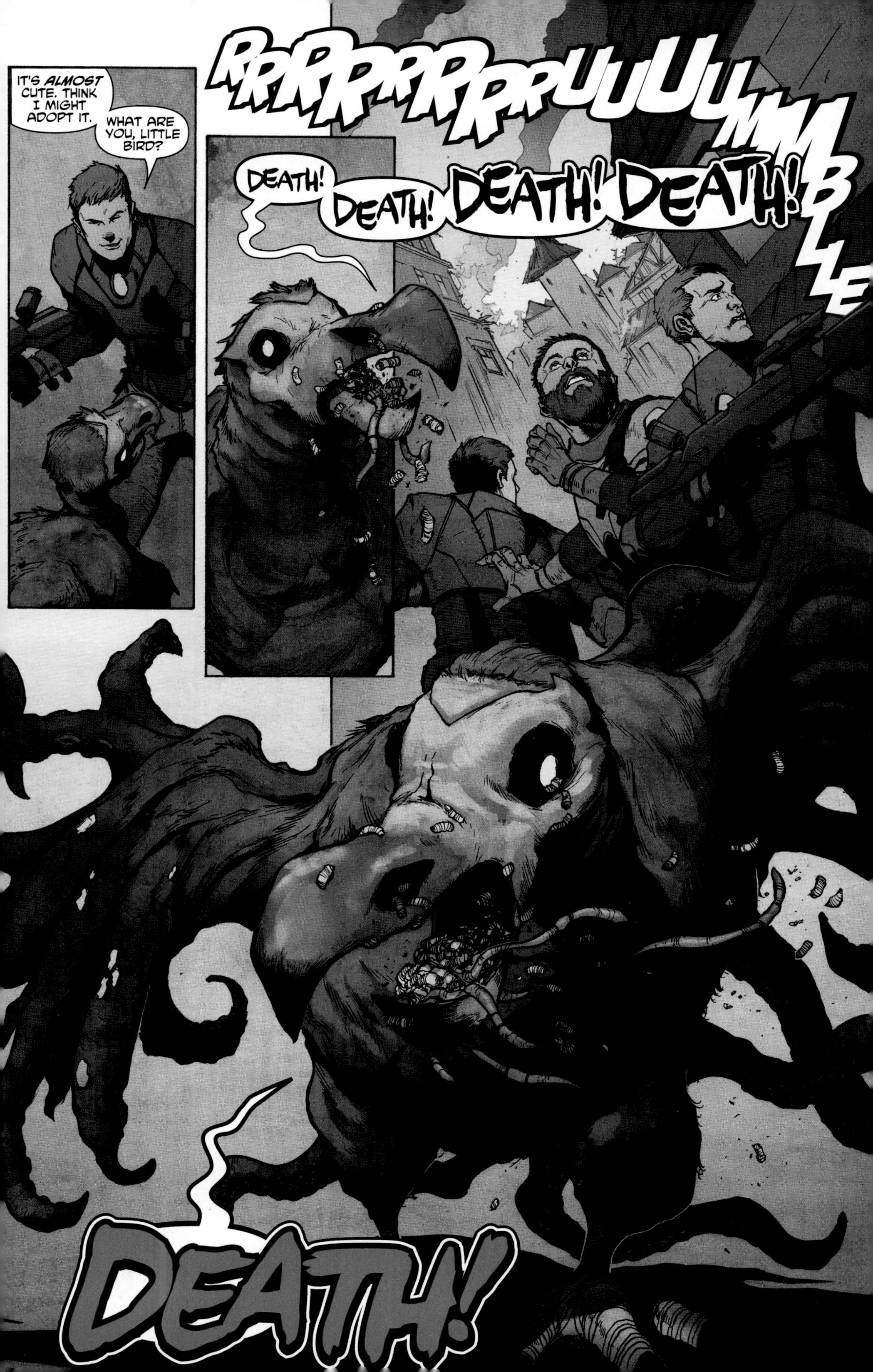
IT'S *ALMOST* CUTE. THINK I MIGHT ADOPT IT.
WHAT ARE YOU, LITTLE BIRD?
RRRRRRRRRRRRUUUUUMMBLE
DEATH!
DEATH!
DEATH!
DEATH!
DEATH!

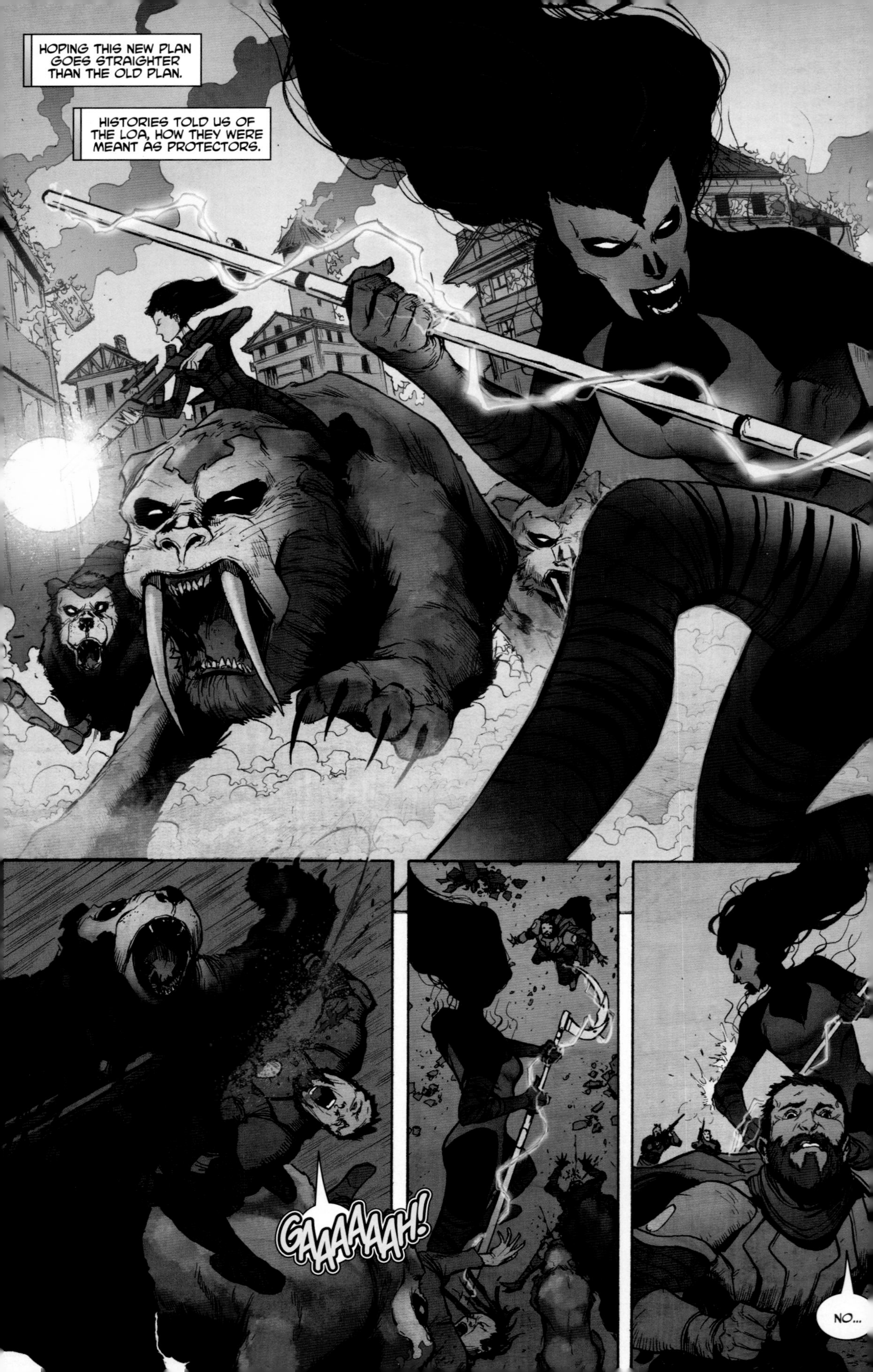
HOPING THIS NEW PLAN GOES STRAIGHTER THAN THE OLD PLAN.
HISTORIES TOLD US OF THE LOA, HOW THEY WERE MEANT AS PROTECTORS.
GAAAAAAH!
NO...

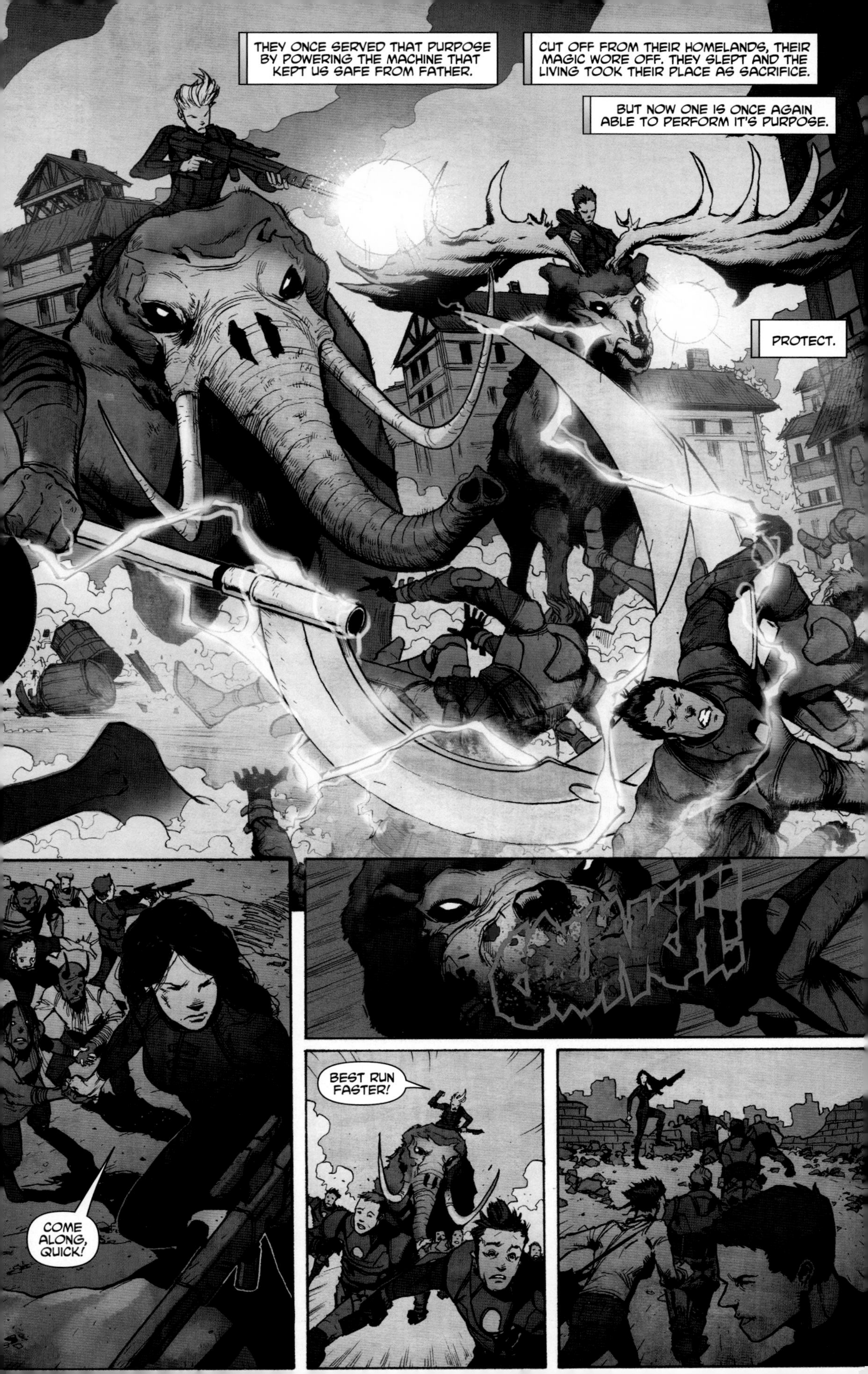
THEY ONCE SERVED THAT PURPOSE BY POWERING THE MACHINE THAT KEPT US SAFE FROM FATHER.
CUT OFF FROM THEIR HOMELANDS, THEIR MAGIC WORE OFF. THEY SLEPT AND THE LIVING TOOK THEIR PLACE AS SACRIFICE.
BUT NOW ONE IS ONCE AGAIN ABLE TO PERFORM IT'S PURPOSE.
PROTECT.
COME ALONG, QUICK!
BEST RUN FASTER!

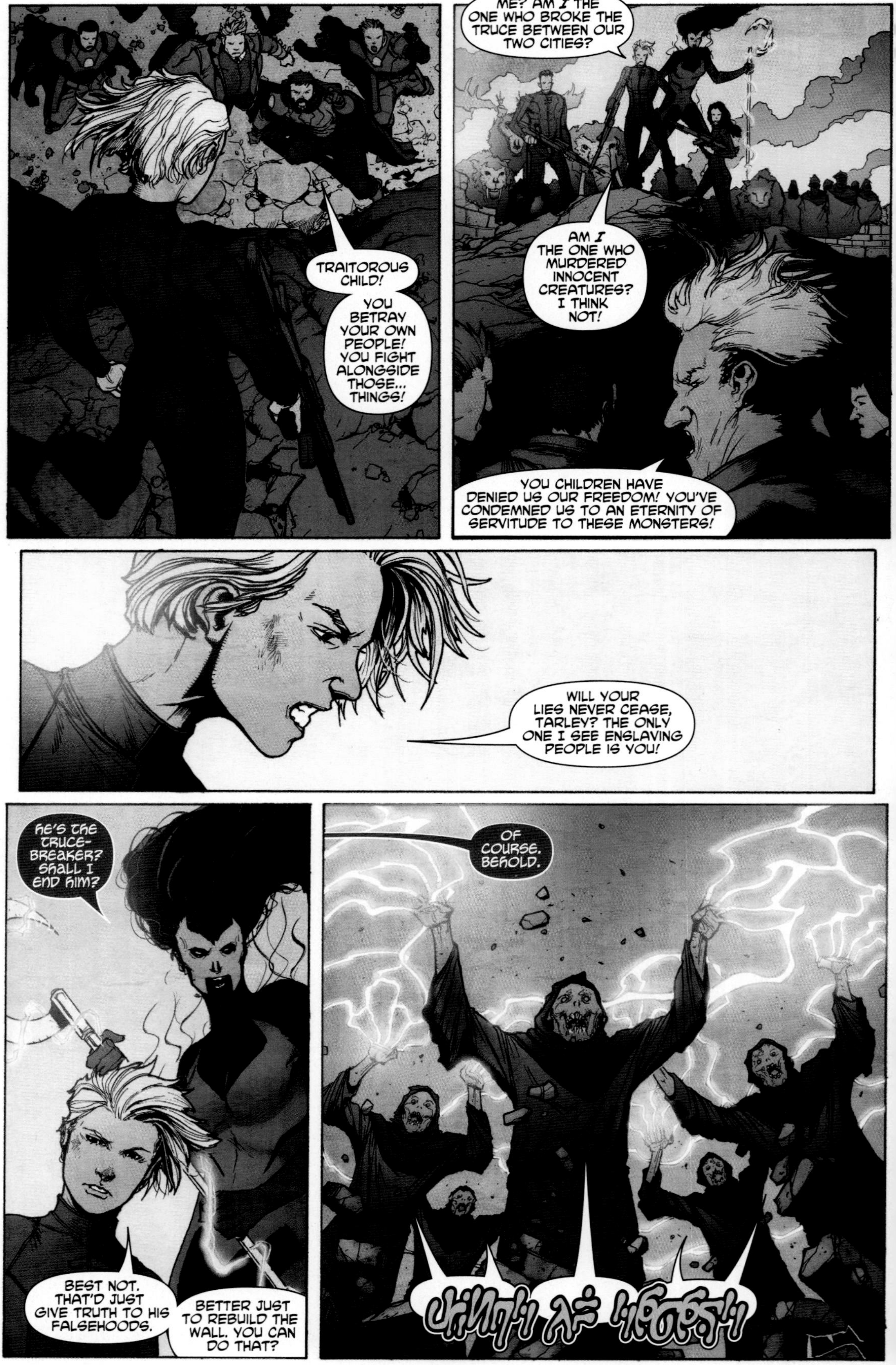
TRAITOROUS CHILD!
YOU BETRAY YOUR OWN PEOPLE! YOU FIGHT ALONGSIDE THOSE... THINGS!
ME? AM I THE ONE WHO BROKE THE TRUCE BETWEEN OUR TWO CITIES?
AM I THE ONE WHO MURDERED INNOCENT CREATURES? I THINK NOT!
YOU CHILDREN HAVE DENIED US OUR FREEDOM! YOU'VE CONDEMNED US TO AN ETERNITY OF SERVITUDE TO THESE MONSTERS!
WILL YOUR LIES NEVER CEASE, TARLEY? THE ONLY ONE I SEE ENSLAVING PEOPLE IS YOU!
HE'S THE TRUCE-BREAKER? SHALL I END HIM?
BEST NOT. THAT'D JUST GIVE TRUTH TO HIS FALSEHOODS.
BETTER JUST TO REBUILD THE WALL. YOU CAN DO THAT?
OF COURSE. BEHOLD.

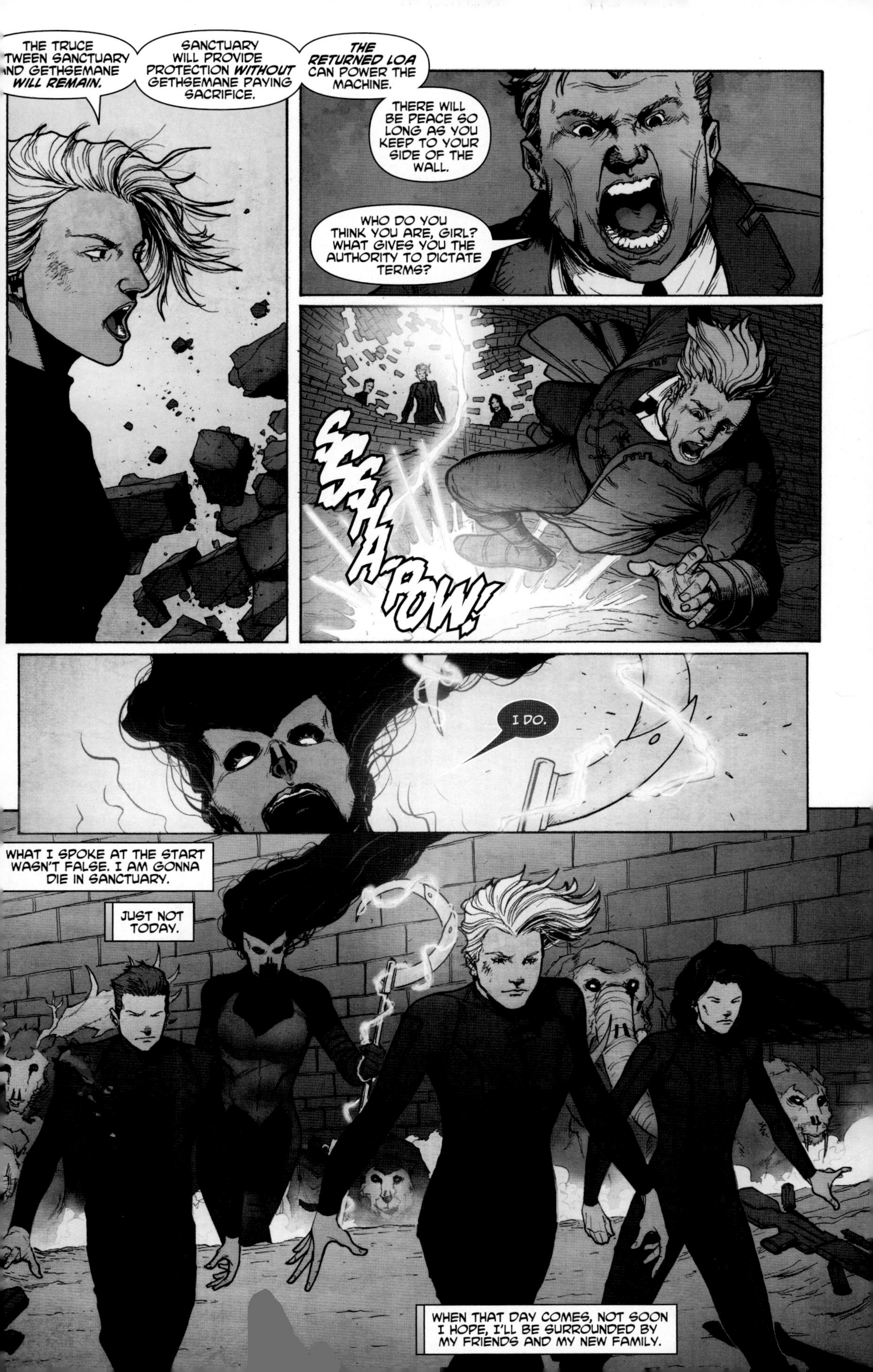
THE TRUCE TWEEN SANCTUARY AND GETHSEMANE WILL REMAIN.
SANCTUARY WILL PROVIDE PROTECTION WITHOUT GETHSEMANE PAYING SACRIFICE.
THE RETURNED LOA CAN POWER THE MACHINE.
THERE WILL BE PEACE SO LONG AS YOU KEEP TO YOUR SIDE OF THE WALL.
WHO DO YOU THINK YOU ARE, GIRL? WHAT GIVES YOU THE AUTHORITY TO DICTATE TERMS?
SSSHA-POW!
I DO.
WHAT I SPOKE AT THE START WASN'T FALSE. I AM GONNA DIE IN SANCTUARY.
JUST NOT TODAY.
WHEN THAT DAY COMES, NOT SOON I HOPE, I'LL BE SURROUNDED BY MY FRIENDS AND MY NEW FAMILY.

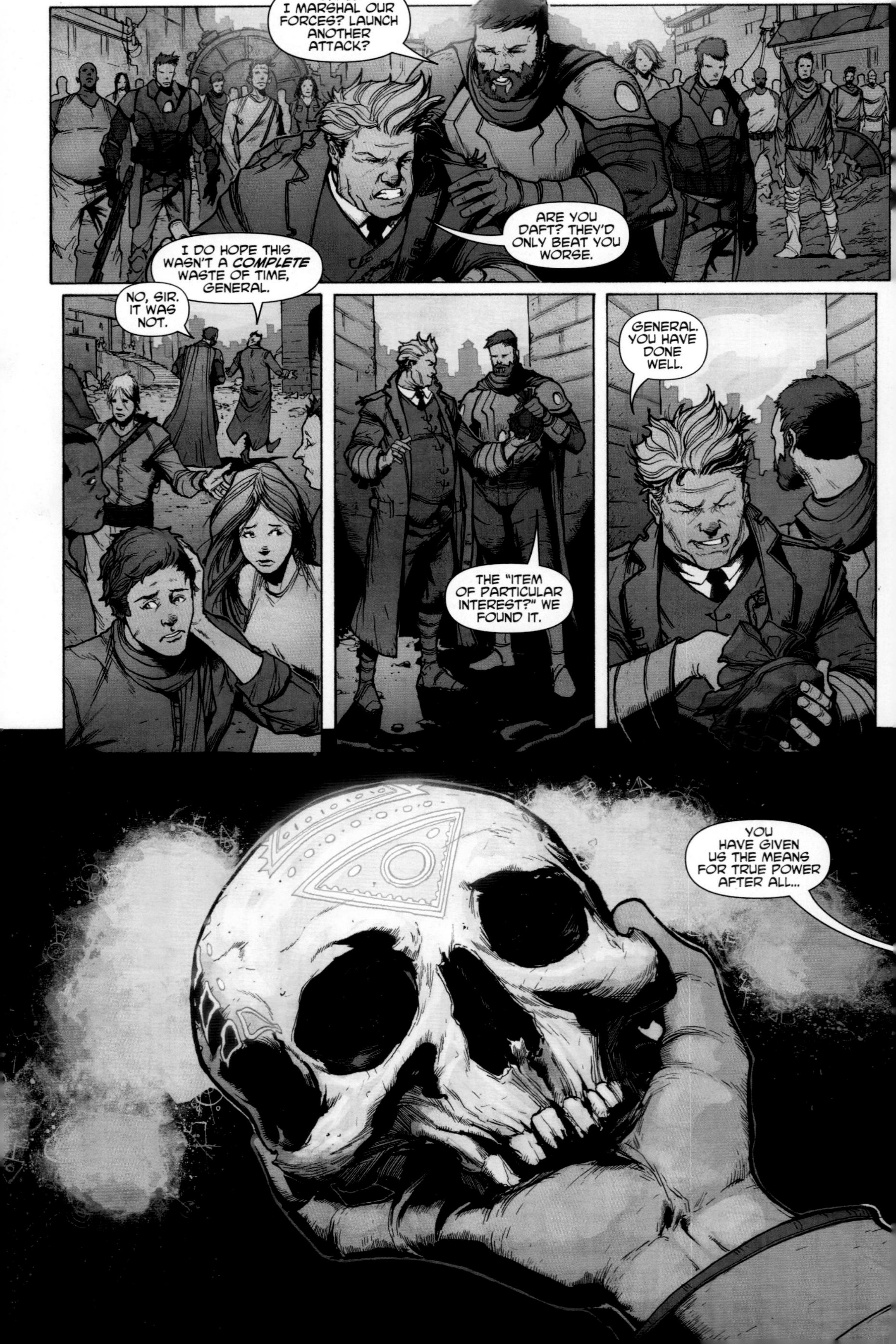
SHALL I MARSHAL OUR FORCES? LAUNCH ANOTHER ATTACK?
ARE YOU DAFT? THEY'D ONLY BEAT YOU WORSE.
I DO HOPE THIS WASN'T A *COMPLETE* WASTE OF TIME, GENERAL.
NO, SIR. IT WAS NOT.
THE "ITEM OF PARTICULAR INTEREST?" WE FOUND IT.
GENERAL. YOU HAVE DONE WELL.
YOU HAVE GIVEN US THE MEANS FOR TRUE POWER AFTER ALL...

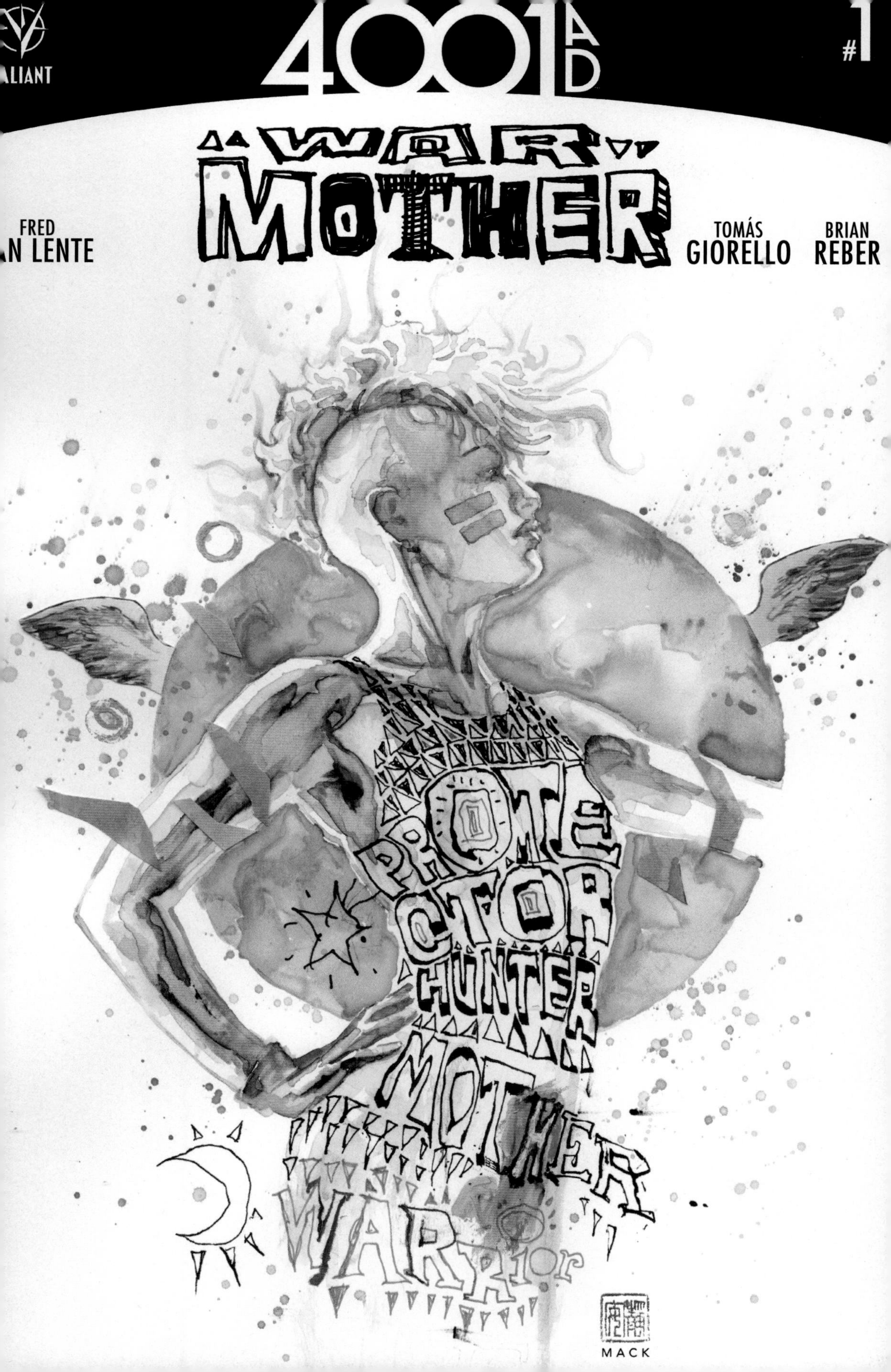

ALIANT
4001 AD
#1
WAR
MOTHER
FRED
N LENTE
TOMÁS
GIORELLO
BRIAN
REBER
PROTECTOR
HUNTER
MOTHER
WARRIOR
MACK

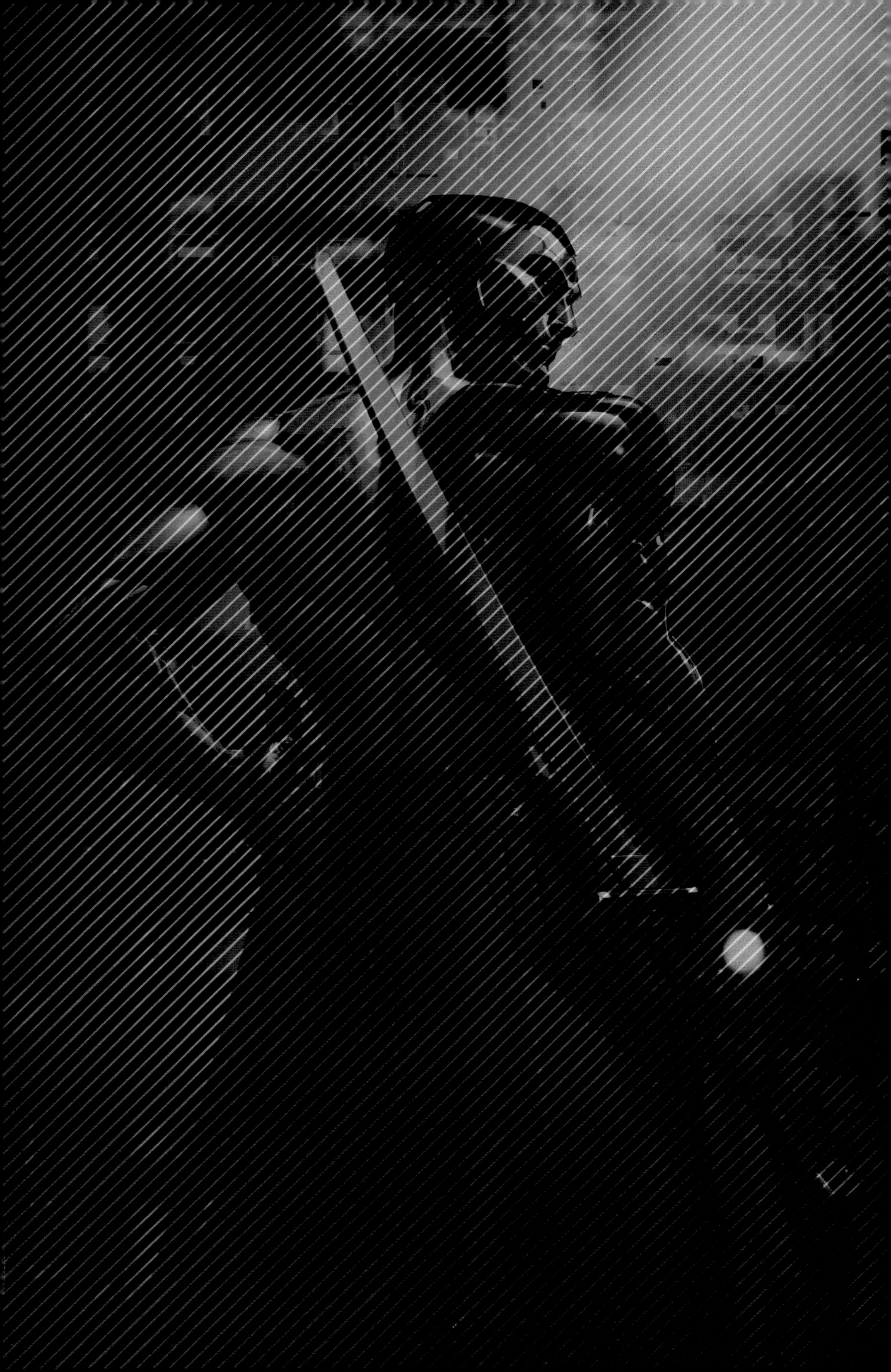

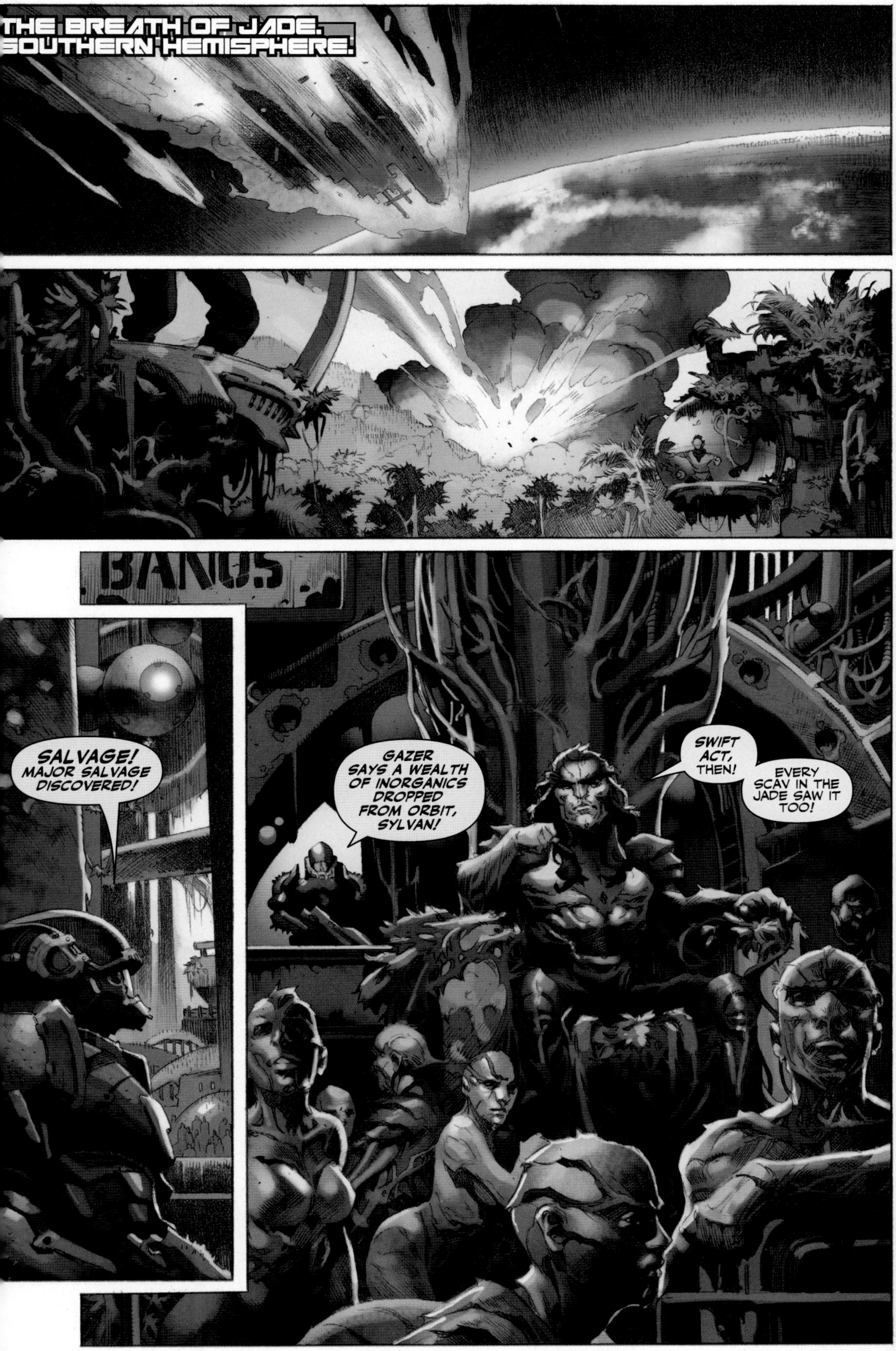
THE BREATH OF JADE. SOUTHERN HEMISPHERE.
BANOS
SALVAGE! MAJOR SALVAGE DISCOVERED!
GAZER SAYS A WEALTH OF INORGANICS DROPPED FROM ORBIT, SYLVAN!
SWIFT ACT, THEN!
EVERY SCAV IN THE JADE SAW IT TOO!

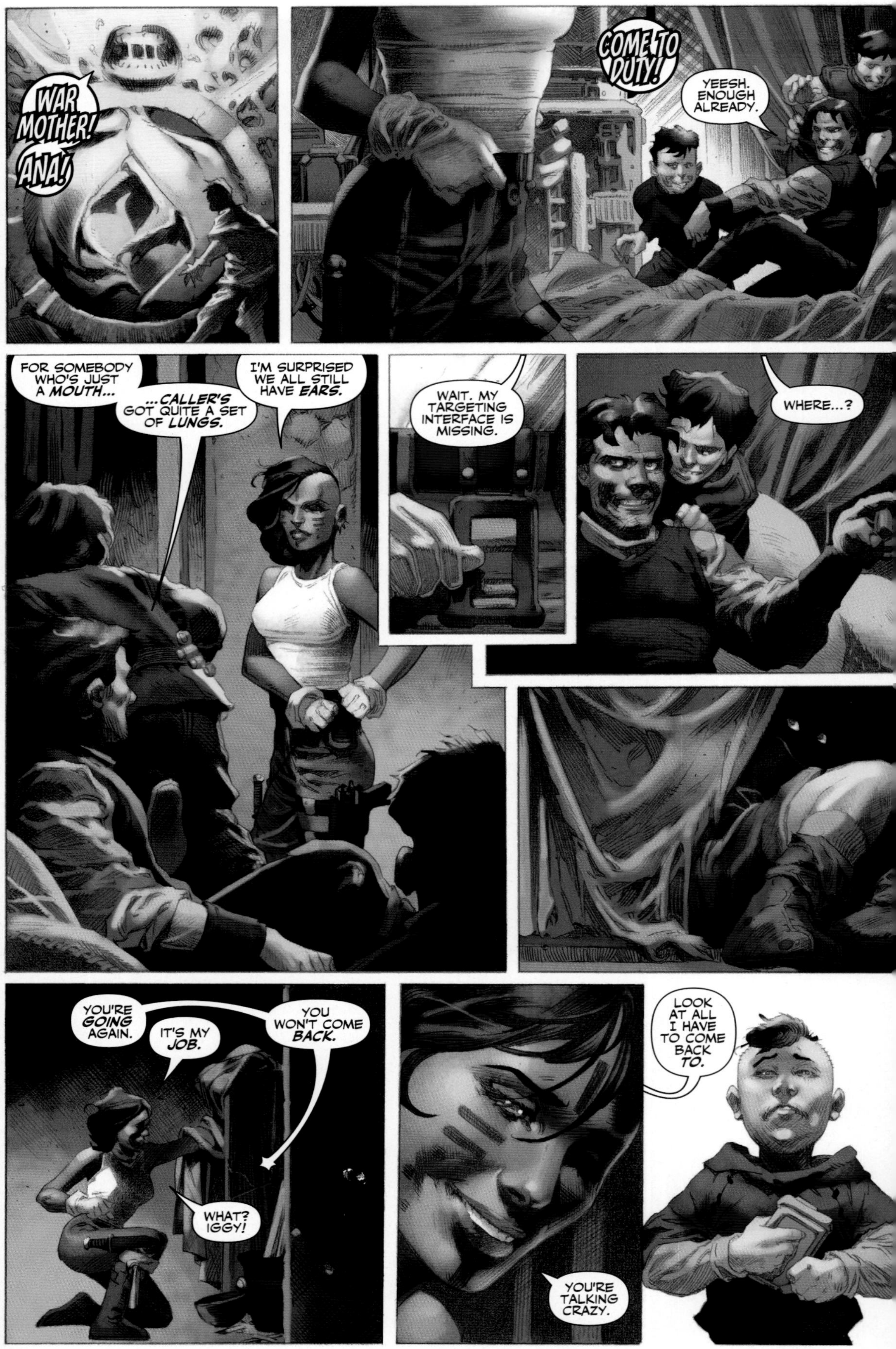
WAR MOTHER! ANA!
COME TO DUTY!
YEESH. ENOUGH ALREADY.
FOR SOMEBODY WHO'S JUST A MOUTH...
...CALLER'S GOT QUITE A SET OF LUNGS.
I'M SURPRISED WE ALL STILL HAVE EARS.
WAIT. MY TARGETING INTERFACE IS MISSING.
WHERE...?
YOU'RE GOING AGAIN.
IT'S MY JOB.
YOU WON'T COME BACK.
WHAT? IGGY!
YOU'RE TALKING CRAZY.
LOOK AT ALL I HAVE TO COME BACK TO.

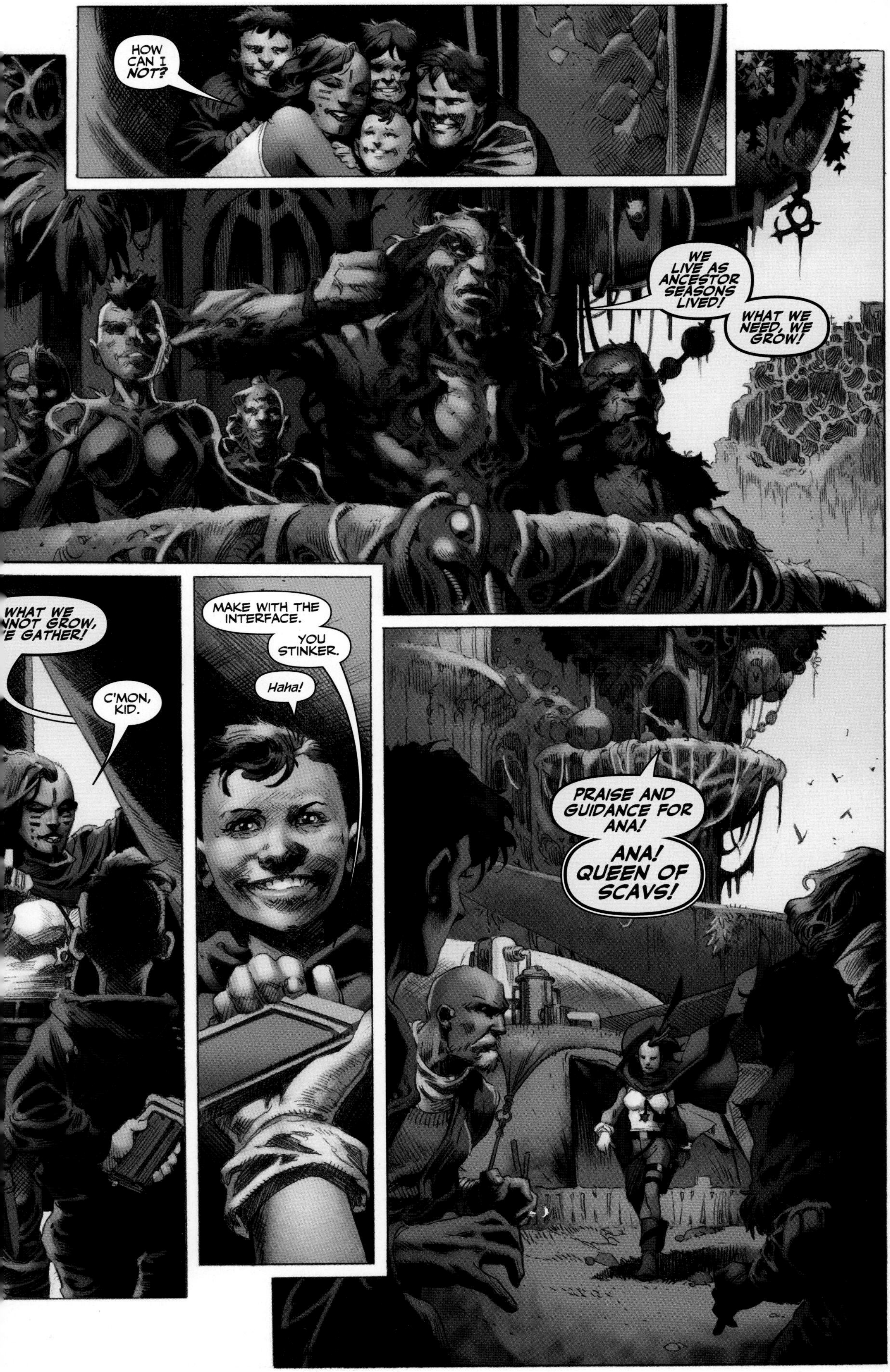
HOW CAN I NOT?
WE LIVE AS ANCESTOR SEASONS LIVED!
WHAT WE NEED, WE GROW!
WHAT WE NNOT GROW, 'E GATHER!
C'MON, KID.
MAKE WITH THE INTERFACE.
YOU STINKER.
Haha!
PRAISE AND GUIDANCE FOR ANA!
ANA! QUEEN OF SCAVS!

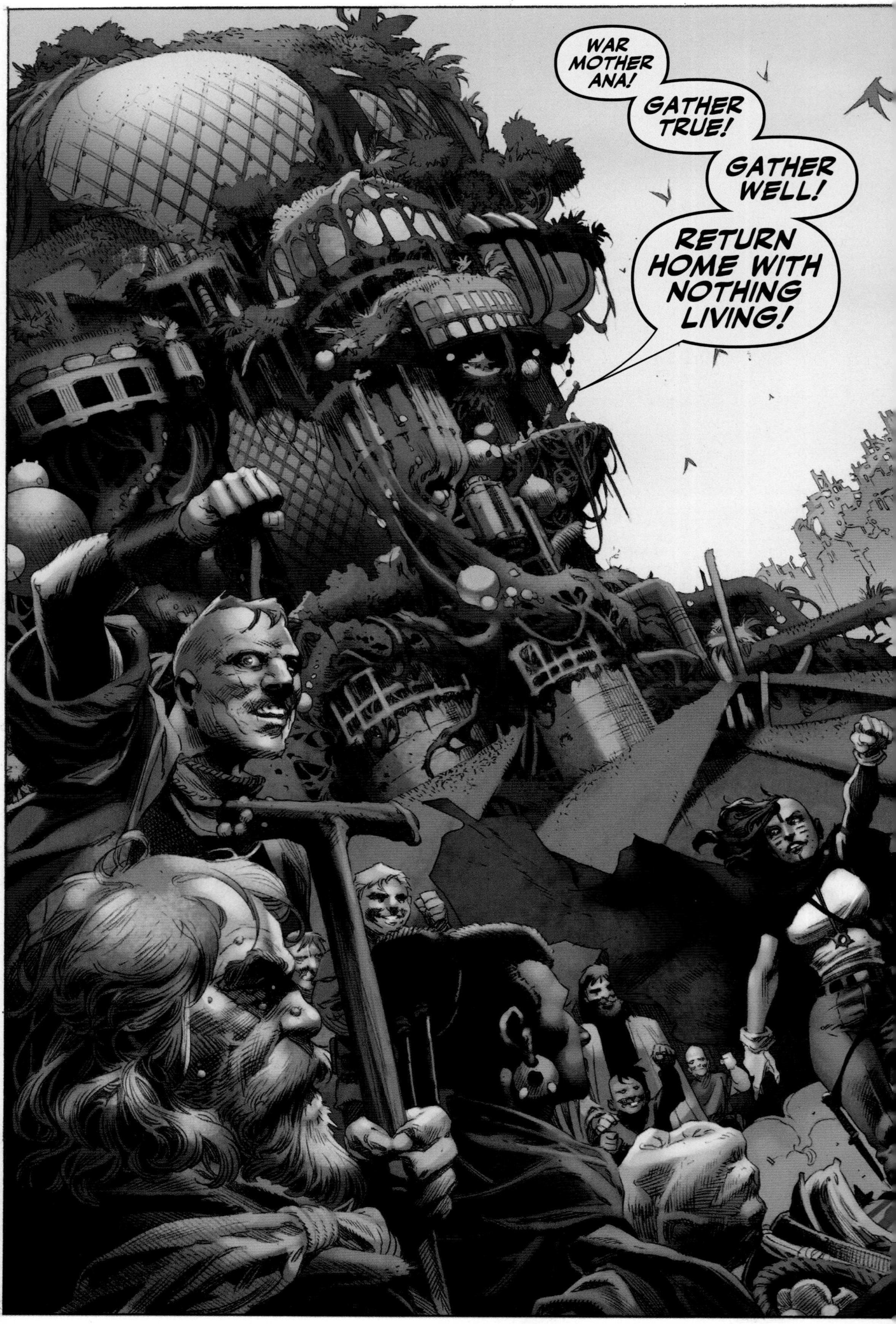
WAR MOTHER ANA!
GATHER TRUE!
GATHER WELL!
RETURN HOME WITH NOTHING LIVING!

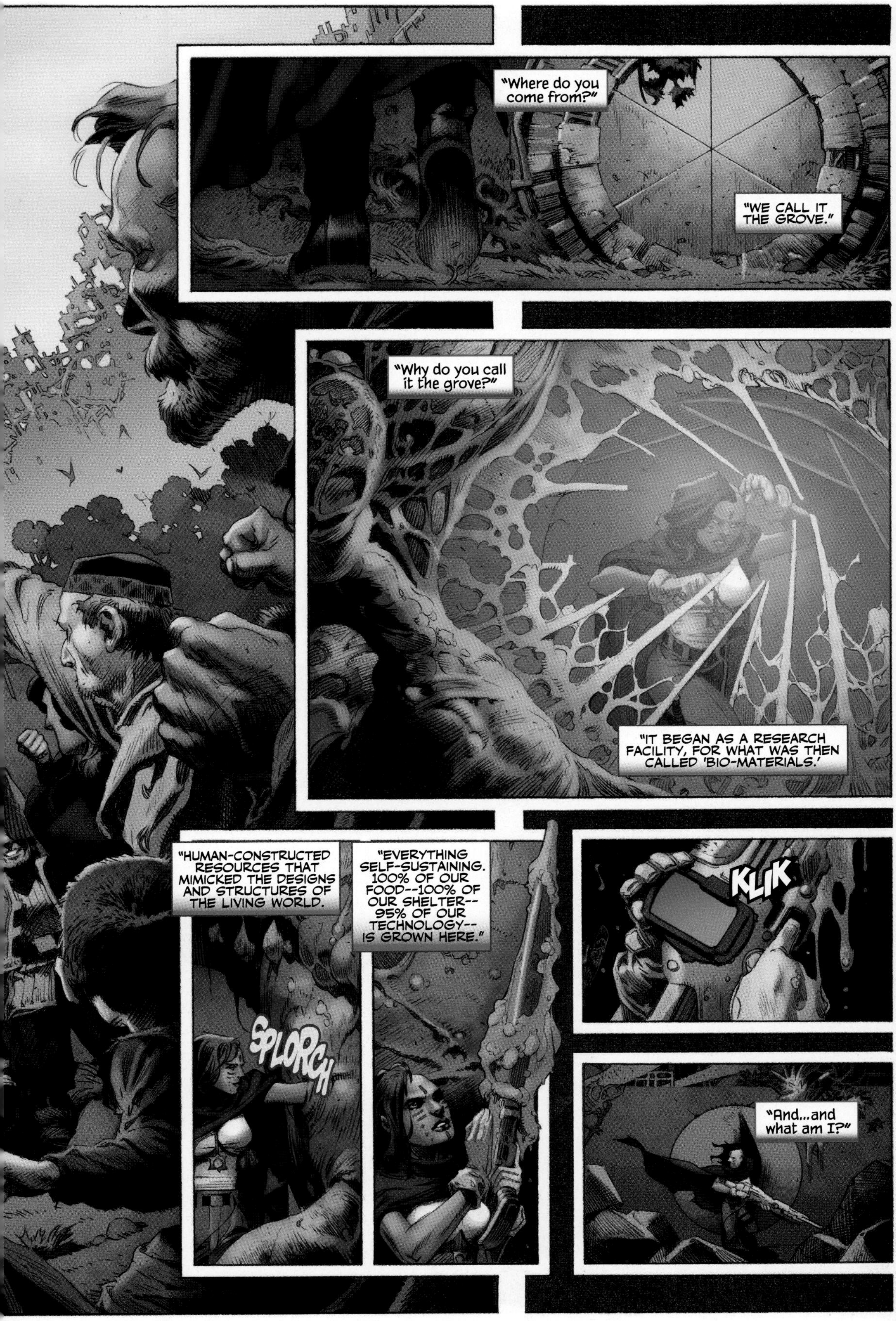
"Where do you come from?"
"WE CALL IT THE GROVE."
"Why do you call it the grove?"
"IT BEGAN AS A RESEARCH FACILITY, FOR WHAT WAS THEN CALLED 'BIO-MATERIALS.'
"HUMAN-CONSTRUCTED RESOURCES THAT MIMICKED THE DESIGNS AND STRUCTURES OF THE LIVING WORLD.
SPLORCH
"EVERYTHING SELF-SUSTAINING. 100% OF OUR FOOD--100% OF OUR SHELTER--95% OF OUR TECHNOLOGY--IS GROWN HERE."
KLIK
"And...and what am I?"

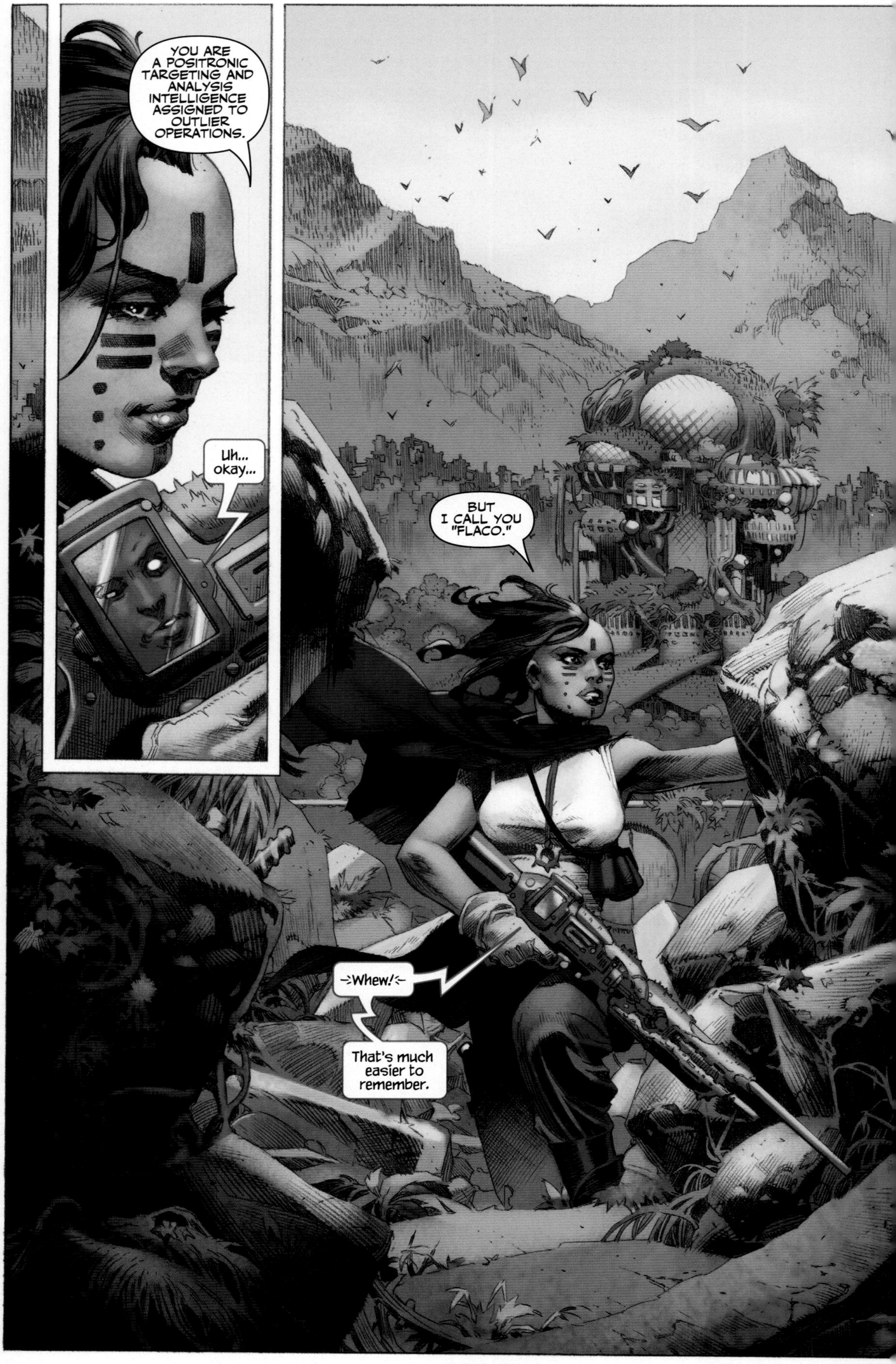
YOU ARE A POSITRONIC TARGETING AND ANALYSIS INTELLIGENCE ASSIGNED TO OUTLIER OPERATIONS.
Uh... okay...
BUT I CALL YOU "FLACO."
-Whew!-
That's much easier to remember.

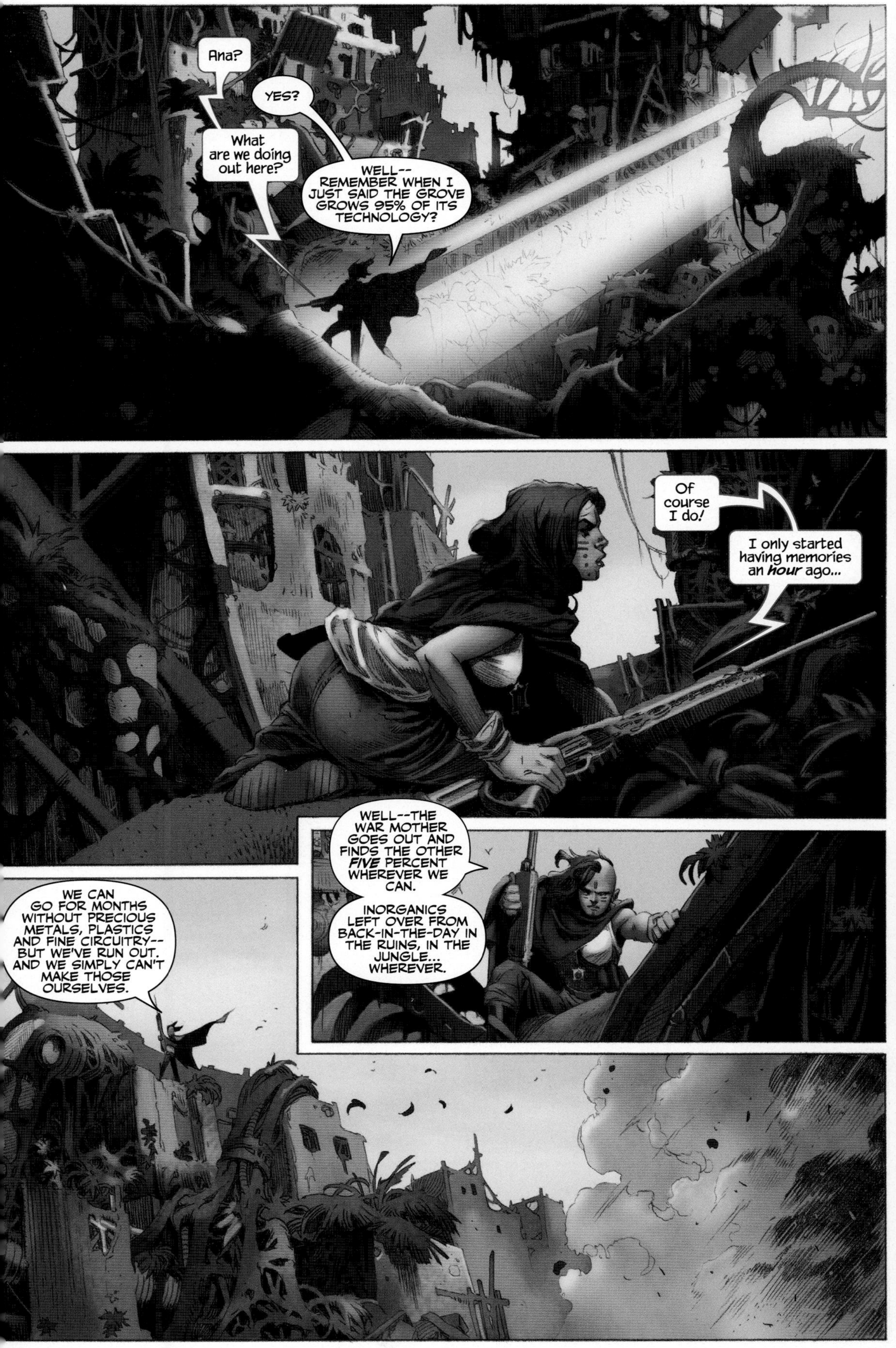
Ana?
YES?
What are we doing out here?
WELL-- REMEMBER WHEN I JUST SAID THE GROVE GROWS 95% OF ITS TECHNOLOGY?
Of course I do!
I only started having memories an *hour* ago...
WELL--THE WAR MOTHER GOES OUT AND FINDS THE OTHER *FIVE* PERCENT WHEREVER WE CAN.
INORGANICS LEFT OVER FROM BACK-IN-THE-DAY IN THE RUINS, IN THE JUNGLE... WHEREVER.
WE CAN GO FOR MONTHS WITHOUT PRECIOUS METALS, PLASTICS AND FINE CIRCUITRY-- BUT WE'VE RUN OUT. AND WE SIMPLY CAN'T MAKE THOSE OURSELVES.

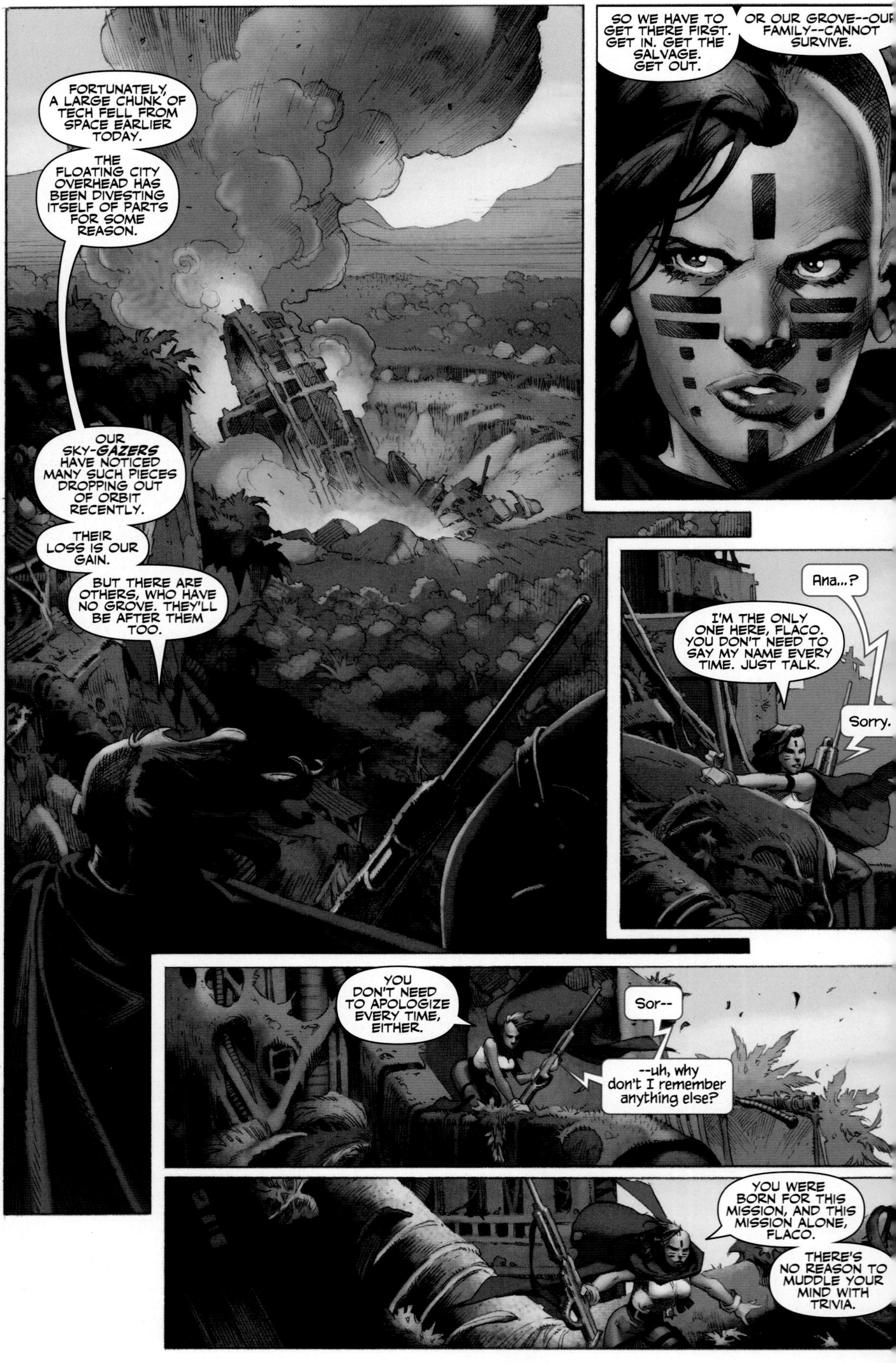
FORTUNATELY, A LARGE CHUNK OF TECH FELL FROM SPACE EARLIER TODAY.
THE FLOATING CITY OVERHEAD HAS BEEN DIVESTING ITSELF OF PARTS FOR SOME REASON.
OUR SKY-GAZERS HAVE NOTICED MANY SUCH PIECES DROPPING OUT OF ORBIT RECENTLY.
THEIR LOSS IS OUR GAIN.
BUT THERE ARE OTHERS, WHO HAVE NO GROVE. THEY'LL BE AFTER THEM TOO.
SO WE HAVE TO GET THERE FIRST. GET IN. GET THE SALVAGE. GET OUT.
OR OUR GROVE--OUR FAMILY--CANNOT SURVIVE.
Ana...?
I'M THE ONLY ONE HERE, FLACO. YOU DON'T NEED TO SAY MY NAME EVERY TIME. JUST TALK.
Sorry.
YOU DON'T NEED TO APOLOGIZE EVERY TIME, EITHER.
Sor--
--uh, why don't I remember anything else?
YOU WERE BORN FOR THIS MISSION, AND THIS MISSION ALONE, FLACO.
THERE'S NO REASON TO MUDDLE YOUR MIND WITH TRIVIA.

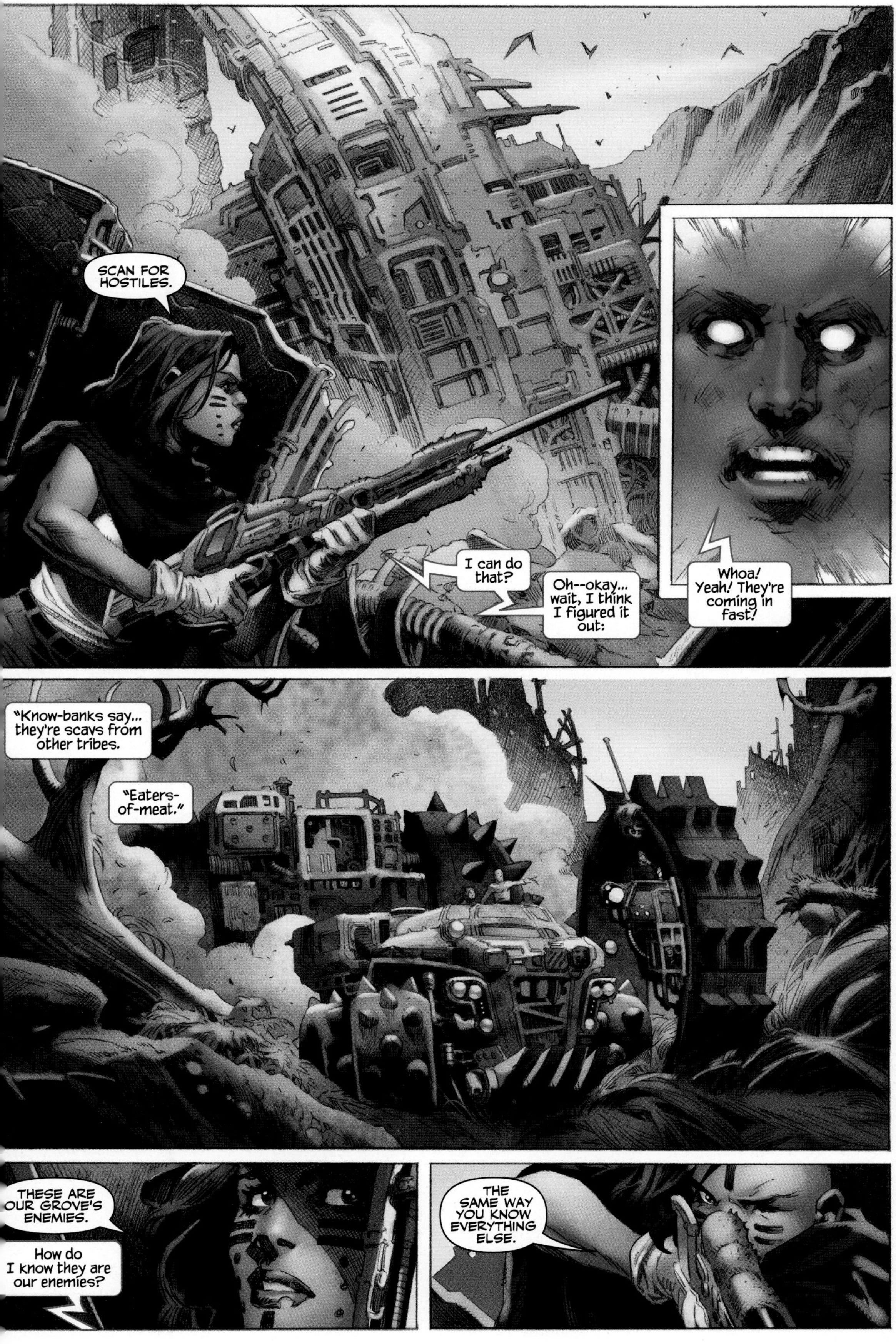
SCAN FOR HOSTILES.
I can do that?
Oh--okay... wait, I think I figured it out:
Whoa! Yeah! They're coming in fast!
"Know-banks say... they're scavs from other tribes.
"Eaters-of-meat."
THESE ARE OUR GROVE'S ENEMIES.
How do I know they are our enemies?
THE SAME WAY YOU KNOW EVERYTHING ELSE.

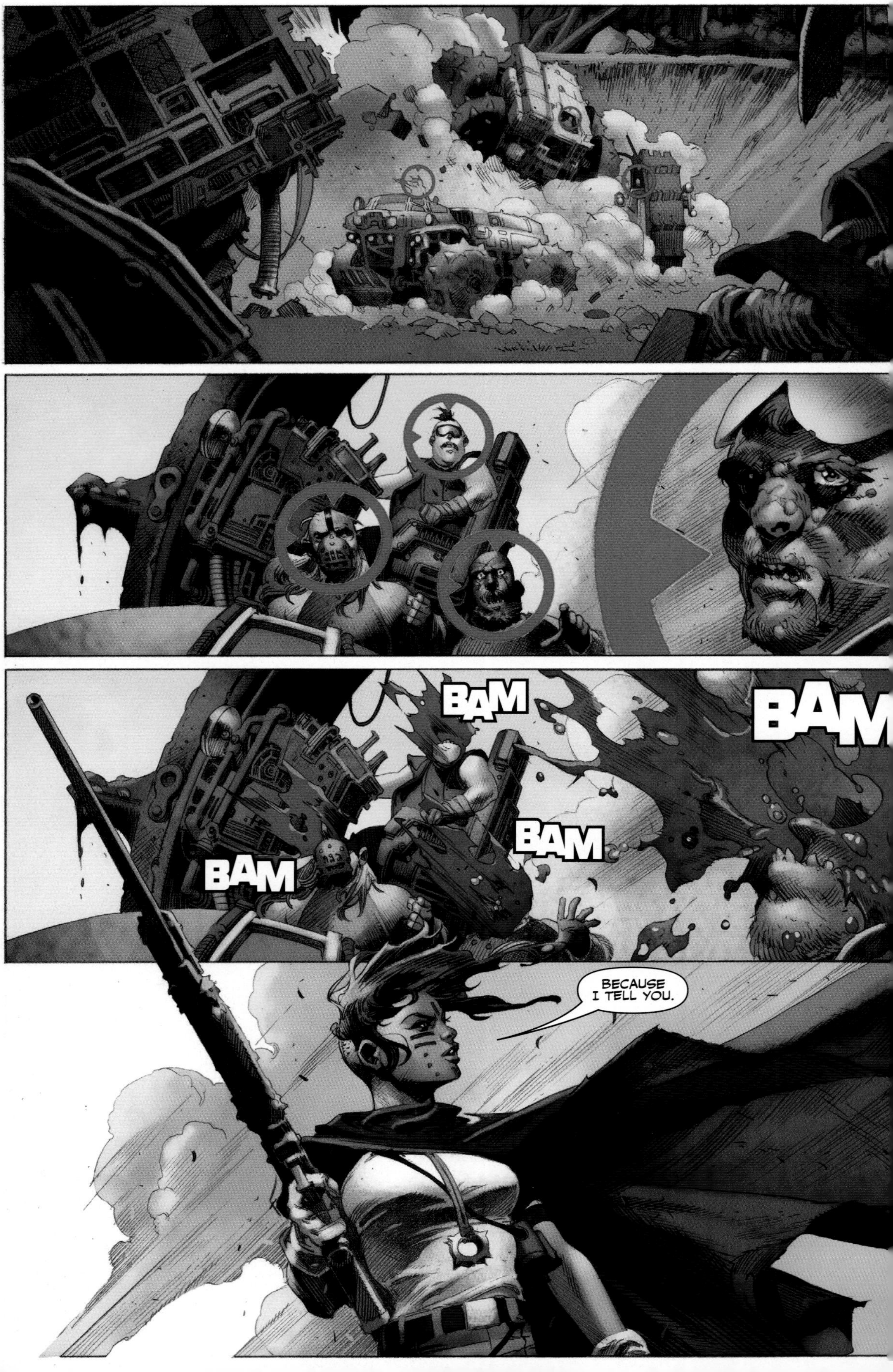
BAM
BAM
BAM
BAM
BECAUSE I TELL YOU.

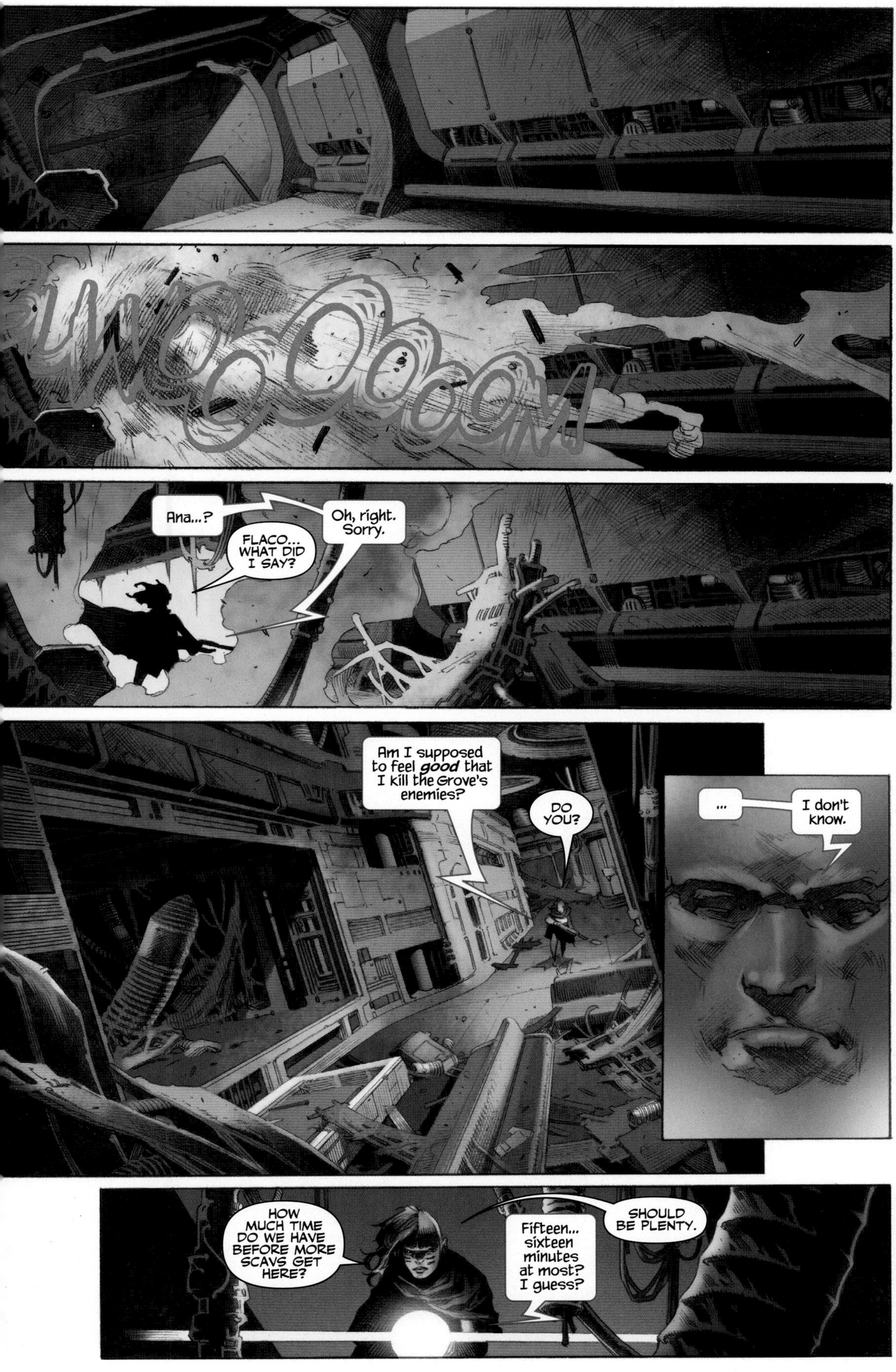
WOOOOOOM
Ana...?
FLACO... WHAT DID I SAY?
Oh, right. Sorry.
Am I supposed to feel *good* that I kill the Grove's enemies?
DO YOU?
...
I don't know.
HOW MUCH TIME DO WE HAVE BEFORE MORE SCAVS GET HERE?
Fifteen... sixteen minutes at most? I guess?
SHOULD BE PLENTY.

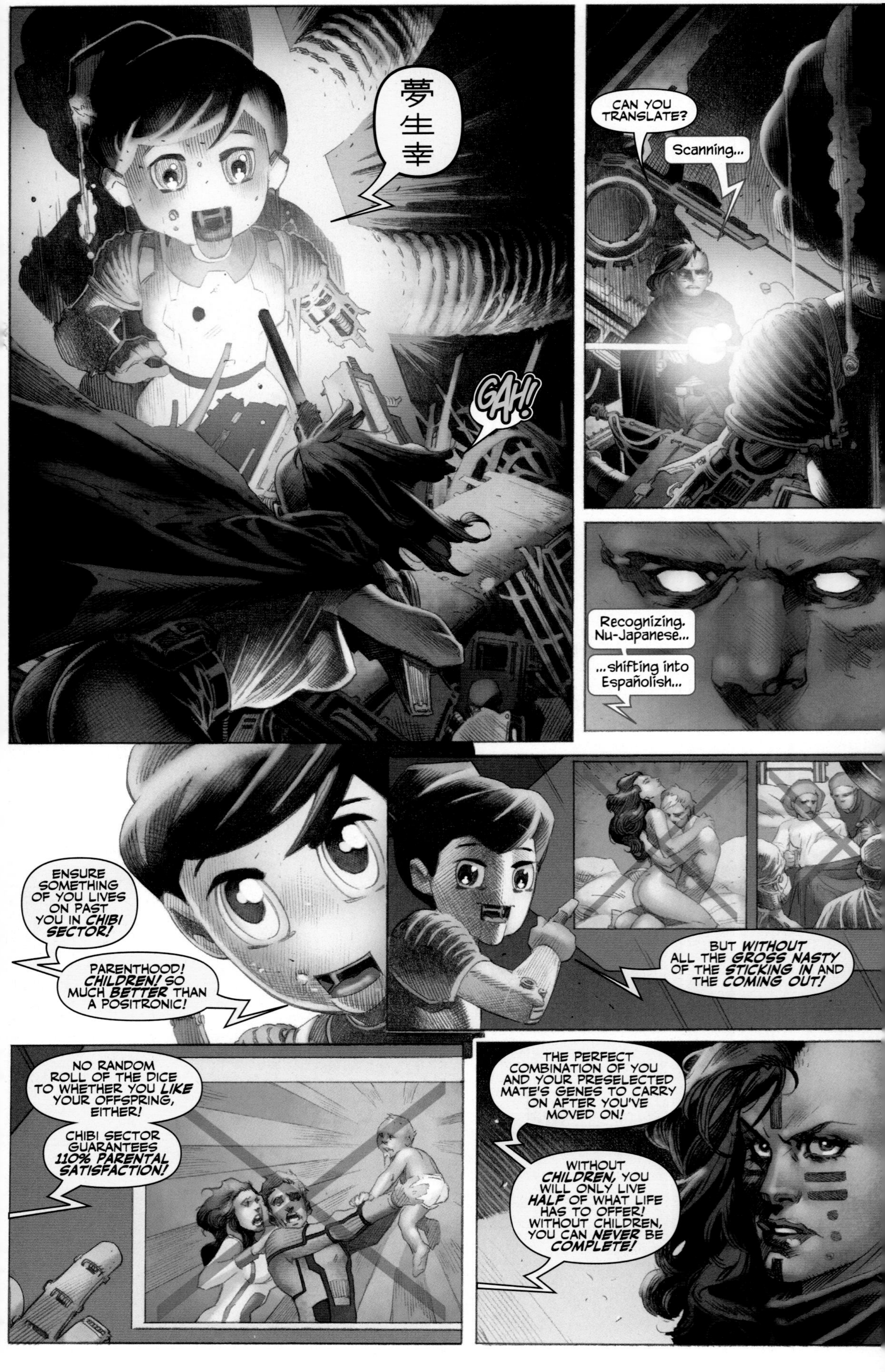

夢生幸
GAH!
CAN YOU TRANSLATE?
Scanning...
Recognizing. Nu-Japanese...
...shifting into Españolish...
ENSURE SOMETHING OF YOU LIVES ON PAST YOU IN CHIBI SECTOR!
PARENTHOOD! CHILDREN! SO MUCH BETTER THAN A POSITRONIC!
BUT WITHOUT ALL THE GROSS NASTY OF THE STICKING IN AND THE COMING OUT!
NO RANDOM ROLL OF THE DICE TO WHETHER YOU LIKE YOUR OFFSPRING, EITHER!
CHIBI SECTOR GUARANTEES 110% PARENTAL SATISFACTION!
THE PERFECT COMBINATION OF YOU AND YOUR PRESELECTED MATE'S GENES TO CARRY ON AFTER YOU'VE MOVED ON!
WITHOUT CHILDREN, YOU WILL ONLY LIVE HALF OF WHAT LIFE HAS TO OFFER! WITHOUT CHILDREN, YOU CAN NEVER BE COMPLETE!

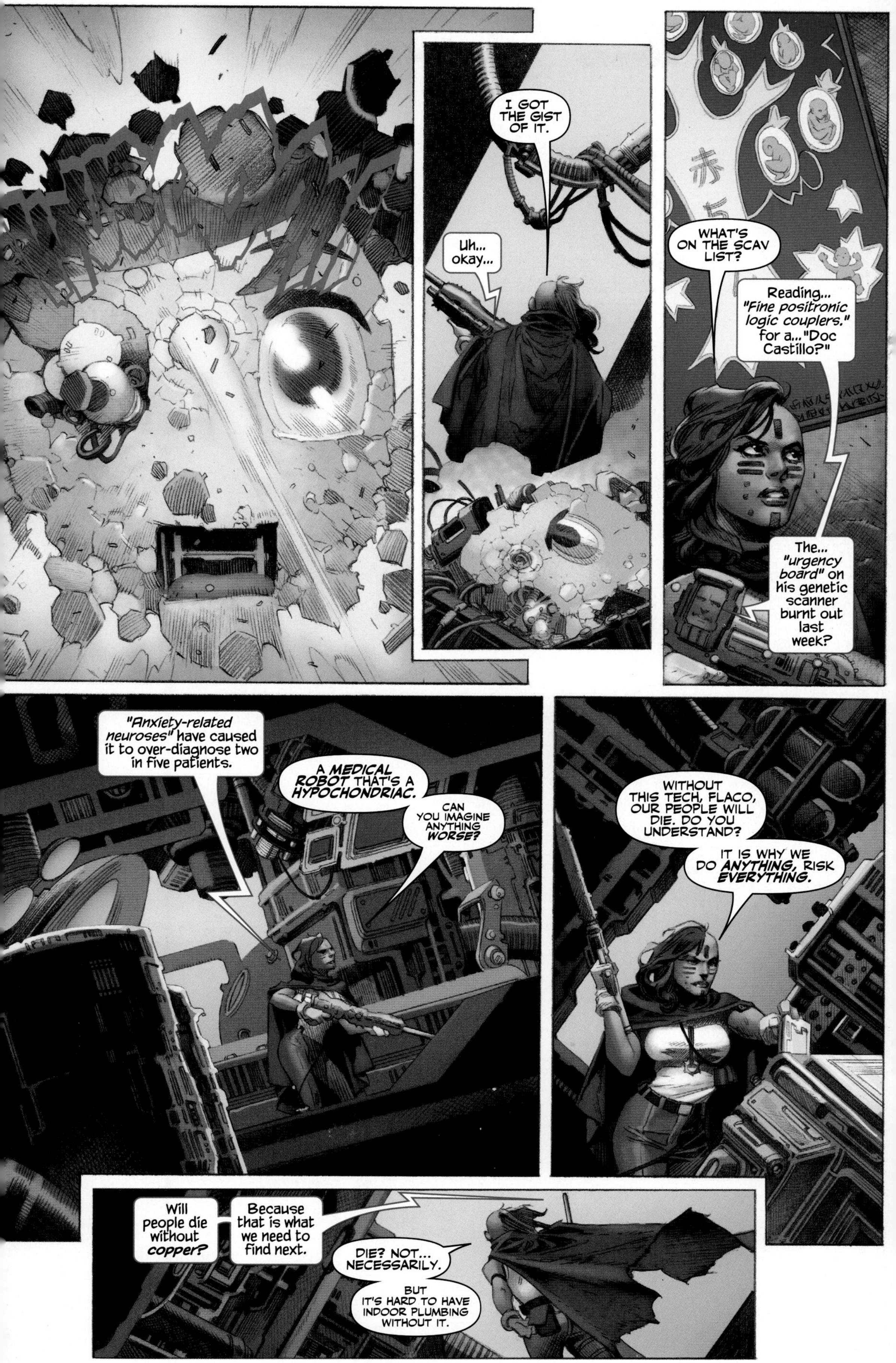
I GOT THE GIST OF IT.
Uh... okay...
WHAT'S ON THE SCAV LIST?
Reading... "Fine positronic logic couplers." for a... "Doc Castillo?"
The... "urgency board" on his genetic scanner burnt out last week?
"Anxiety-related neuroses" have caused it to over-diagnose two in five patients.
A MEDICAL ROBOT THAT'S A HYPOCHONDRIAC.
CAN YOU IMAGINE ANYTHING WORSE?
WITHOUT THIS TECH, FLACO, OUR PEOPLE WILL DIE. DO YOU UNDERSTAND?
IT IS WHY WE DO ANYTHING, RISK EVERYTHING.
Will people die without copper?
Because that is what we need to find next.
DIE? NOT... NECESSARILY.
BUT IT'S HARD TO HAVE INDOOR PLUMBING WITHOUT IT.

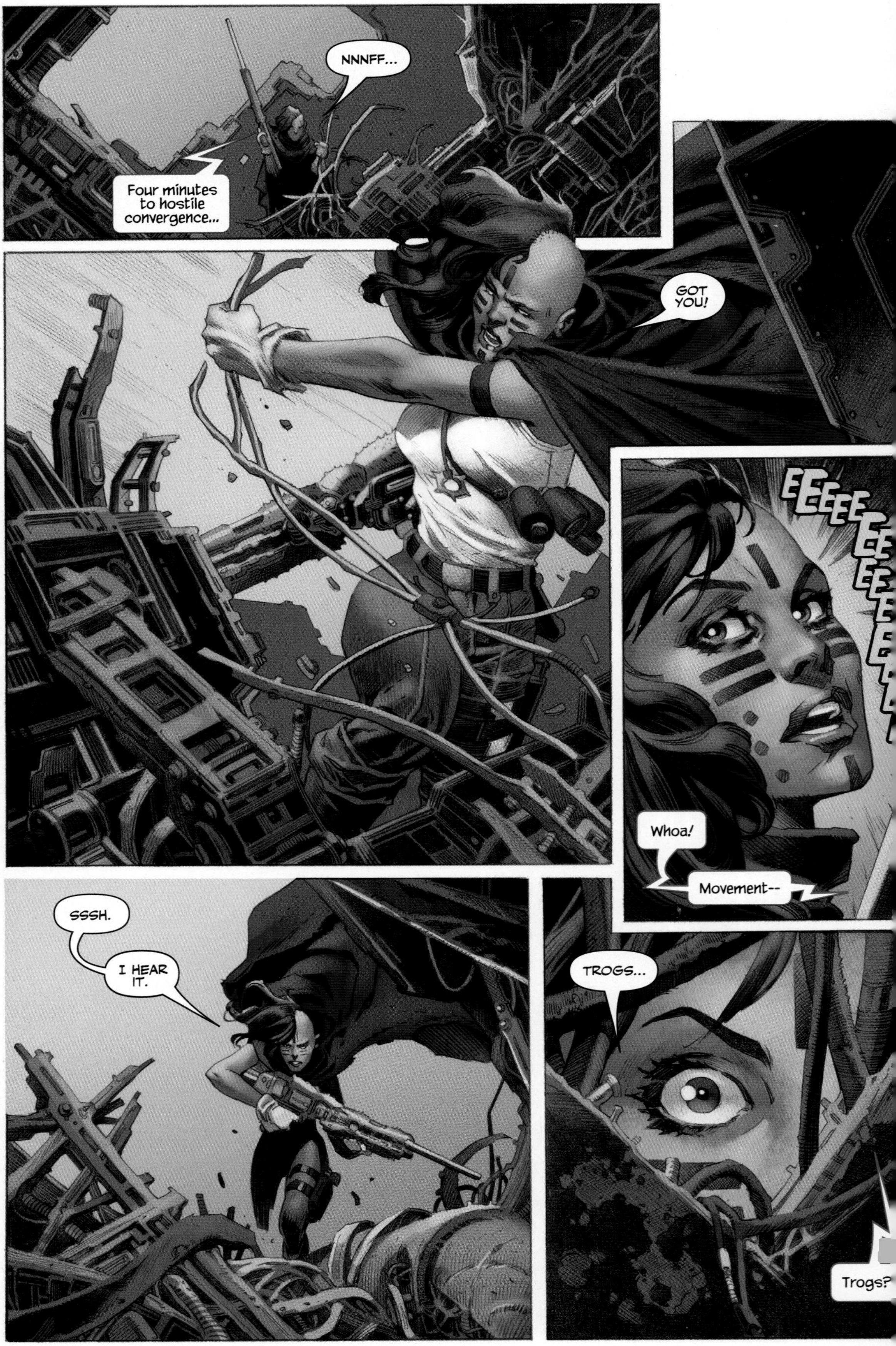
NNNFF...
Four minutes to hostile convergence...
GOT YOU!
EEEEEEEEEE
Whoa!
Movement--
SSSH.
I HEAR IT.
TROGS...
Trogs?

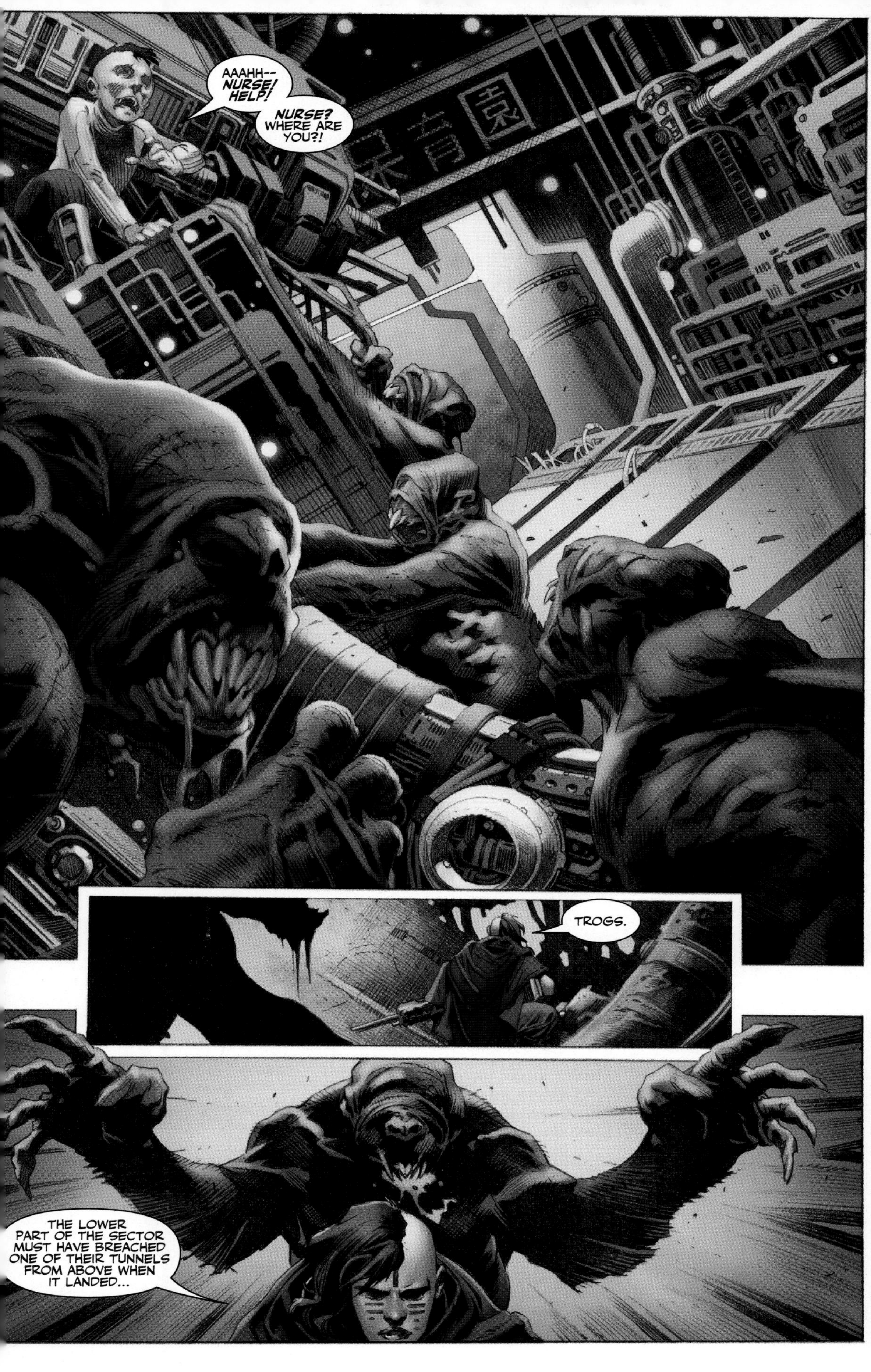
AAAHH-- NURSE! HELP!
NURSE? WHERE ARE YOU?!
TROGS.
THE LOWER PART OF THE SECTOR MUST HAVE BREACHED ONE OF THEIR TUNNELS FROM ABOVE WHEN IT LANDED...

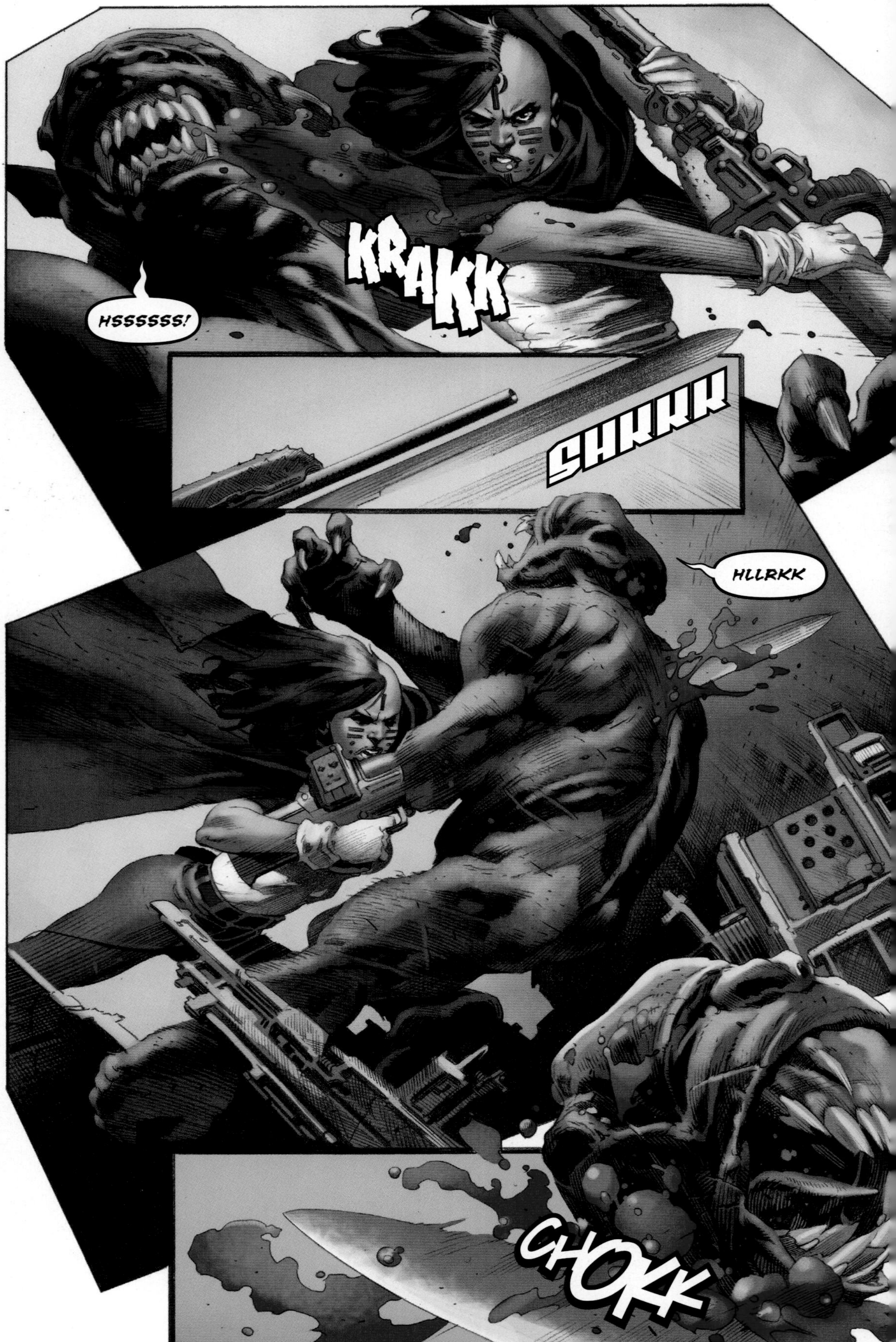
KRAKK
HSSSSSS!
SHKKK
HLLRKK
CHOKK

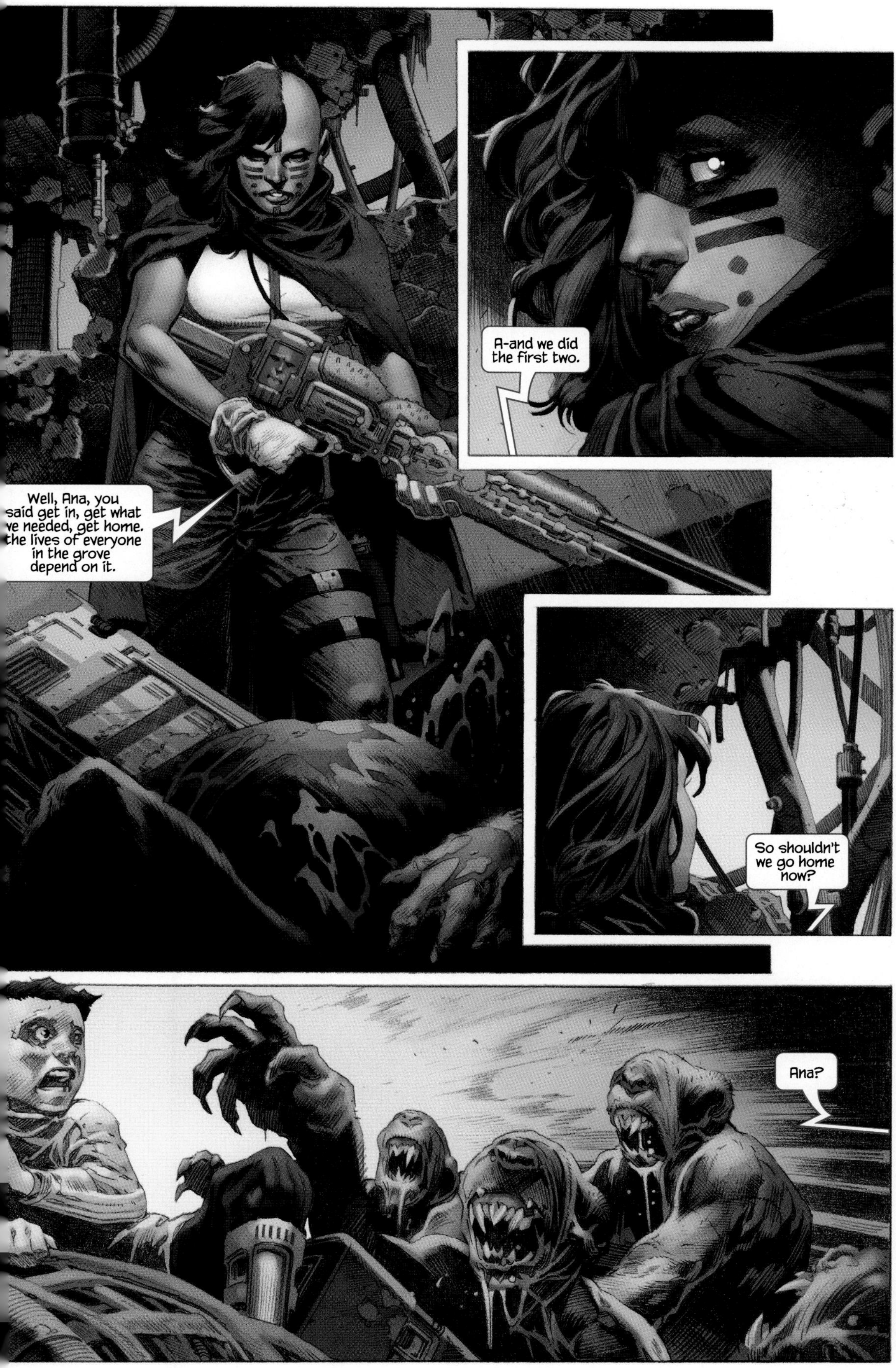
A-and we did the first two.
Well, Ana, you said get in, get what we needed, get home. the lives of everyone in the grove depend on it.
So shouldn't we go home now?
Ana?

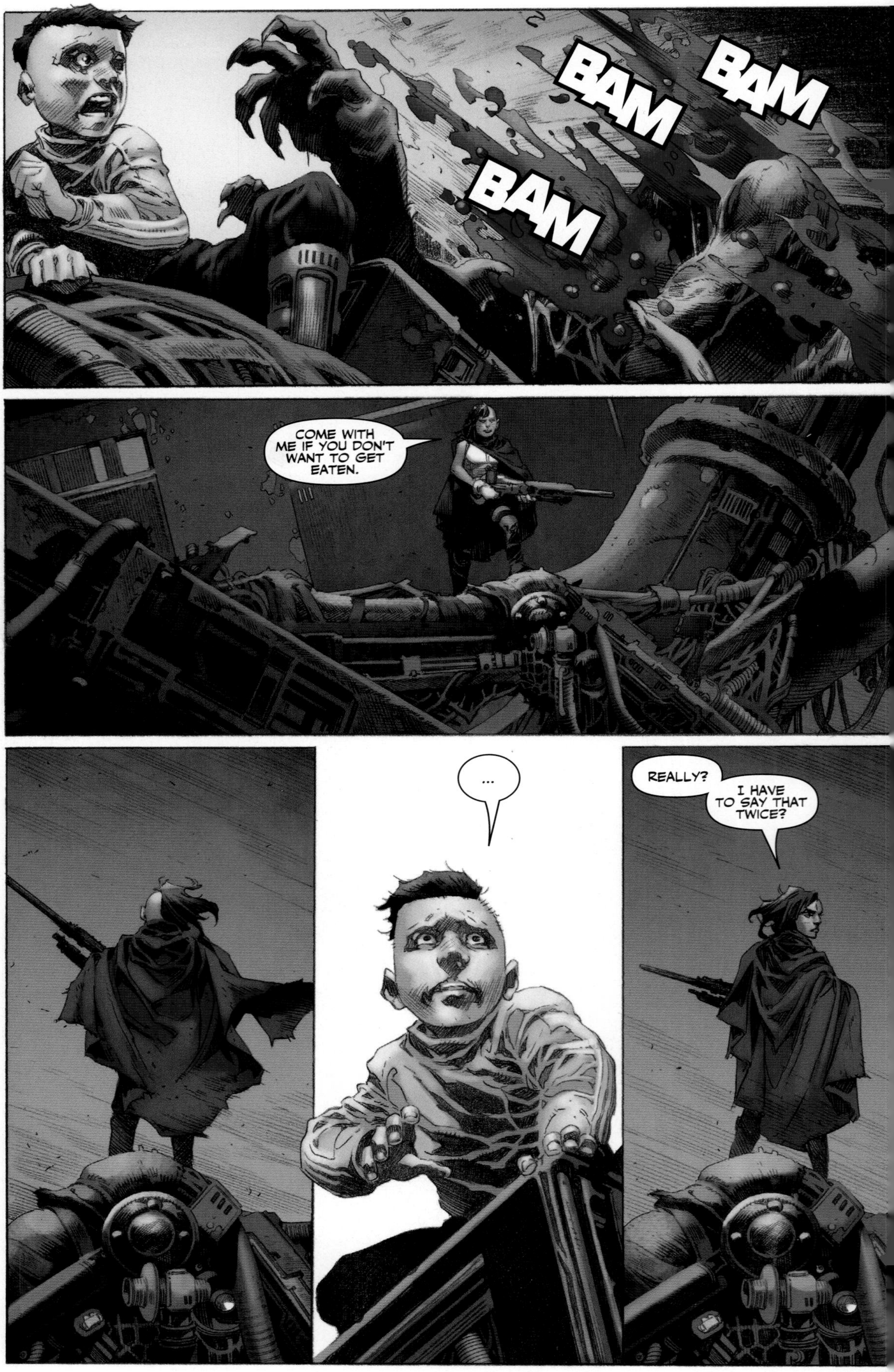
BAM
BAM
BAM
COME WITH ME IF YOU DON'T WANT TO GET EATEN.
...
REALLY?
I HAVE TO SAY THAT TWICE?

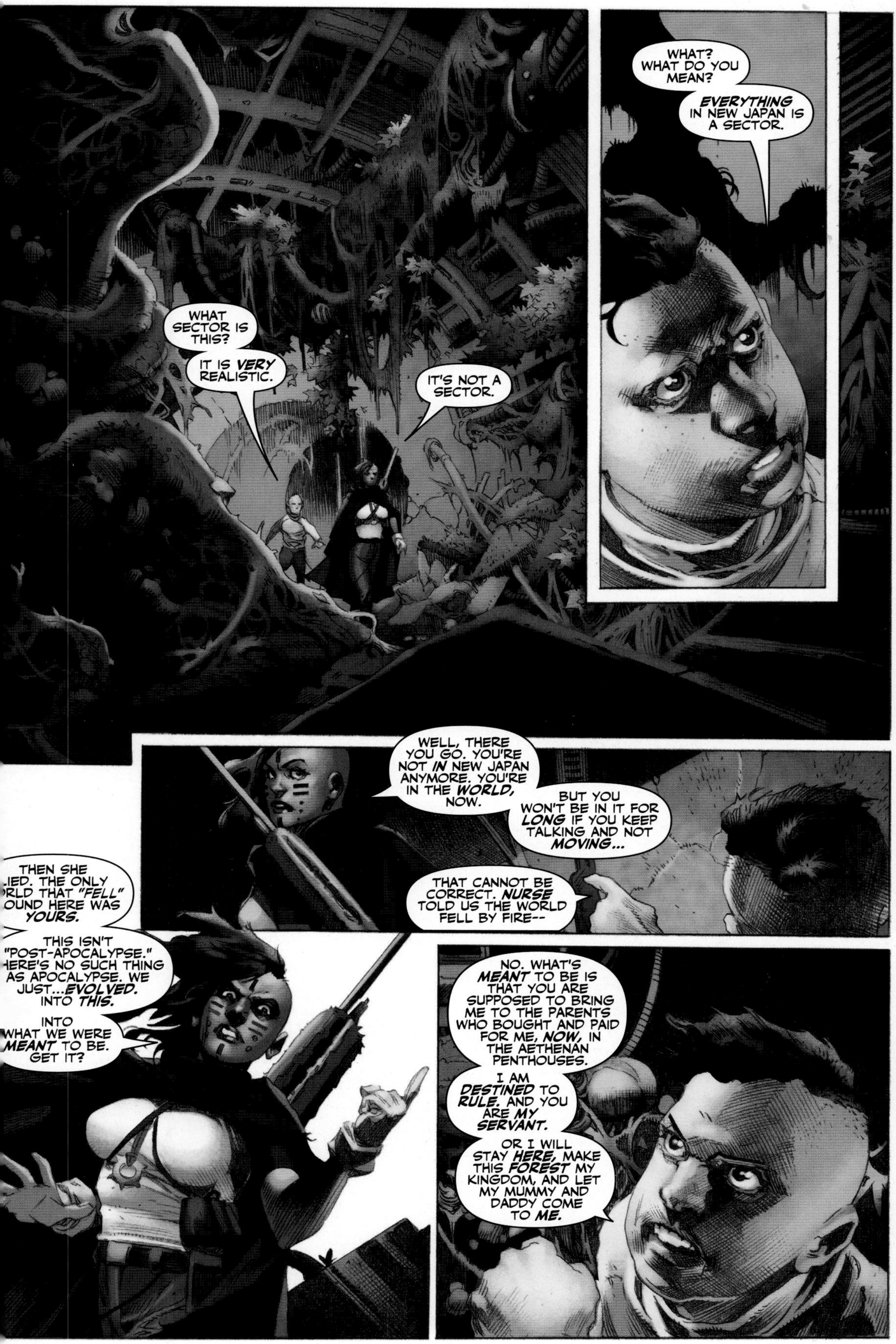
WHAT SECTOR IS THIS?
IT IS VERY REALISTIC.
IT'S NOT A SECTOR.
WHAT? WHAT DO YOU MEAN?
EVERYTHING IN NEW JAPAN IS A SECTOR.
WELL, THERE YOU GO. YOU'RE NOT IN NEW JAPAN ANYMORE. YOU'RE IN THE WORLD, NOW.
BUT YOU WON'T BE IN IT FOR LONG IF YOU KEEP TALKING AND NOT MOVING...
THAT CANNOT BE CORRECT. NURSE TOLD US THE WORLD FELL BY FIRE--
THEN SHE LIED. THE ONLY ORLD THAT "FELL" OUND HERE WAS YOURS.
THIS ISN'T "POST-APOCALYPSE." HERE'S NO SUCH THING AS APOCALYPSE. WE JUST...EVOLVED. INTO THIS.
INTO WHAT WE WERE MEANT TO BE. GET IT?
NO. WHAT'S MEANT TO BE IS THAT YOU ARE SUPPOSED TO BRING ME TO THE PARENTS WHO BOUGHT AND PAID FOR ME, NOW, IN THE AETHENAN PENTHOUSES.
I AM DESTINED TO RULE. AND YOU ARE MY SERVANT.
OR I WILL STAY HERE, MAKE THIS FOREST MY KINGDOM, AND LET MY MUMMY AND DADDY COME TO ME.

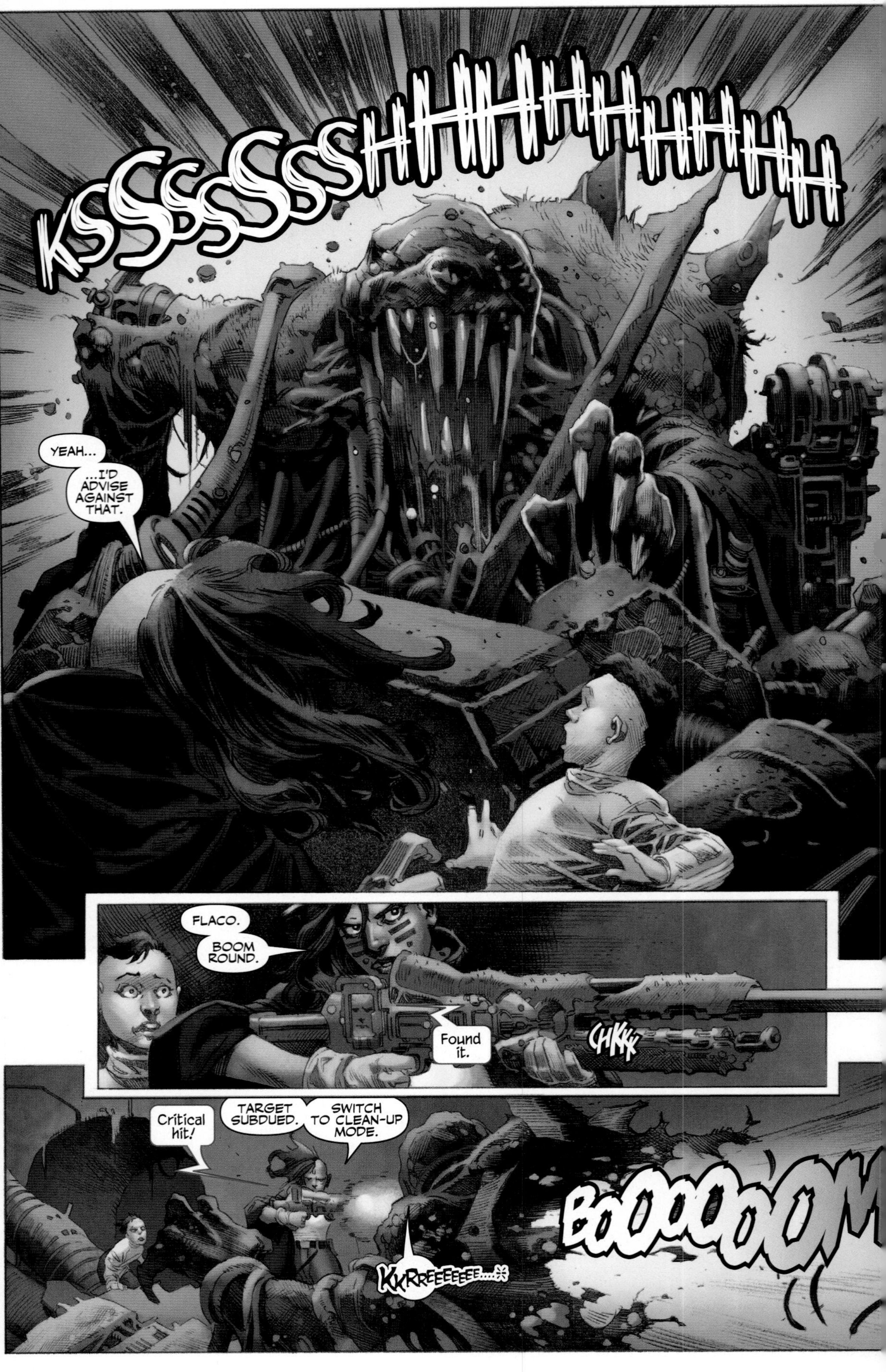
KSSSSSSSHHHHHHHHHHHHHHH
YEAH...
...I'D ADVISE AGAINST THAT.
FLACO.
BOOM ROUND.
Found it.
CHKKK
Critical hit!
TARGET SUBDUED.
SWITCH TO CLEAN-UP MODE.
BOOOOOOM
KKRREEEEEEE....

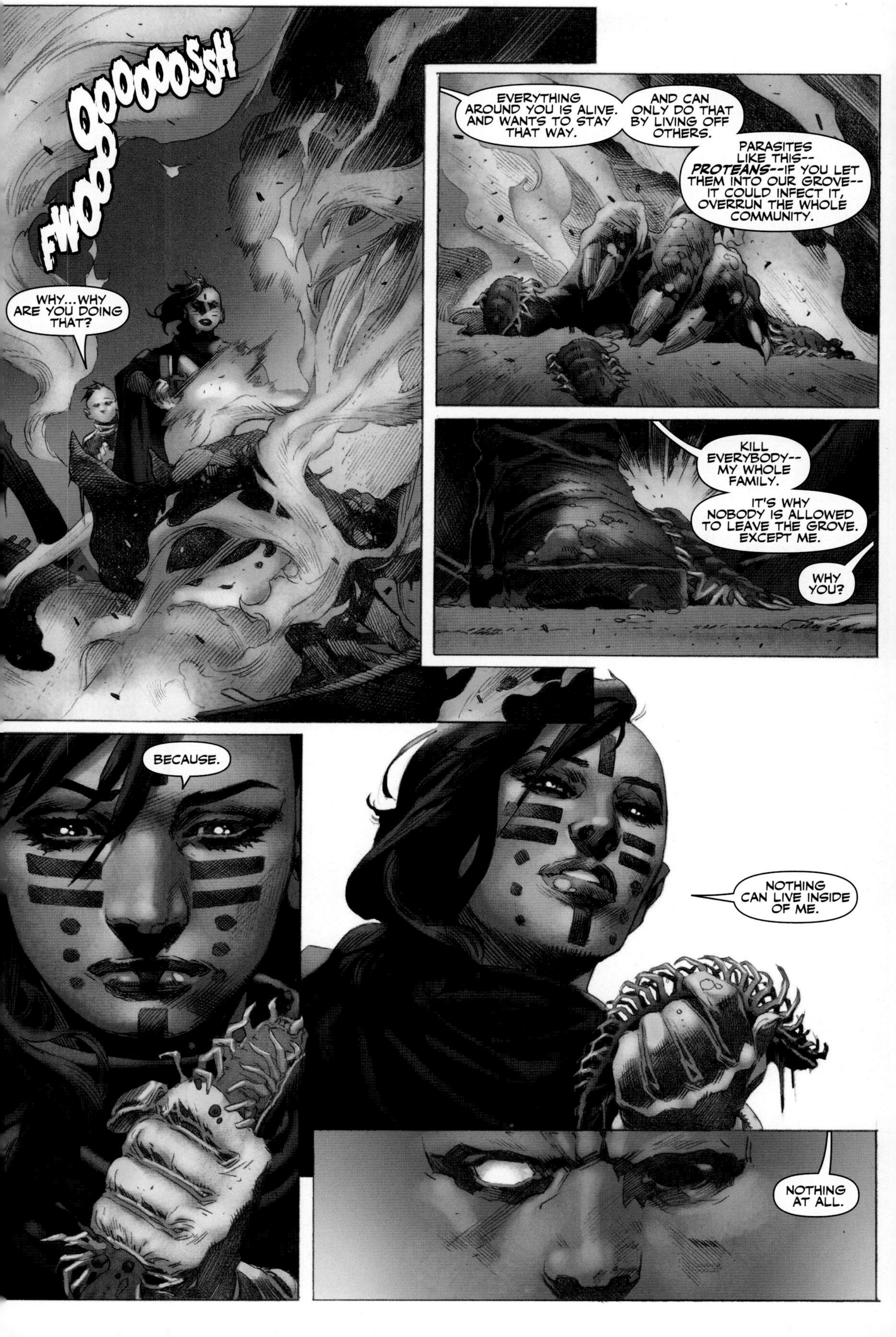
FWOOOOOOOOOSSH
WHY...WHY ARE YOU DOING THAT?
EVERYTHING AROUND YOU IS ALIVE. AND WANTS TO STAY THAT WAY.
AND CAN ONLY DO THAT BY LIVING OFF OTHERS.
PARASITES LIKE THIS--PROTEANS--IF YOU LET THEM INTO OUR GROVE--IT COULD INFECT IT, OVERRUN THE WHOLE COMMUNITY.
KILL EVERYBODY--MY WHOLE FAMILY.
IT'S WHY NOBODY IS ALLOWED TO LEAVE THE GROVE. EXCEPT ME.
WHY YOU?
BECAUSE.
NOTHING CAN LIVE INSIDE OF ME.
NOTHING AT ALL.

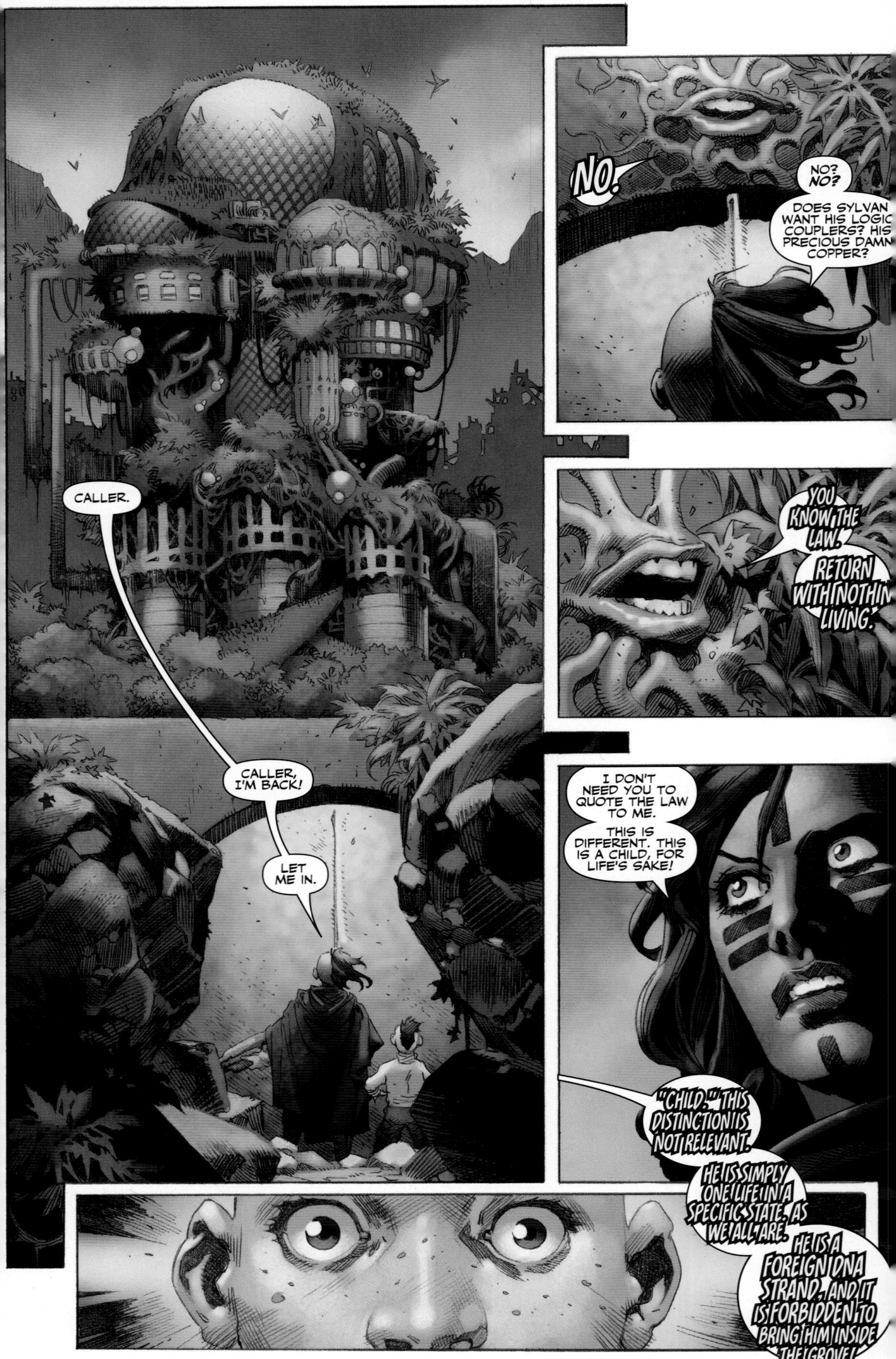
CALLER.
NO.
NO? NO?
DOES SYLVAN WANT HIS LOGIC COUPLERS? HIS PRECIOUS DAMN COPPER?
YOU KNOW THE LAW.
RETURN WITH NOTHIN LIVING.
CALLER, I'M BACK!
LET ME IN.
I DON'T NEED YOU TO QUOTE THE LAW TO ME.
THIS IS DIFFERENT. THIS IS A CHILD, FOR LIFE'S SAKE!
"CHILD." THIS DISTINCTION IS NOT RELEVANT.
HE IS SIMPLY ONE LIFE IN A SPECIFIC STATE, AS WE ALL ARE.
HE IS A FOREIGN DNA STRAND, AND IT IS FORBIDDEN TO BRING HIM INSIDE THE GROVE!

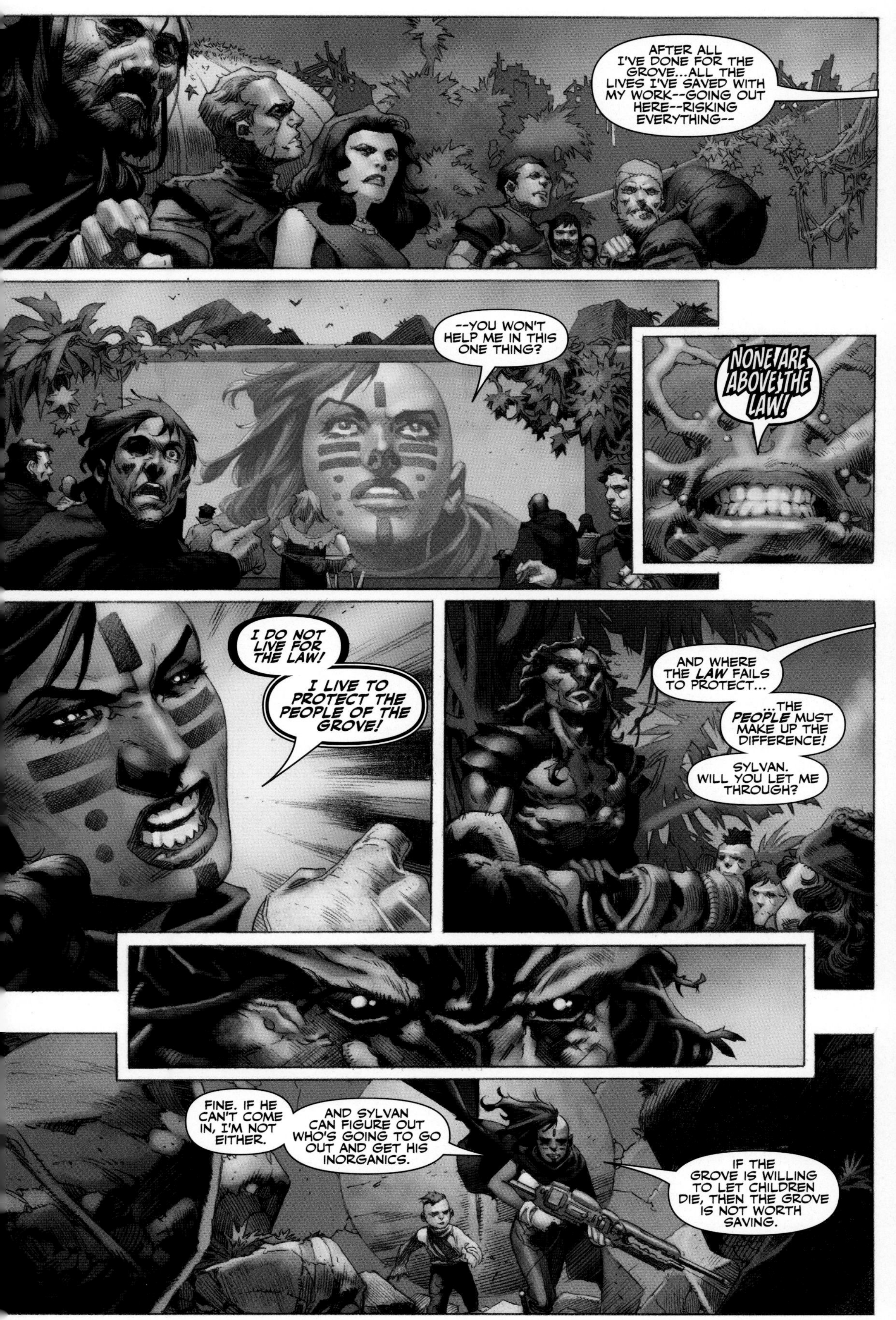
AFTER ALL I'VE DONE FOR THE GROVE...ALL THE LIVES I'VE SAVED WITH MY WORK--GOING OUT HERE--RISKING EVERYTHING--
--YOU WON'T HELP ME IN THIS ONE THING?
NONE ARE ABOVE THE LAW!
I DO NOT LIVE FOR THE LAW!
I LIVE TO PROTECT THE PEOPLE OF THE GROVE!
AND WHERE THE LAW FAILS TO PROTECT...
...THE PEOPLE MUST MAKE UP THE DIFFERENCE!
SYLVAN. WILL YOU LET ME THROUGH?
FINE. IF HE CAN'T COME IN, I'M NOT EITHER.
AND SYLVAN CAN FIGURE OUT WHO'S GOING TO GO OUT AND GET HIS INORGANICS.
IF THE GROVE IS WILLING TO LET CHILDREN DIE, THEN THE GROVE IS NOT WORTH SAVING.

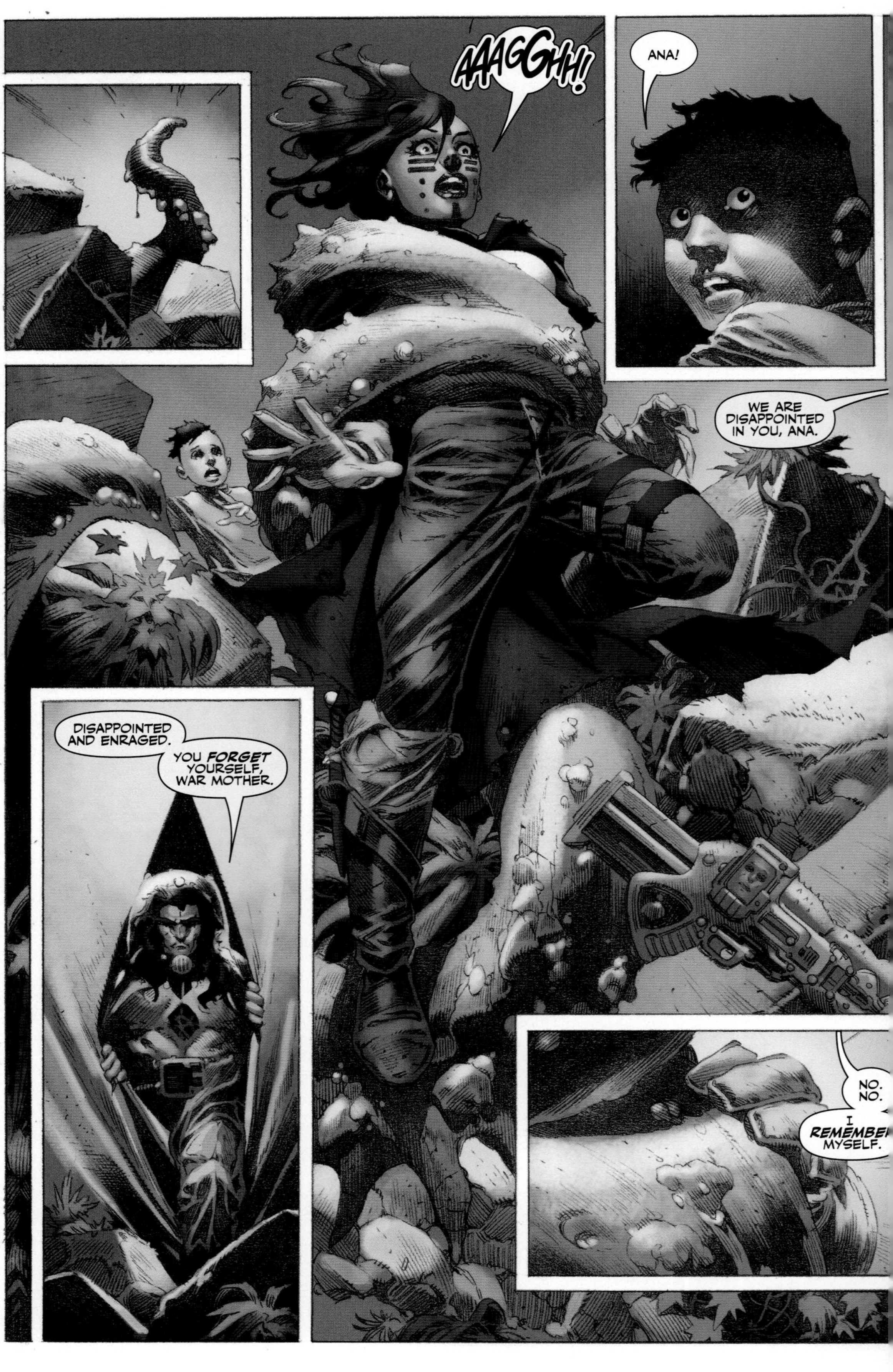
AAAGGHH!
ANA!
WE ARE DISAPPOINTED IN YOU, ANA.
DISAPPOINTED AND ENRAGED.
YOU FORGET YOURSELF, WAR MOTHER.
NO. NO.
I REMEMBE
MYSELF.

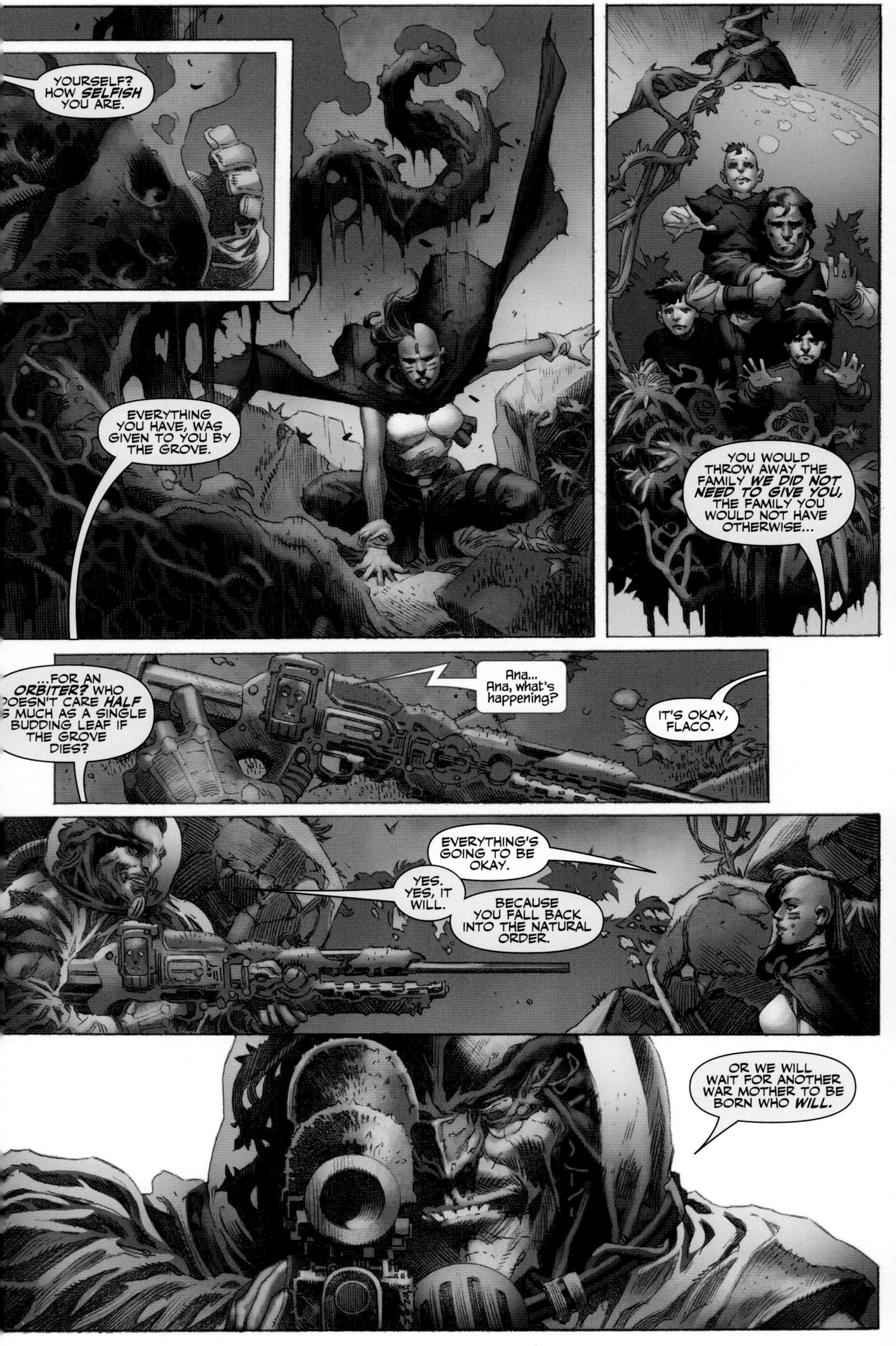
YOURSELF? HOW SELFISH YOU ARE.
EVERYTHING YOU HAVE, WAS GIVEN TO YOU BY THE GROVE.
YOU WOULD THROW AWAY THE FAMILY WE DID NOT NEED TO GIVE YOU, THE FAMILY YOU WOULD NOT HAVE OTHERWISE...
...FOR AN ORBITER? WHO DOESN'T CARE HALF AS MUCH AS A SINGLE BUDDING LEAF IF THE GROVE DIES?
Ana... Ana, what's happening?
IT'S OKAY, FLACO.
EVERYTHING'S GOING TO BE OKAY.
YES. YES, IT WILL.
BECAUSE YOU FALL BACK INTO THE NATURAL ORDER.
OR WE WILL WAIT FOR ANOTHER WAR MOTHER TO BE BORN WHO WILL.

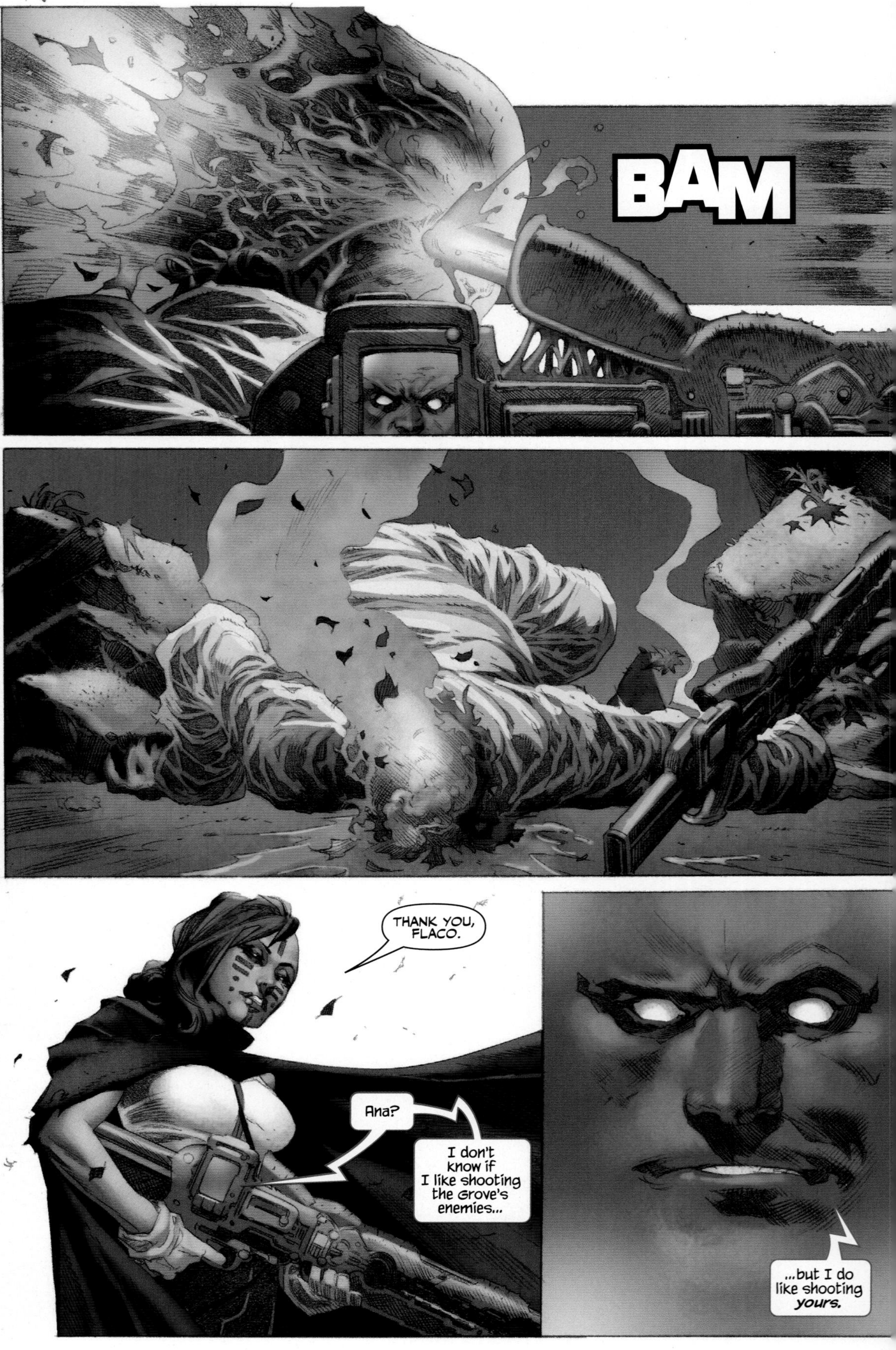
BAM
THANK YOU, FLACO.
Ana?
I don't know if I like shooting the Grove's enemies...
...but I do like shooting *yours.*

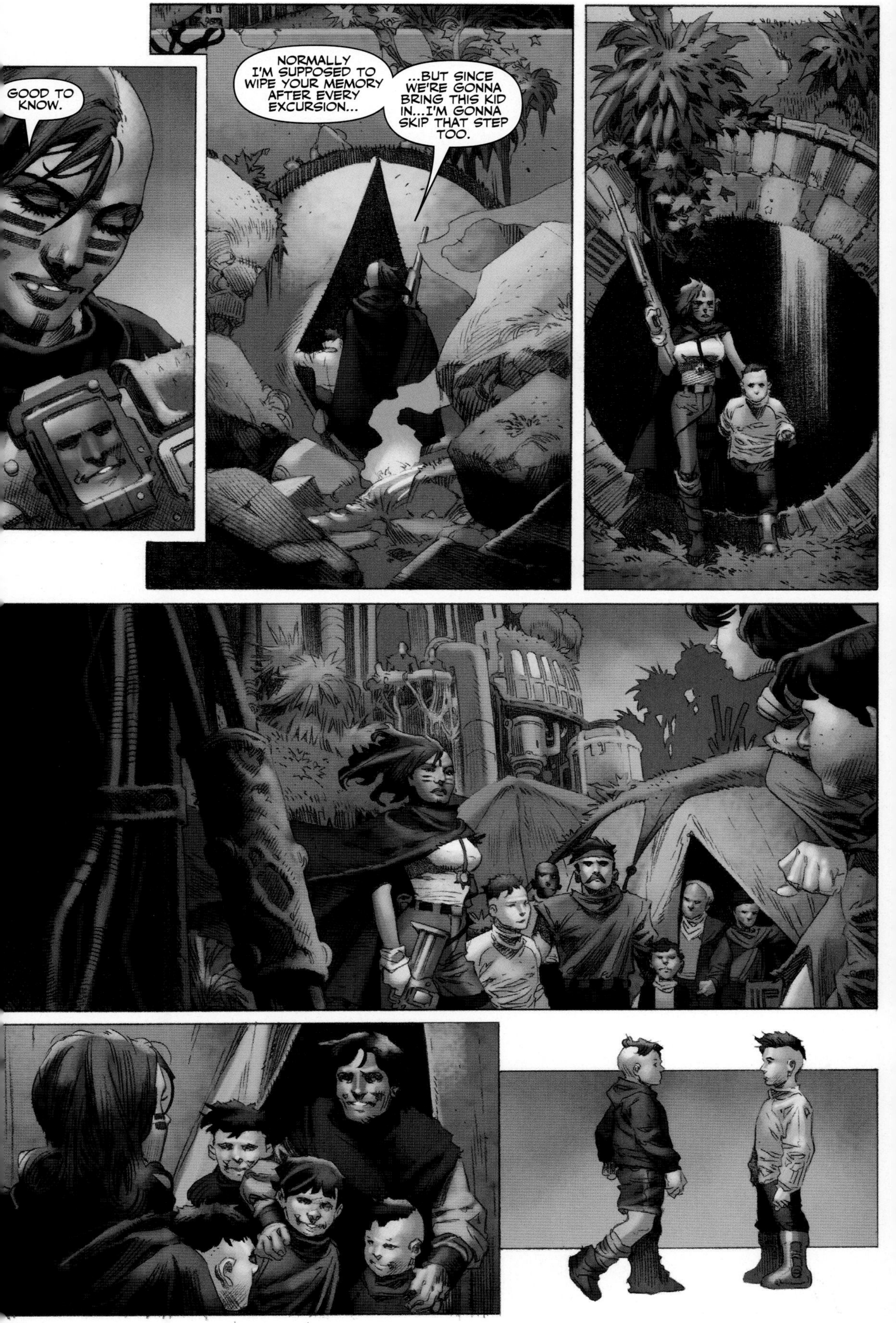
GOOD TO KNOW.
NORMALLY I'M SUPPOSED TO WIPE YOUR MEMORY AFTER EVERY EXCURSION...
...BUT SINCE WE'RE GONNA BRING THIS KID IN...I'M GONNA SKIP THAT STEP TOO.

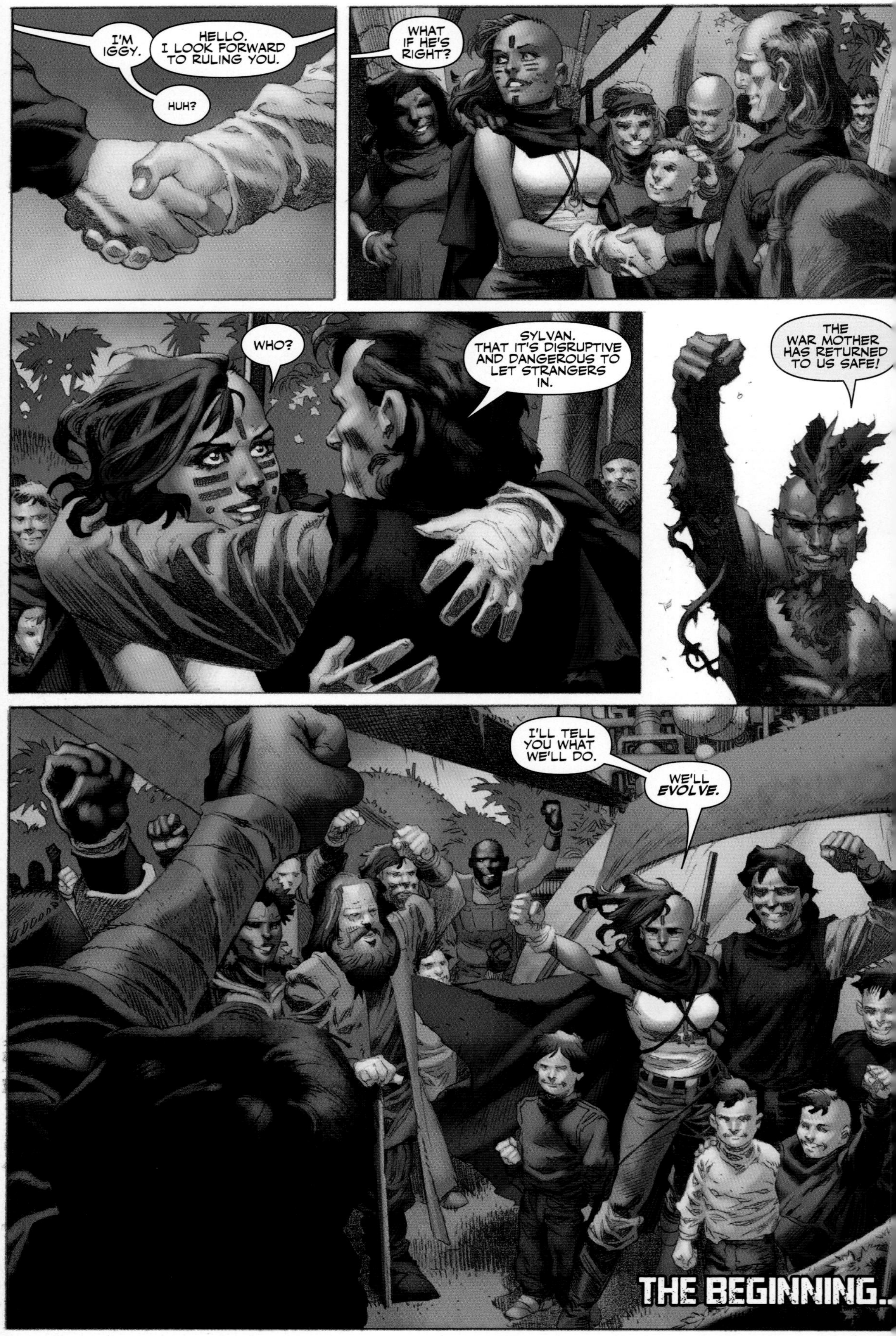

I'M IGGY.
HELLO. I LOOK FORWARD TO RULING YOU.
HUH?
WHAT IF HE'S RIGHT?
WHO?
SYLVAN. THAT IT'S DISRUPTIVE AND DANGEROUS TO LET STRANGERS IN.
THE WAR MOTHER HAS RETURNED TO US SAFE!
I'LL TELL YOU WHAT WE'LL DO.
WE'LL EVOLVE.
THE BEGINNING...

GALLERY

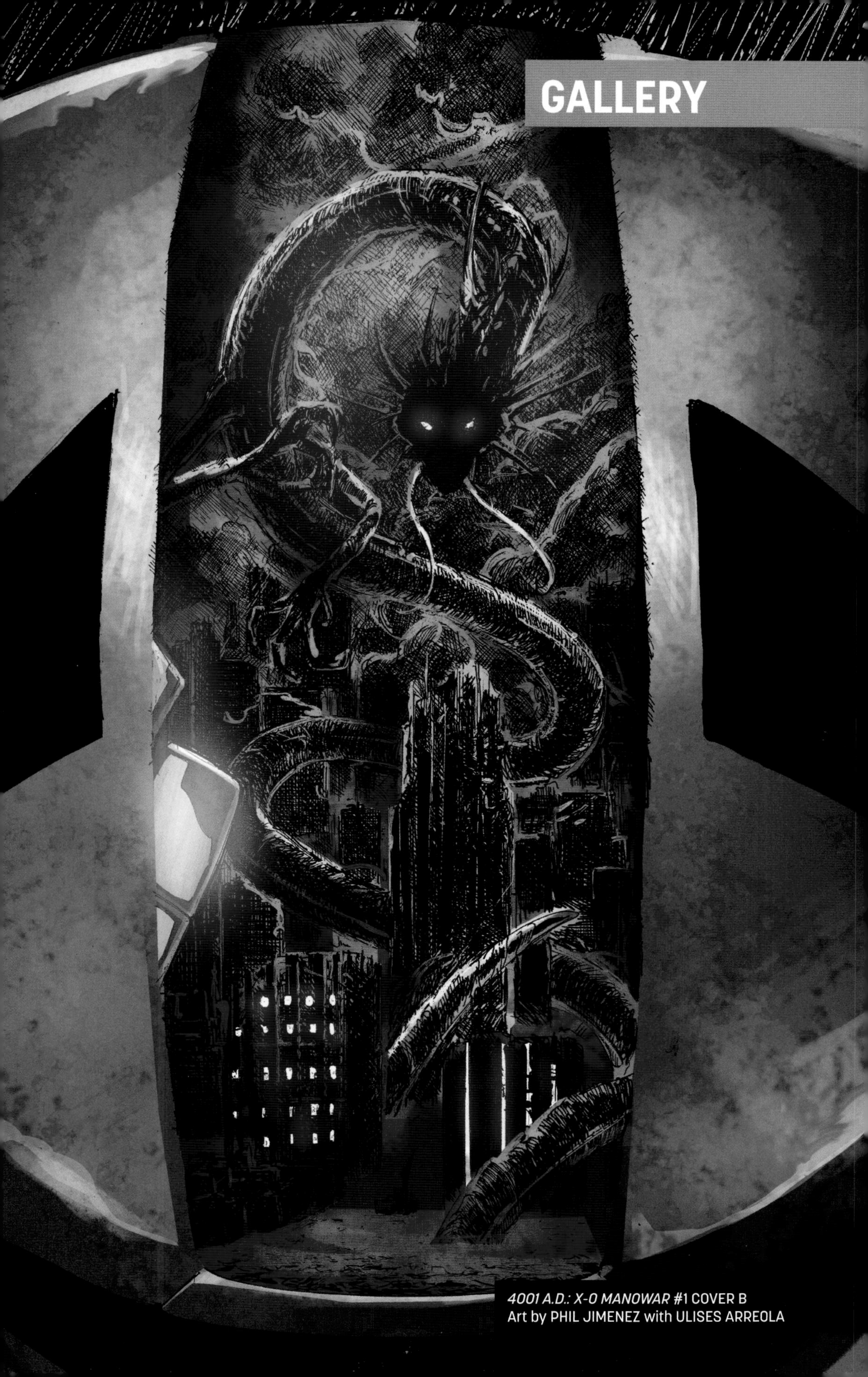

4001 A.D.: X-O MANOWAR #1 COVER B
Art by PHIL JIMENEZ with ULISES ARREOLA

4001 A.D.: BLOODSHOT #1 COVER B
Art by CAFU

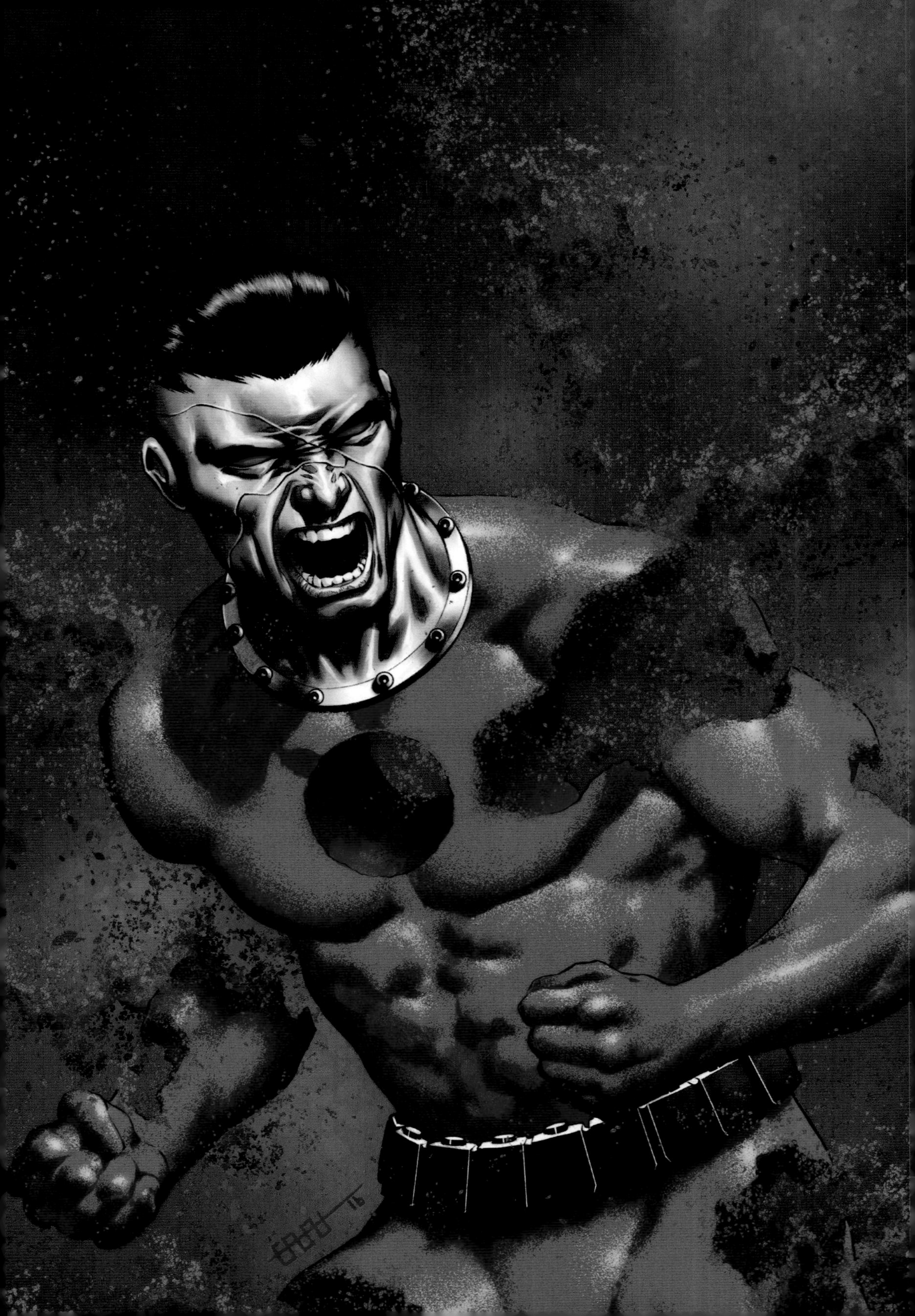

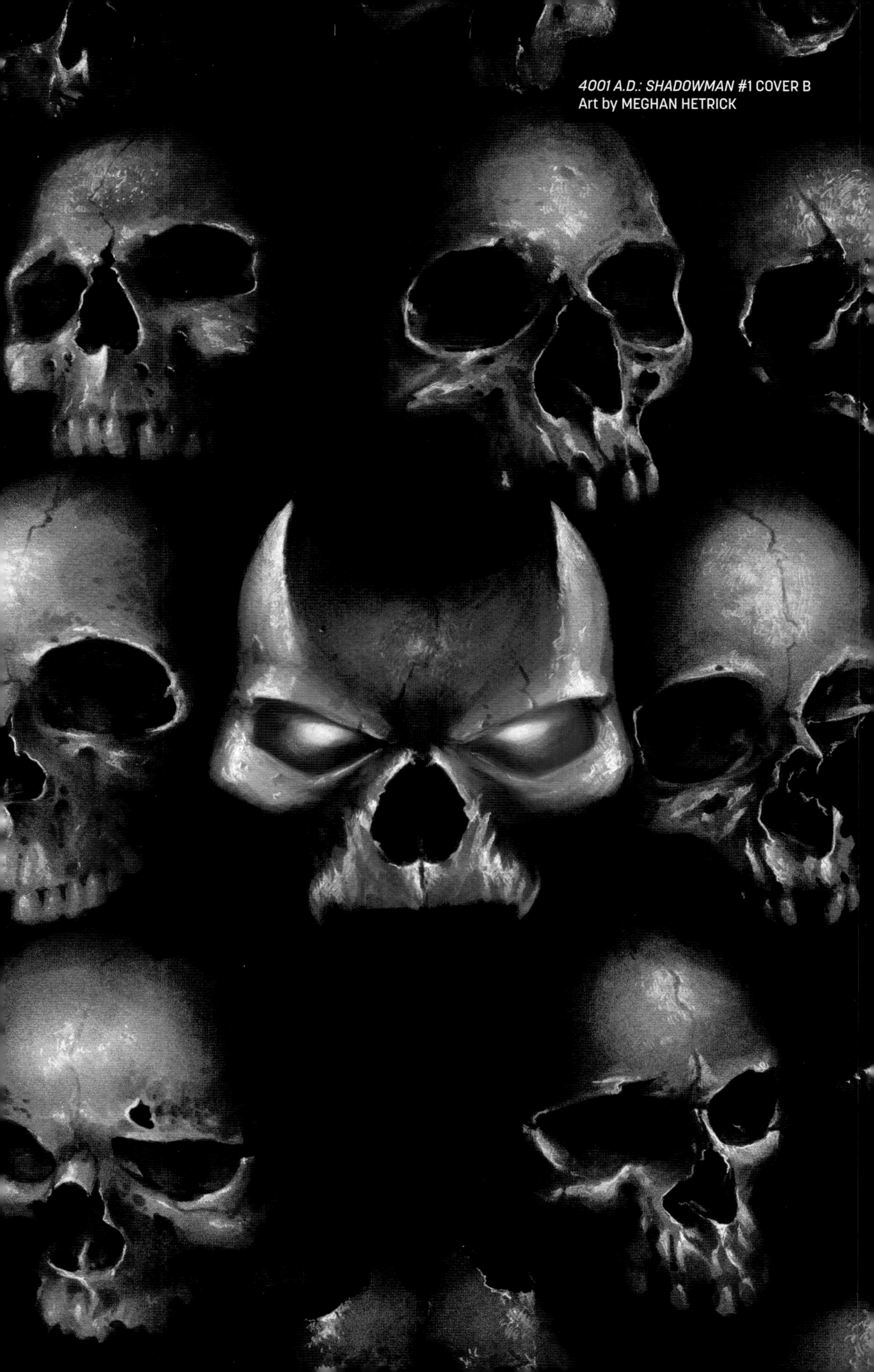

4001 A.D.: SHADOWMAN #1 COVER B
Art by MEGHAN HETRICK

4001 A.D.: WAR MOTHER #1 COVER B
Art by JELENA KEVIC-DJURDJEVIC

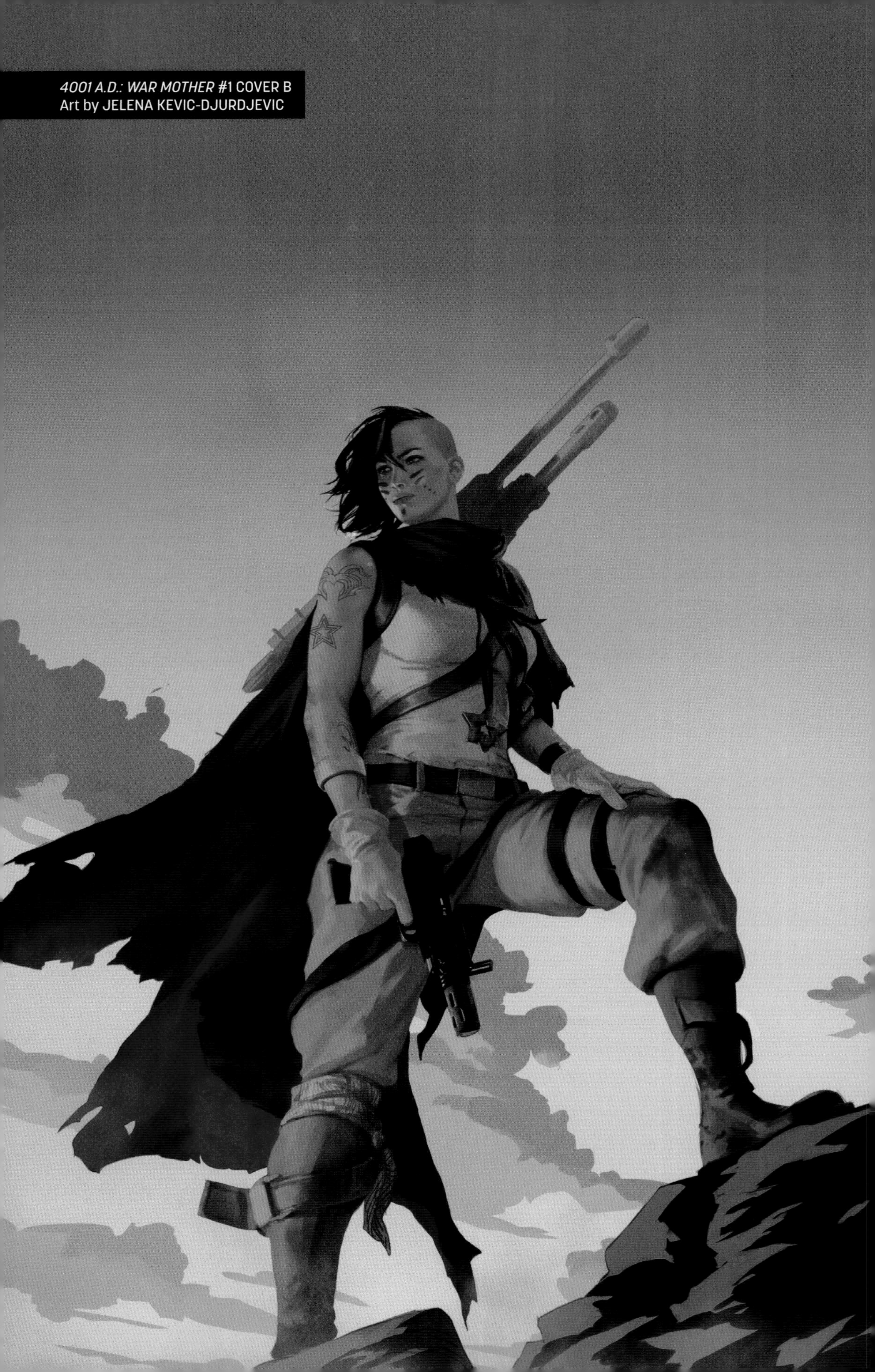

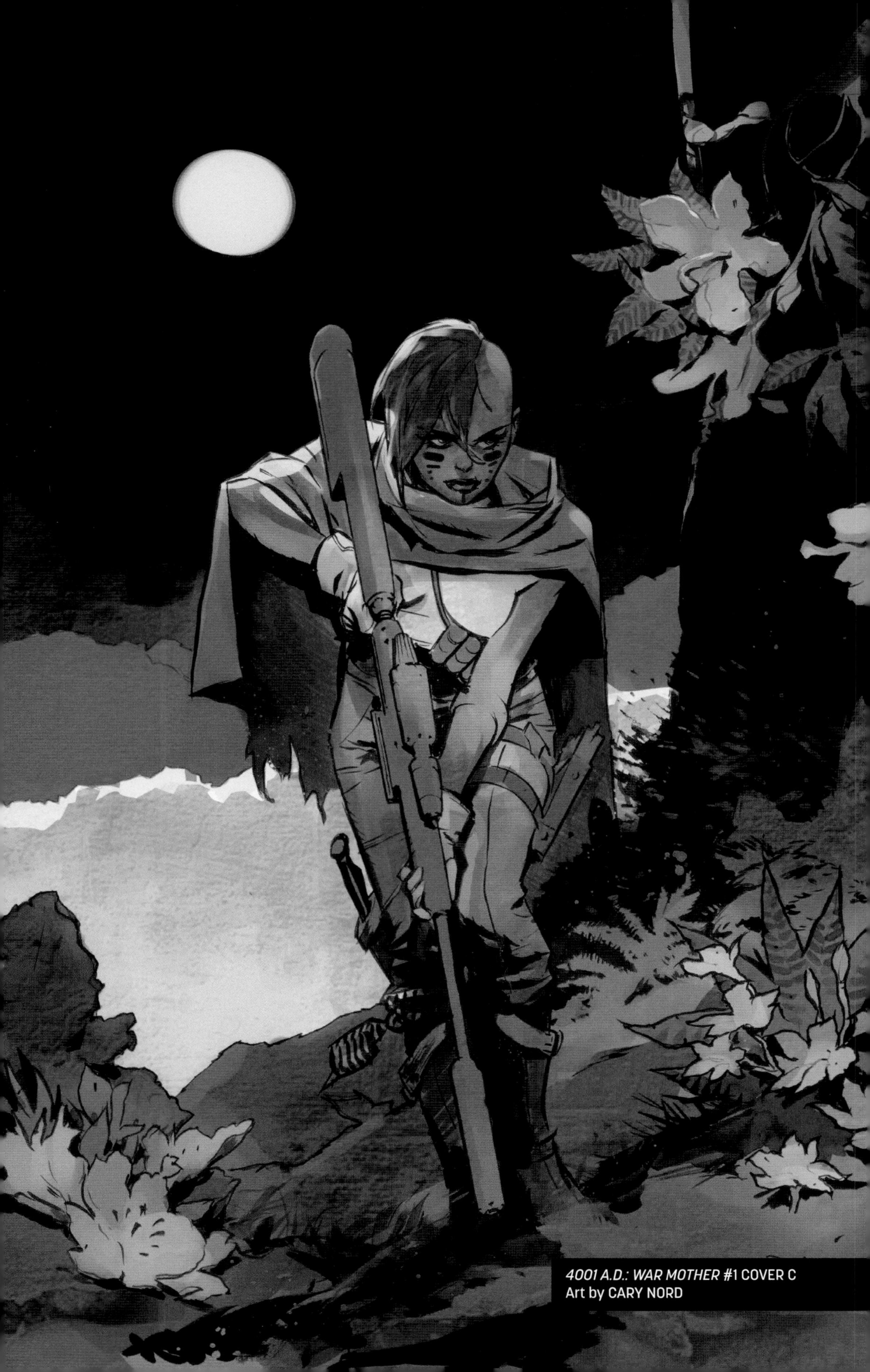

4001 A.D.: WAR MOTHER #1 COVER C
Art by CARY NORD

4001 A.D.: WAR MOTHER #1 CHARACTER DESIGN VARIANT COVER
Art by ANDRES GUINALDO with MICHAEL SPICER

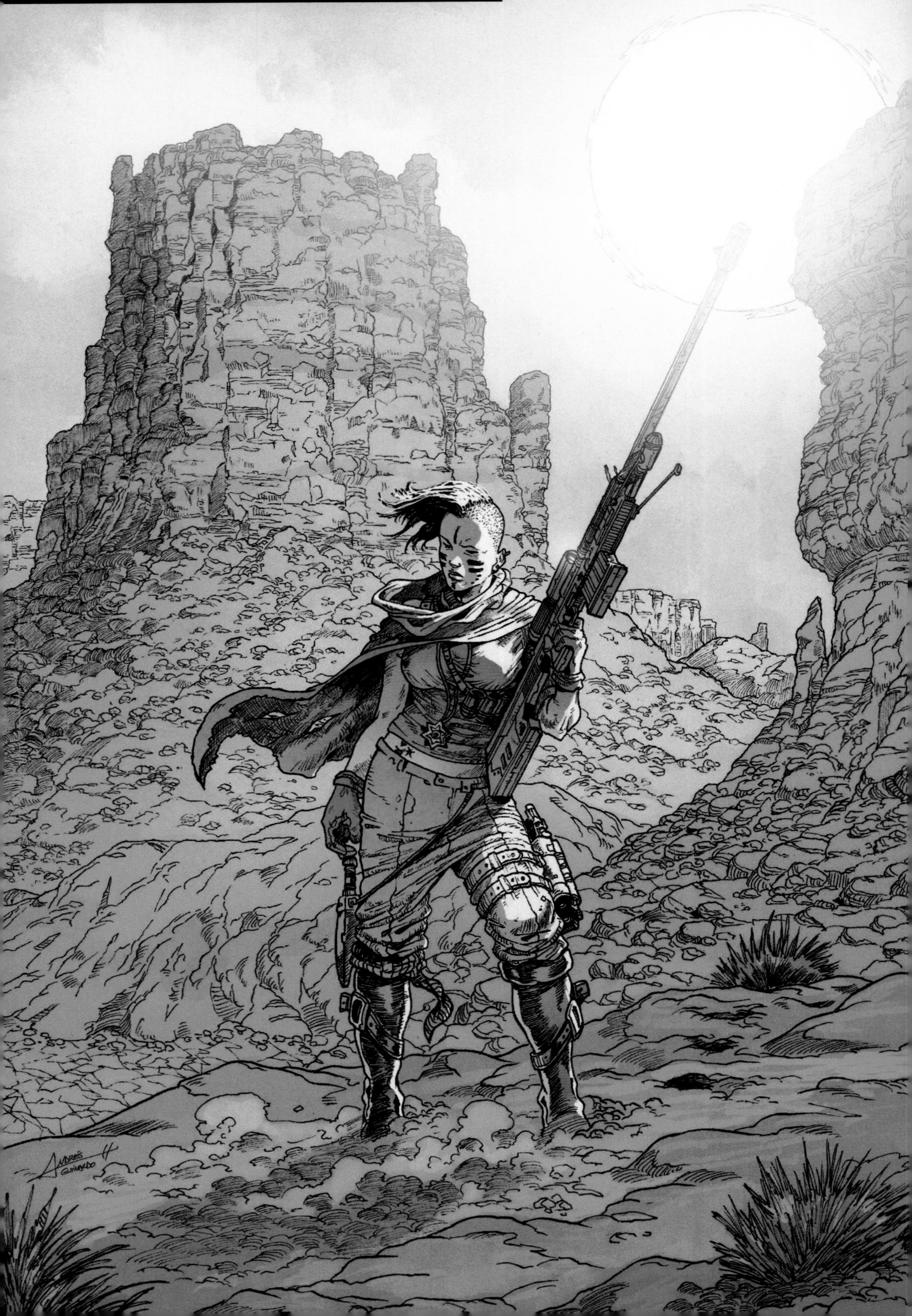

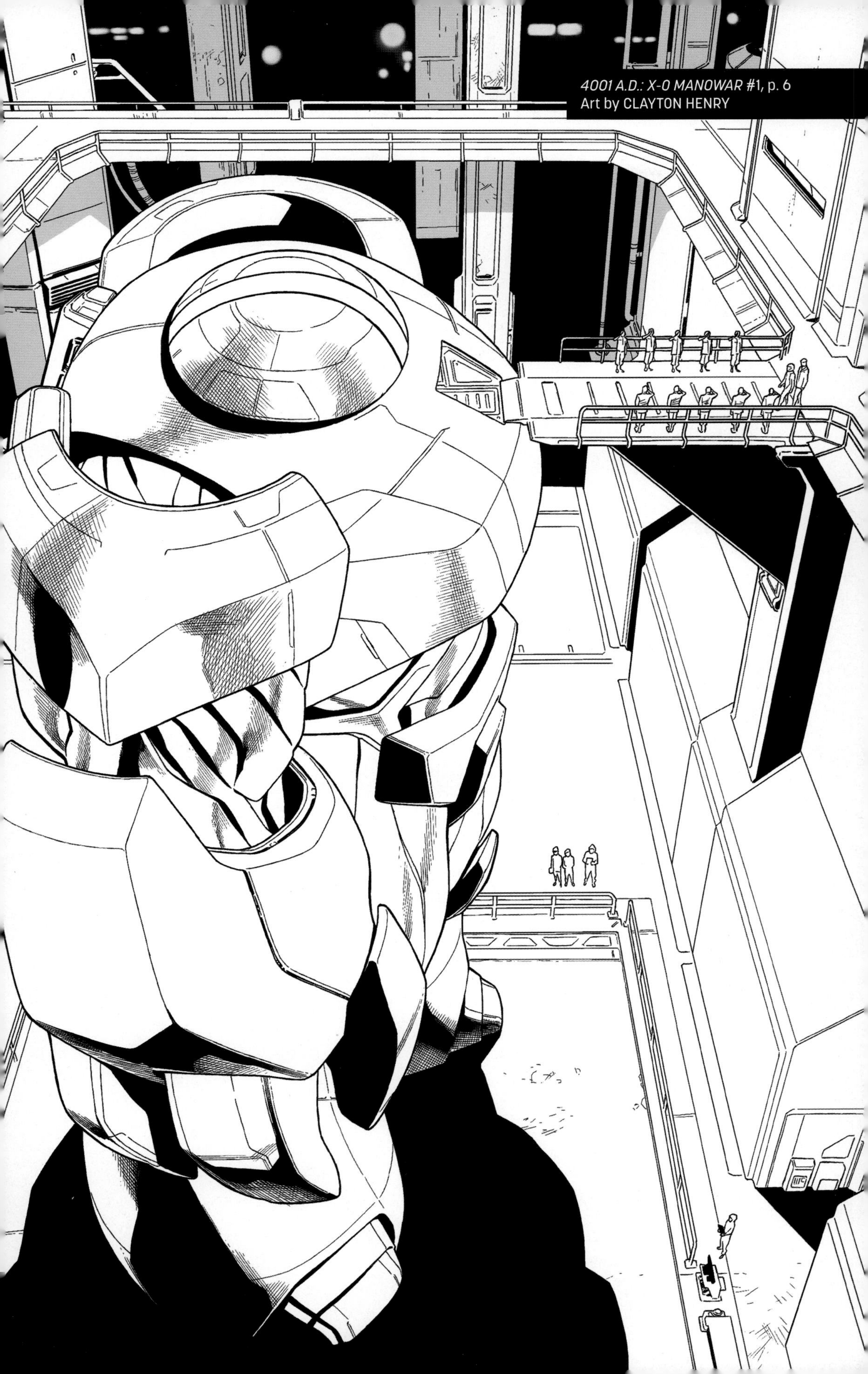

4001 A.D.: X-O MANOWAR #1, p. 6
Art by CLAYTON HENRY

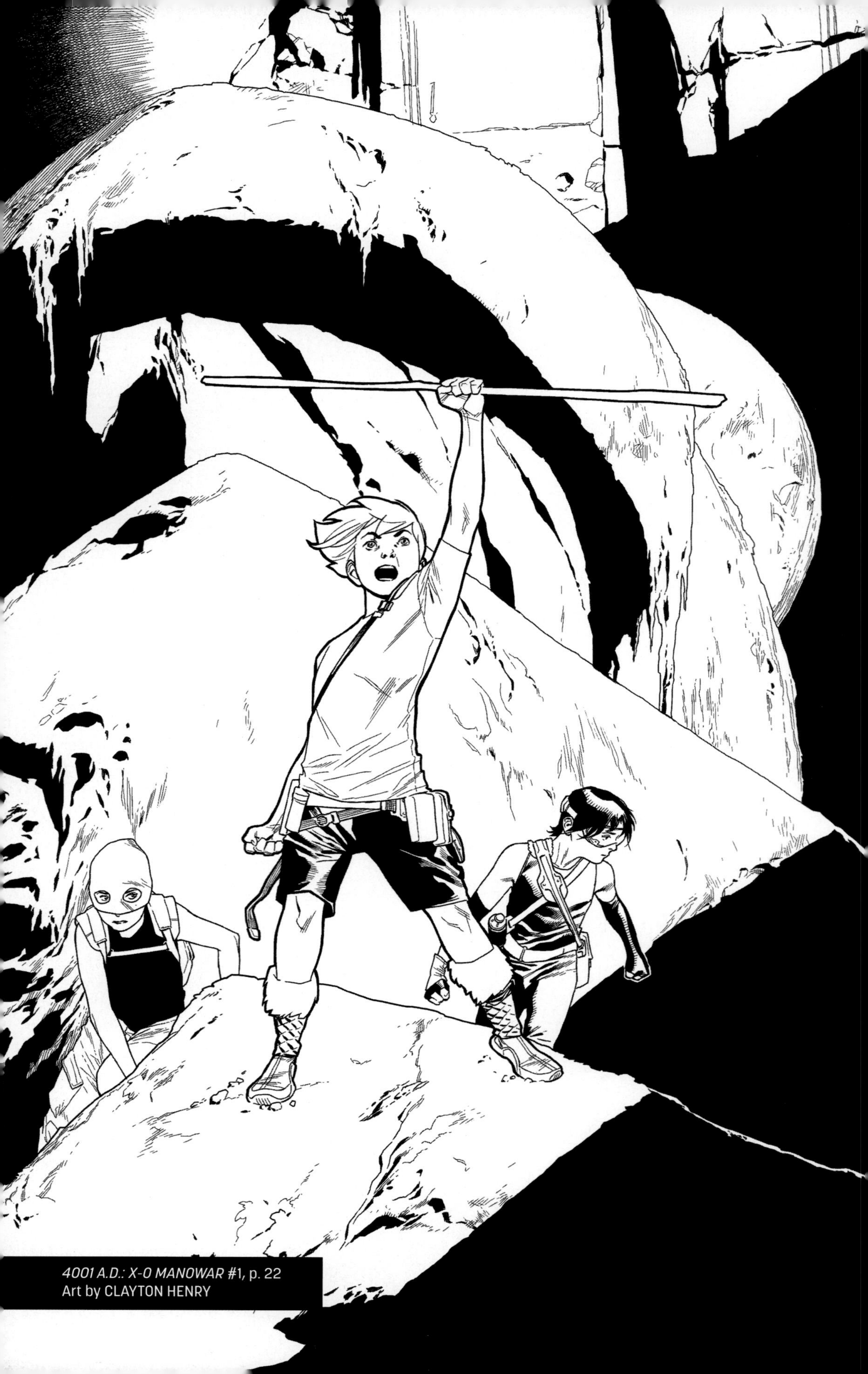

4001 A.D.: X-O MANOWAR #1, p. 22
Art by CLAYTON HENRY

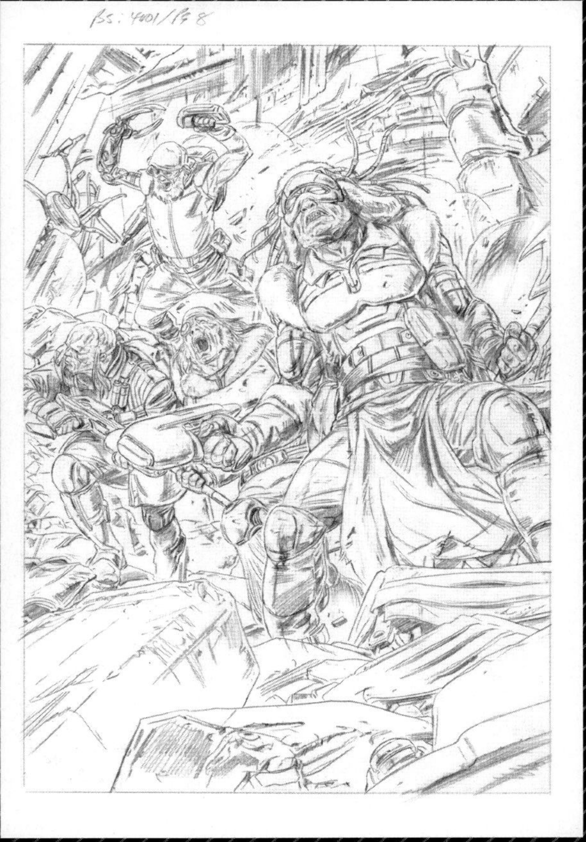

4001 A.D.: BLOODSHOT #1, p. 8
Art by DOUG BRAITHWAITE

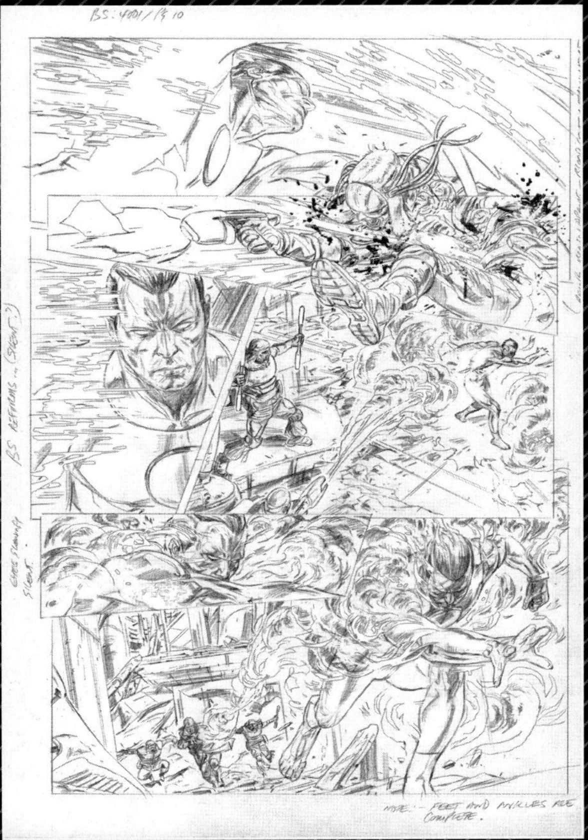
NOTE – FEET AND ANKLES ARE COMPLETE.

4001 A.D.: BLOODSHOT #1, p. 10
Art by DOUG BRAITHWAITE

4001 A.D.: BLOODSHOT #1, p. 11
Art by DOUG BRAITHWAITE

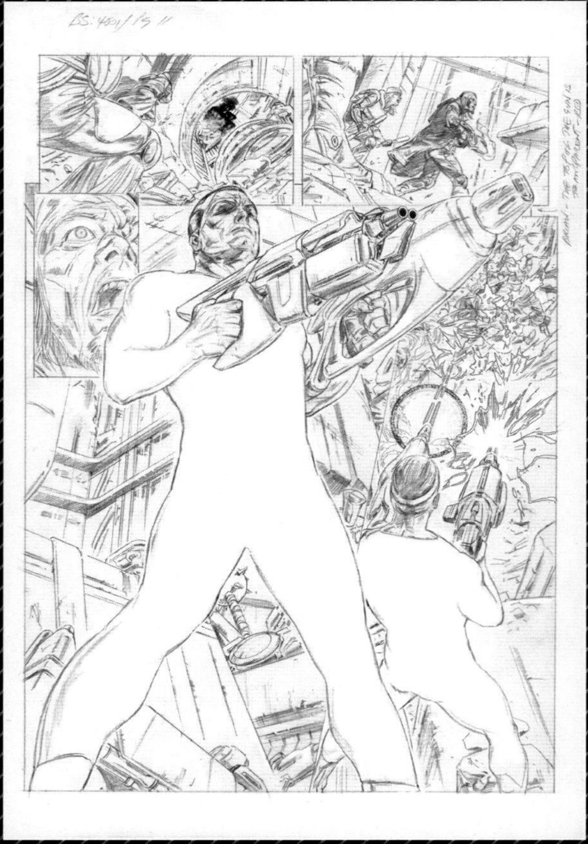
BS:4001 / Pg 11

4001 A.D.: BLOODSHOT #1, p. 14
Art by DOUG BRAITHWAITE

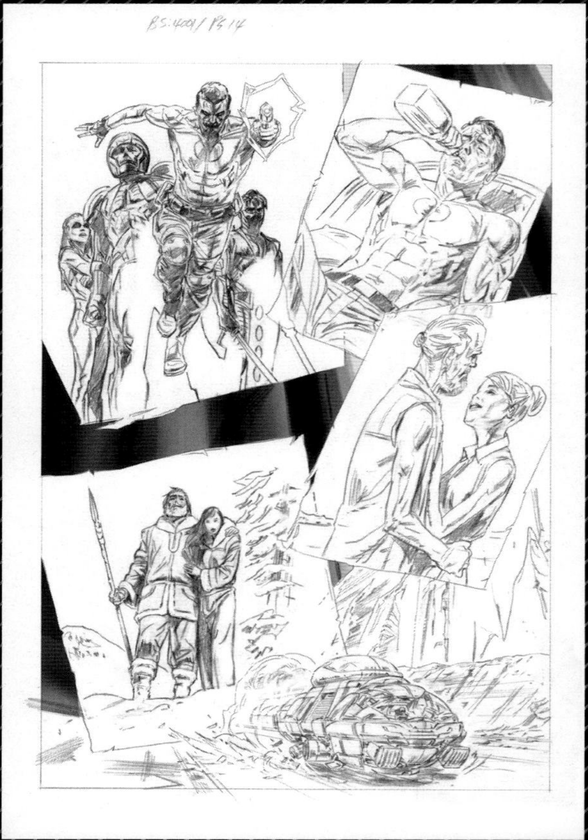
BS:4001 / Pg 14

BS!4001/PG 22

4001 A.D.: BLOODSHOT #1, p. 22
Art by DOUG BRAITHWAITE

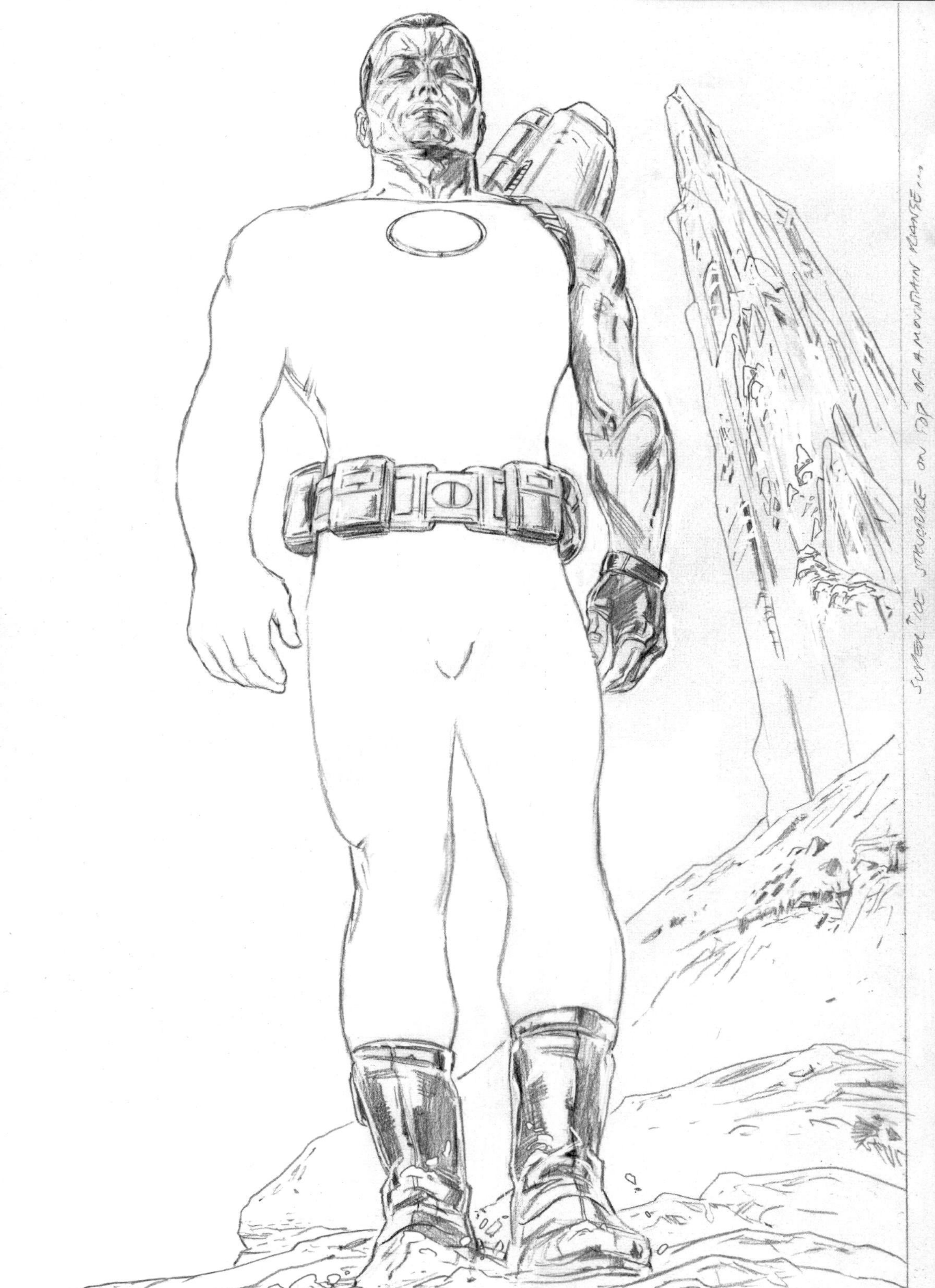

SUPER ICE STRUCTURE ON TOP OF A MOUNTAIN RANGE...

4001 A.D.: SHADOWMAN #1, p. 1
Art by ROBERT GILL

4001 A.D.: SHADOWMAN #1, p. 2
Art by ROBERT GILL

4001 A.D.: WAR MOTHER #1, p. 1
Art by TOMÁS GIORELLO

4001 A.D.: WAR MOTHER #1, p. 3
Art by TOMÁS GIORELLO

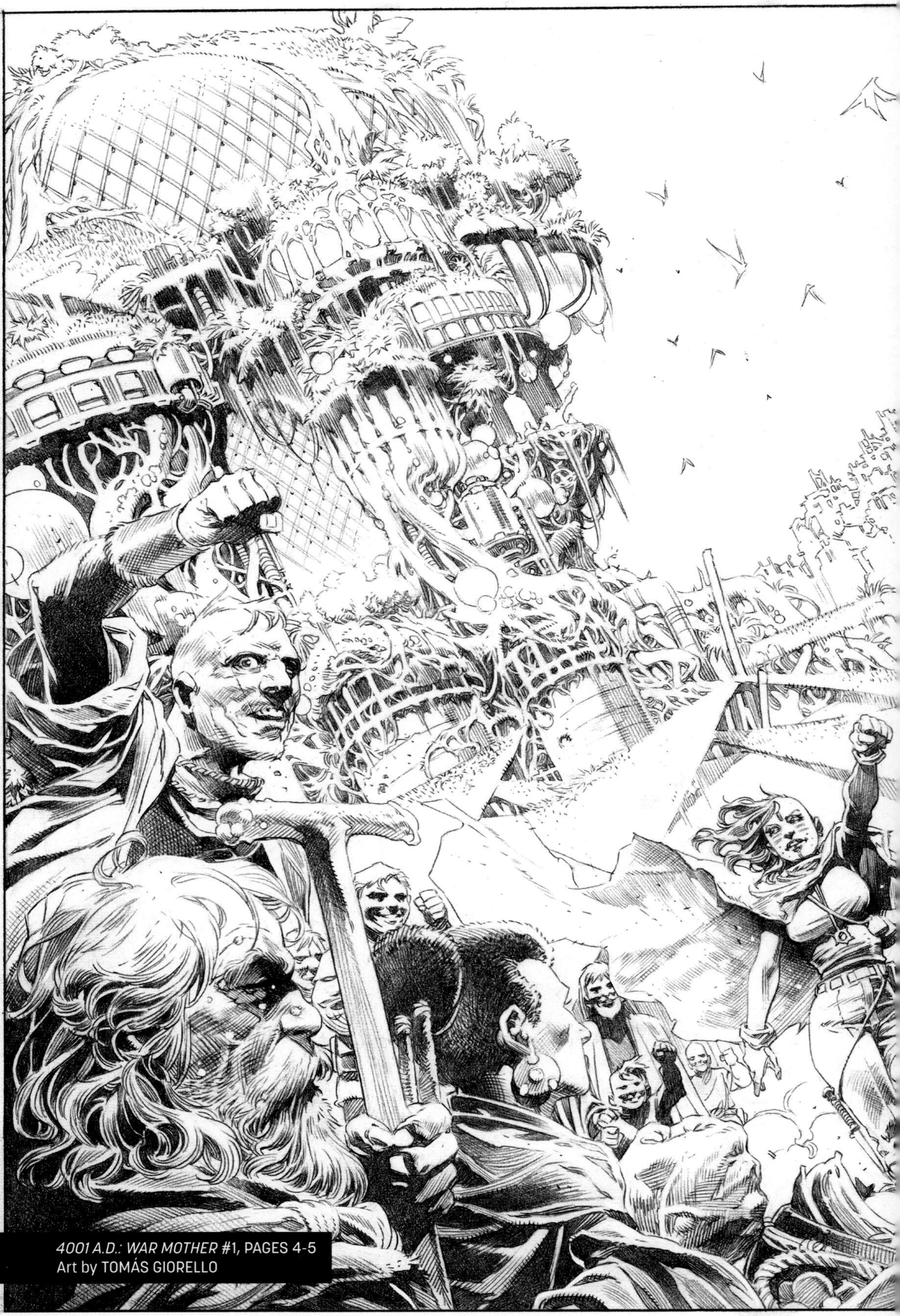

4001 A.D.: WAR MOTHER #1, PAGES 4-5
Art by TOMÁS GIORELLO

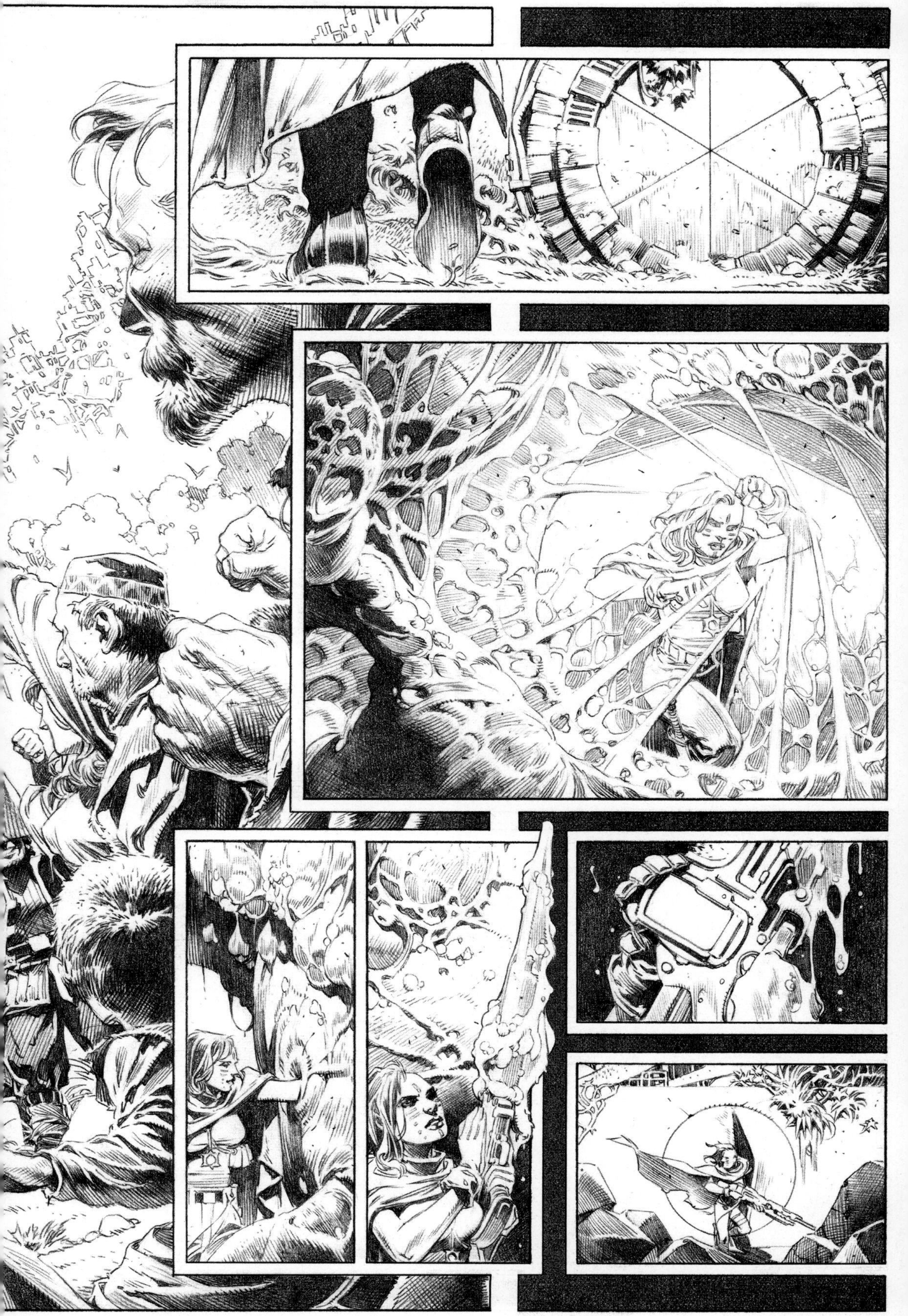

4001 A.D.: WAR MOTHER #1, p. 15
Art by TOMÁS GIORELLO

4001 A.D.: WAR MOTHER #1, p. 16
Art by TOMÁS GIORELLO

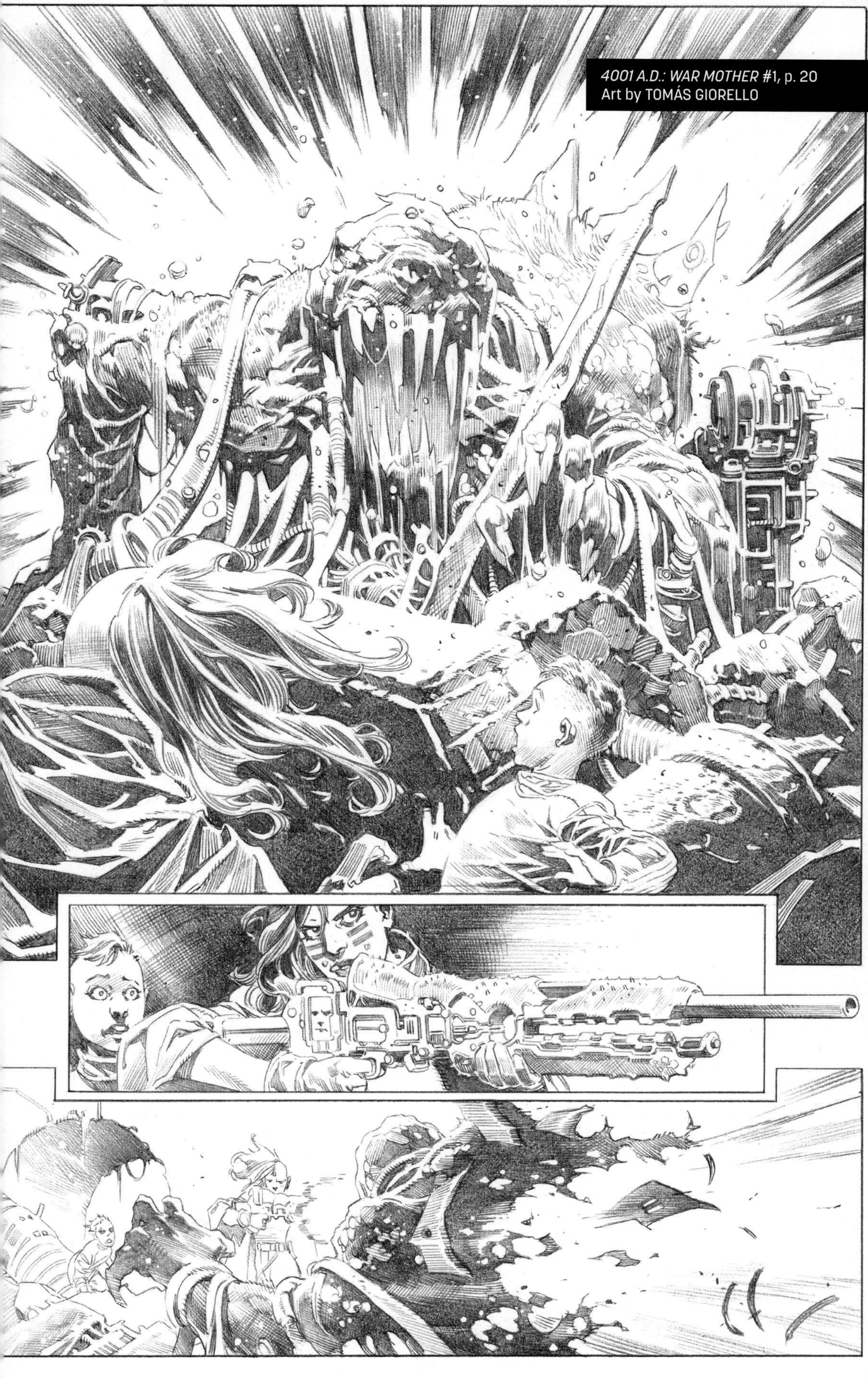

4001 A.D.: WAR MOTHER #1, p. 20
Art by TOMÁS GIORELLO

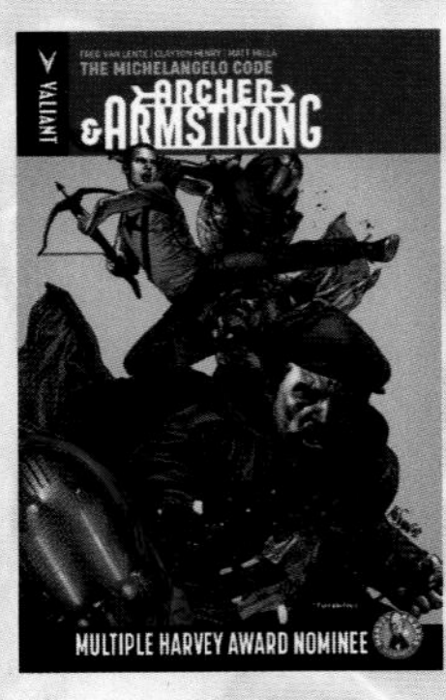
VALIANT
THE MICHELANGELO CODE
ARCHER & ARMSTRONG
MULTIPLE HARVEY AWARD NOMINEE
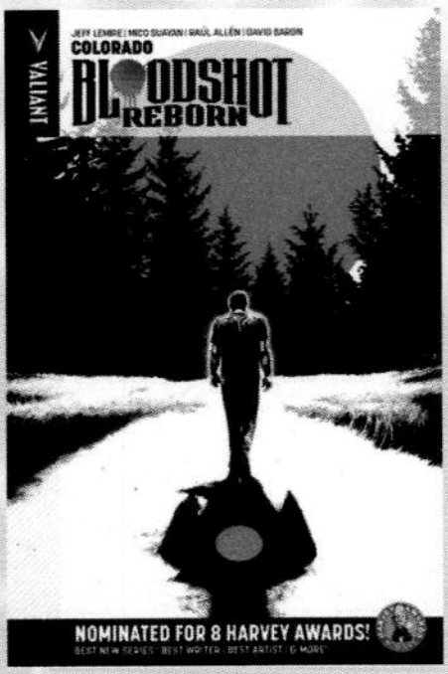
VALIANT
COLORADO
BLOODSHOT REBORN
NOMINATED FOR 8 HARVEY AWARDS!
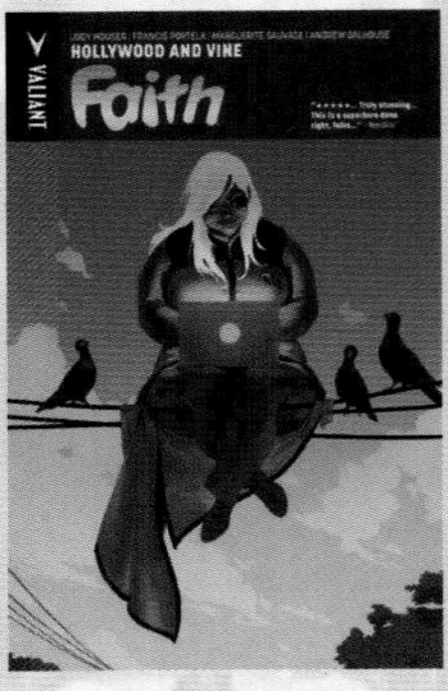
VALIANT
HOLLYWOOD AND VINE
Faith
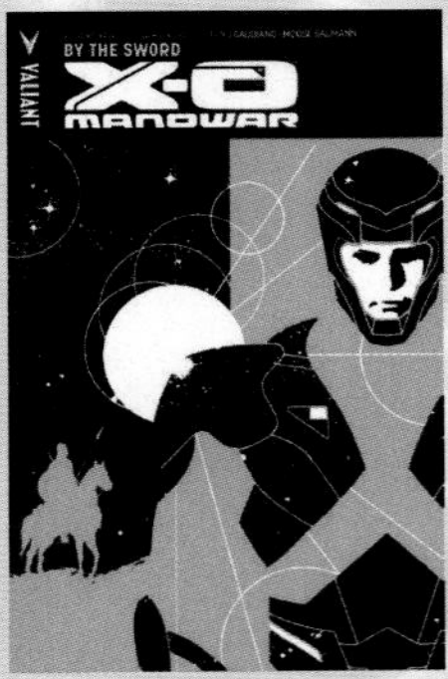
VALIANT
BY THE SWORD
X-O MANOWAR
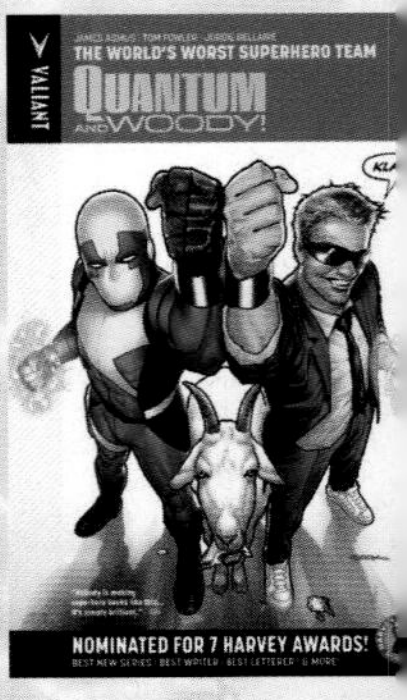
VALIANT
THE WORLD'S WORST SUPERHERO TEAM
QUANTUM AND WOODY!
NOMINATED FOR 7 HARVEY AWARDS!

4001 A.D.

4001 A.D.
ISBN: 9781682151433

4001 A.D.: Beyond New Japan
ISBN: 9781682151464

Rai Vol 4: 4001 A.D.
ISBN: 9781682151471

A&A: THE ADVENTURES OF ARCHER AND ARMSTRONG

Volume 1: In the Bag
ISBN: 9781682151495

ARCHER & ARMSTRONG

Volume 1: The Michelangelo Code
ISBN: 9780979640988

Volume 2: Wrath of the Eternal Warrior
ISBN: 9781939346049

Volume 3: Far Faraway
ISBN: 9781939346148

Volume 4: Sect Civil War
ISBN: 9781939346254

Volume 5: Mission: Improbable
ISBN: 9781939346353

Volume 6: American Wasteland
ISBN: 9781939346421

Volume 7: The One Percent and Other Tales
ISBN: 9781939346537

ARMOR HUNTERS

Armor Hunters
ISBN: 9781939346452

Armor Hunters: Bloodshot
ISBN: 9781939346469

Armor Hunters: Harbinger
ISBN: 9781939346506

Unity Vol. 3: Armor Hunters
ISBN: 9781939346445

X-O Manowar Vol. 7: Armor Hunters
ISBN: 9781939346476

BLOODSHOT

Volume 1: Setting the World on Fire
ISBN: 9780979640964

Volume 2: The Rise and the Fall
ISBN: 9781939346032

Volume 3: Harbinger Wars
ISBN: 9781939346124

Volume 4: H.A.R.D. Corps
ISBN: 9781939346193

Volume 5: Get Some!
ISBN: 9781939346315

Volume 6: The Glitch and Other Tales
ISBN: 9781939346711

BLOODSHOT REBORN

Volume 1: Colorado
ISBN: 9781939346674

Volume 2: The Hunt
ISBN: 9781939346827

Volume 3: The Analog Man
ISBN: 9781682151334

BOOK OF DEATH

Book of Death
ISBN: 9781939346971

Book of Death: The Fall of the Valiant Universe
ISBN: 9781939346988

DEAD DROP

ISBN: 9781939346858

THE DEATH-DEFYING DOCTOR MIRAGE

Volume 1
ISBN: 9781939346490

Volume 2: Second Lives
ISBN: 9781682151297

THE DELINQUENTS

ISBN: 9781939346513

DIVINITY

Volume 1
ISBN: 9781939346766

Volume 2
ISBN: 9781682151518

ETERNAL WARRIOR

Volume 1: Sword of the Wild
ISBN: 9781939346209

Volume 2: Eternal Emperor
ISBN: 9781939346292

Volume 3: Days of Steel
ISBN: 9781939346742

WRATH OF THE ETERNAL WARRIOR

Volume 1: Risen
ISBN: 9781682151235

Volumel 2: Labyrinth
ISBN: 9781682151594

FAITH

Faith Vol 1: Hollywood and Vine
ISBN: 9781682151402

Faith Vol 2: California Scheming
ISBN: 9781682151631

HARBINGER

Volume 1: Omega Rising
ISBN: 9780979640957

Volume 2: Renegades
ISBN: 9781939346025

Volume 3: Harbinger Wars
ISBN: 9781939346117

Volume 4: Perfect Day
ISBN: 9781939346155

Volume 5: Death of a Renegade
ISBN: 9781939346339

Volume 6: Omegas
ISBN: 9781939346384

HARBINGER WARS

Harbinger Wars
ISBN: 9781939346094

Bloodshot Vol. 3: Harbinger Wars
ISBN: 9781939346124

Harbinger Vol. 3: Harbinger Wars
ISBN: 9781939346117

EXPLORE THE VALIANT UNIVERSE

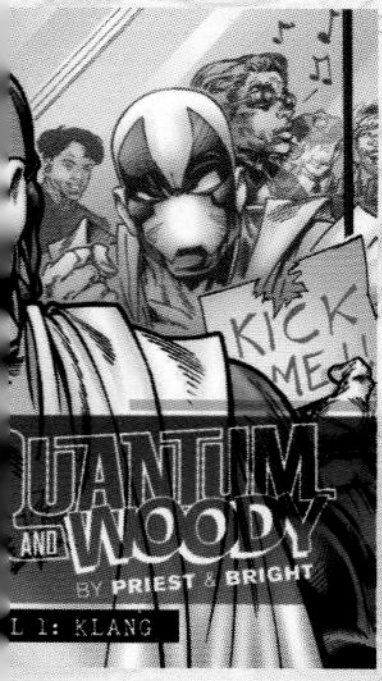

KICK ME
UANTUM AND WOODY
BY PRIEST & BRIGHT
L 1: KLANG

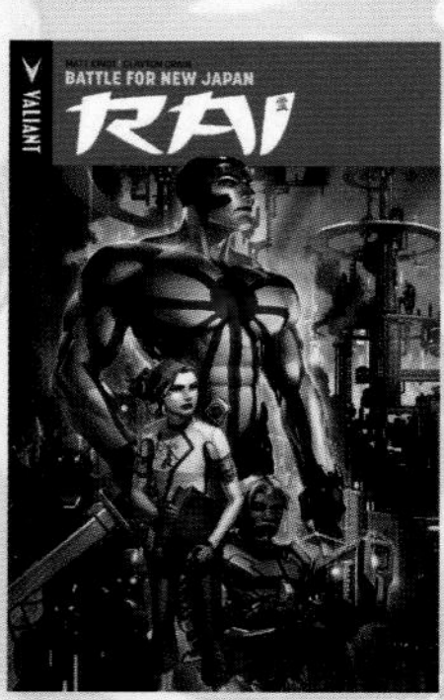

VALIANT
BATTLE FOR NEW JAPAN
RAI

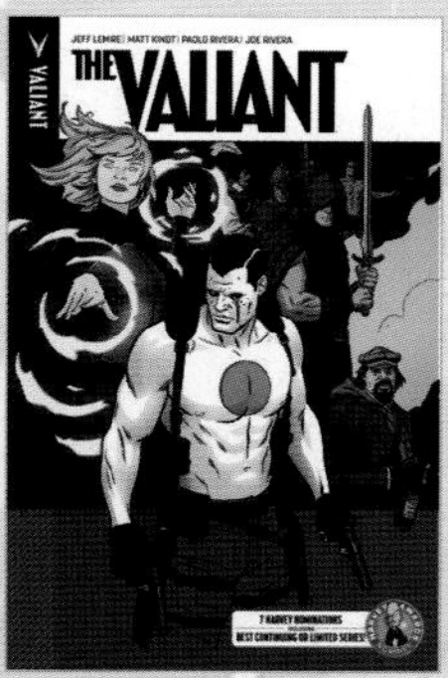

VALIANT
THE VALIANT

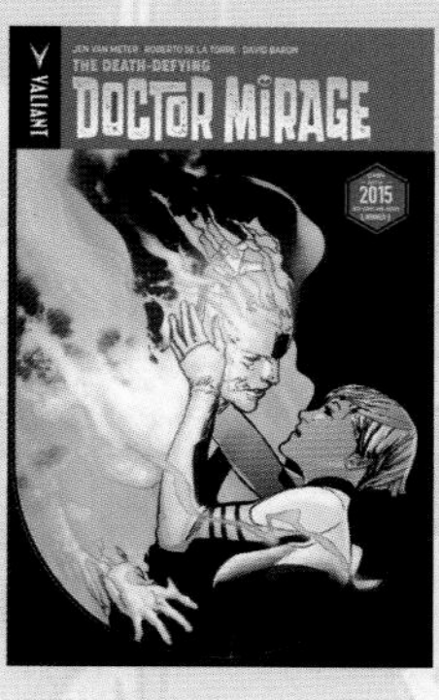

VALIANT
THE DEATH-DEFYING
DOCTOR MIRAGE
2015

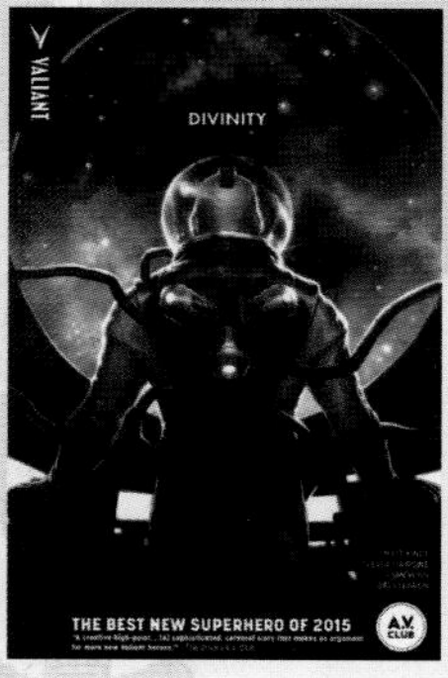

VALIANT
DIVINITY
THE BEST NEW SUPERHERO OF 2015
A.V. CLUB

RBINGER WARS

inger Wars
: 9781939346094

dshot Vol. 3: Harbinger Wars
: 9781939346124

inger Vol. 3: Harbinger Wars
: 9781939346117

PERIUM

me 1: Collecting Monsters
: 9781939346759

me 2: Broken Angels
: 9781939346896

me 3: The Vine Imperative
: 9781682151112

me 4: Stormbreak
: 9781682151372

NJAK

me 1: Weaponeer
: 9781939346667

me 2: The Shadow Wars
: 9781939346940

me 3: Operation: Deadside
9781682151259

me 4: The Siege of King's Castle
: 9781682151617

ANTUM AND WOODY

me 1: The World's Worst Superhero Team
: 9781939346186

me 2: In Security
: 9781939346230

me 3: Crooked Pasts, Present Tense
9781939346391

me 4: Quantum and Woody Must Die!
: 9781939346629

ANTUM AND WOODY BY IEST & BRIGHT

me 1: Klang
9781939346780

me 2: Switch
9781939346803

Volume 3: And So...
ISBN: 9781939346865

Volume 4: Q2 - The Return
ISBN: 9781682151099

RAI

Volume 1: Welcome to New Japan
ISBN: 9781939346414

Volume 2: Battle for New Japan
ISBN: 9781939346612

Volume 3: The Orphan
ISBN: 9781939346841

Rai Vol 4: 4001 A.D.
ISBN: 9781682151471

SHADOWMAN

Volume 1: Birth Rites
ISBN: 9781939346001

Volume 2: Darque Reckoning
ISBN: 9781939346056

Volume 3: Deadside Blues
ISBN: 9781939346162

Volume 4: Fear, Blood, And Shadows
ISBN: 9781939346278

Volume 5: End Times
ISBN: 9781939346377

SHADOWMAN BY ENNIS & WOOD

ISBN: 9781682151358

IVAR, TIMEWALKER

Volume 1: Making History
ISBN: 9781939346636

Volume 2: Breaking History
ISBN: 9781939346834

Volume 3: Ending History
ISBN: 9781939346995

UNITY

Volume 1: To Kill a King
ISBN: 9781939346261

Volume 2: Trapped by Webnet
ISBN: 9781939346346

Volume 3: Armor Hunters
ISBN: 9781939346445

Volume 4: The United
ISBN: 9781939346544

Volume 5: Homefront
ISBN: 9781939346797

Volume 6: The War-Monger
ISBN: 9781939346902

Volume 7: Revenge of the Armor Hunters
ISBN: 9781682151136

THE VALIANT

ISBN: 9781939346605

VALIANT ZEROES AND ORIGINS

ISBN: 9781939346582

X-O MANOWAR

Volume 1: By the Sword
ISBN: 9780979640940

Volume 2: Enter Ninjak
ISBN: 9780979640995

Volume 3: Planet Death
ISBN: 9781939346087

Volume 4: Homecoming
ISBN: 9781939346179

Volume 5: At War With Unity
ISBN: 9781939346247

Volume 6: Prelude to Armor Hunters
ISBN: 9781939346407

Volume 7: Armor Hunters
ISBN: 9781939346476

Volume 8: Enter: Armorines
ISBN: 9781939346551

Volume 9: Dead Hand
ISBN: 9781939346650

Volume 10: Exodus
ISBN: 9781939346933

Volume 11: The Kill List
ISBN: 9781682151273

JOSHUA DYSART | BARRY KITSON | CLAYTON HENRY | KHARI EVANS | RAFA SANDOVAL
VALIANT
HARBINGER
DELUXE EDITION 2

ROBERT VENDITTI MATT KINDT JOSHUA DYSART JOE HARRIS ROBERT GILL DOUG BRAITHWAITE DIEGO BERNARD TREVOR HAIRSINE STEPHEN SEGOVIA
VALIANT
ARMOR HUNTERS
DELUXE EDITION

JIM SHOOTER DAVID LAPHAM
VALIANT
CHILDREN OF THE EIGHTH DAY
HARBINGER
VALIANT MASTERS

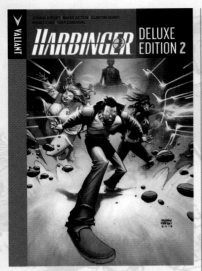

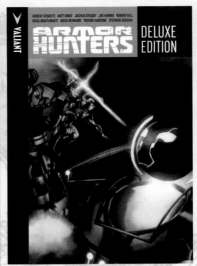

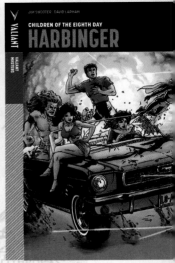

Omnibuses

Archer & Armstrong: The Complete Classic Omnibus
ISBN: 9781939346872
Collecting ARCHER & ARMSTRONG (1992) #0-26, ETERNAL WARRIOR (1992) #25 along with ARCHER & ARMSTRONG: THE FORMATION OF THE SECT.

Quantum and Woody: The Complete Classic Omnibus
ISBN: 9781939346360
Collecting QUANTUM AND WOODY (1997) #0, 1-21 and #32, THE GOAT: H.A.E.D.U.S. #1, and X-O MANOWAR (1996) #16

X-O Manowar Classic Omnibus Vol. 1
ISBN: 9781939346308
Collecting X-O MANOWAR (1992) #0-30, ARMORINES #0, X-O DATABASE #1, as well as material from SECRETS OF THE VALIANT UNIVERSE #1

Deluxe Editions

Archer & Armstrong Deluxe Edition Book 1
ISBN: 9781939346223
Collecting ARCHER & ARMSTRONG #0-13

Archer & Armstrong Deluxe Edition Book 2
ISBN: 9781939346957
Collecting ARCHER & ARMSTRONG #14-25, ARCHER & ARMSTRONG: ARCHER #0 and BLOODSHOT AND H.A.R.D. CORPS #20-21.

Armor Hunters Deluxe Edition
ISBN: 9781939346728
Collecting Armor Hunters #1-4, Armor Hunters: Aftermath #1, Armor Hunters: Bloodshot #1-3, Armor Hunters: Harbinger #1-3, Unity #8-11, and X-O MANOWAR #23-29

Bloodshot Deluxe Edition Book 1
ISBN: 9781939346216
Collecting BLOODSHOT #1-13

Bloodshot Deluxe Edition Book 2
ISBN: 9781939346810
Collecting BLOODSHOT AND H.A.R.D. CORPS #14-23, BLOODSHOT #24-25, BLOODSHOT #0, BLOODSHOT AND H.A.R.D. CORPS: H.A.R.D. CORPS #0, along with ARCHER & ARMSTRONG #18-19

Book of Death Deluxe Edition
ISBN: 9781682151150
Collecting BOOK OF DEATH #1-4, BOOK OF DEATH: THE FALL OF BLOODSHOT #1, BOOK OF DEATH: THE FALL OF NINJAK #1, BOOK OF DEATH: THE FALL OF HARBINGER #1, and BOOK OF DEATH: THE FALL OF X-O MANOWAR #1.

Divinity Deluxe Edition
ISBN: 97819393460993
Collecting DIVNITY #1-4

Harbinger Deluxe Edition Book 1
ISBN: 9781939346131
Collecting HARBINGER #0-14

Harbinger Deluxe Edition Book 2
ISBN: 9781939346773
Collecting HARBINGER #15-25, HARBINGER: OMEGAS #1-3, and HARBINGER: BLEEDING MONK #0

Harbinger Wars Deluxe Edition
ISBN: 9781939346322
Collecting HARBINGER WARS #1-4, HARBINGER #11-14, and BLOODSHOT #10-13

Ivar, Timewalker Deluxe Edition Book 1
ISBN: 9781682151198
Collecting IVAR, TIMEWALKER #1-12

Quantum and Woody Deluxe Edition Book 1
ISBN: 9781939346681
Collecting QUANTUM AND WOODY #1-12 and QUANTUM AND WOODY: THE GOAT #0

Q2: The Return of Quantum and Woody Deluxe Edition
ISBN: 9781939346568
Collecting Q2: THE RETURN OF QUANTUM AND WOODY #1-5

Rai Deluxe Edition Book 1
ISBN: 9781682151174
Collecting RAI #1-12, along with material from RAI #1 PLUS EDITION and RAI #5 PLUS EDITION

Shadowman Deluxe Edition Book 1
ISBN: 9781939346438
Collecting SHADOWMAN #0-10

Shadowman Deluxe Edition Book 2
ISBN: 9781682151075
Collecting SHADOWMAN #11-16, SHADOWMAN #13X, SHADOWMAN: END TIMES #1-3 and PUNK MAMBO #0

Unity Deluxe Edition Book 1
ISBN: 9781939346575
Collecting UNITY #0-14

The Valiant Deluxe Edition
ISBN: 97819393460986
Collecting THE VALIANT #1-4

X-O Manowar Deluxe Edition Book 1
ISBN: 9781939346100
Collecting X-O MANOWAR #1-14

X-O Manowar Deluxe Edition Book 2
ISBN: 9781939346520
Collecting X-O MANOWAR #15-22, and UNITY #

X-O Manowar Deluxe Edition Book 3
ISBN: 9781682151310
Collecting X-O MANOWAR #23-29 and ARMOR HUNTERS #1-4.

Valiant Masters

Bloodshot Vol. 1 - Blood of the Machine
ISBN: 9780979640933

H.A.R.D. Corps Vol. 1 - Search and Destroy
ISBN: 9781939346285

Harbinger Vol. 1 - Children of the Eighth Day
ISBN: 9781939346483

Ninjak Vol. 1 - Black Water
ISBN: 9780979640971

Rai Vol. 1 - From Honor to Strength
ISBN: 9781939346070

Shadowman Vol. 1 - Spirits Within
ISBN: 9781939346018

4001 A.D. | READING ORDER

Read the entirety of the blistering comics event uniting Rai with the greatest heroes of the 41st century!

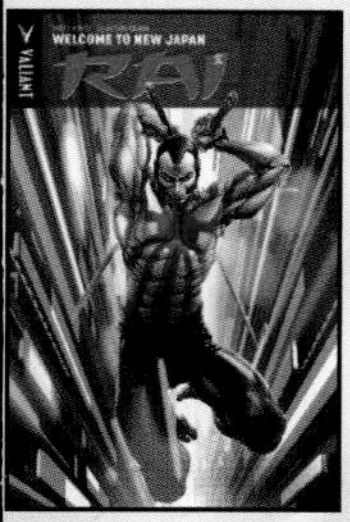
WELCOME TO NEW JAPAN
RAI

Rai Vol. 1: Welcome to New Japan
(OPTIONAL)

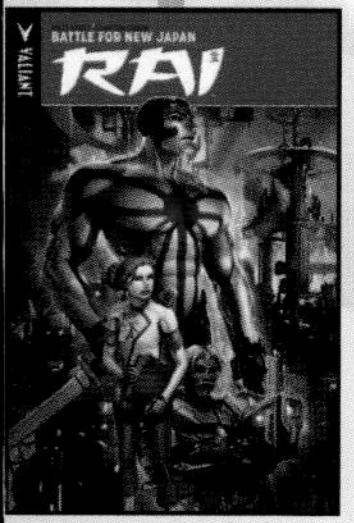
BATTLE FOR NEW JAPAN
RAI

Rai Vol. 2: Battle for New Japan
(OPTIONAL)

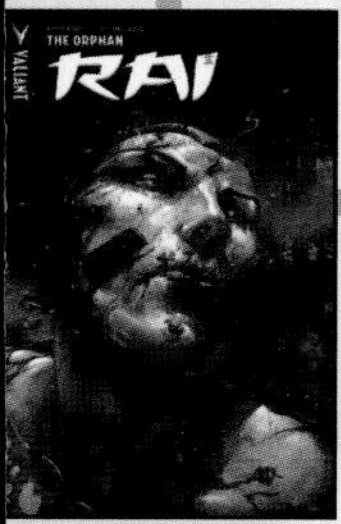
THE ORPHAN
RAI

Rai Vol. 3: The Orphan
(OPTIONAL)

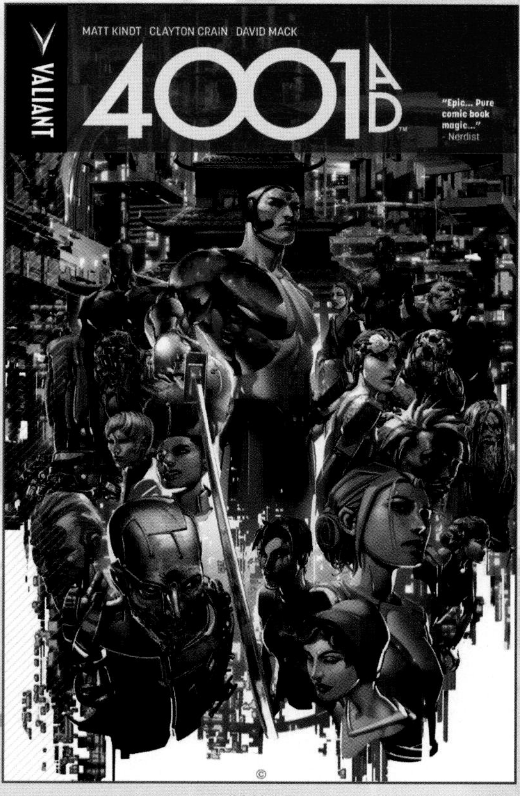
VALIANT
MATT KINDT CLAYTON CRAIN DAVID MACK
4001 A.D.
"Epic... Pure comic book magic..."
- Nerdist

4001 A.D.

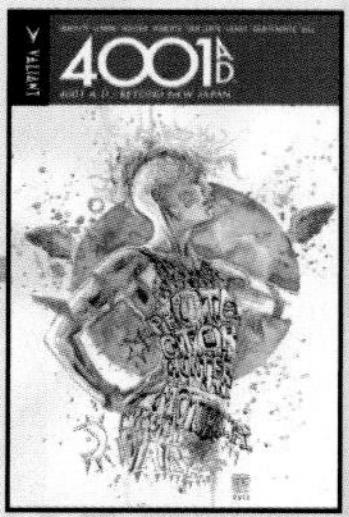
4001 A.D.

4001 A.D.: Beyond New Japan

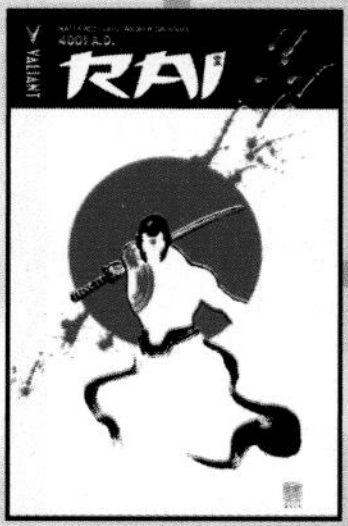
RAI

Rai Vol. 4: 4001 A.D.
(OPTIONAL)